L.R.R.P.:
The Professional

FRANK CAMPER

A DELL BOOK

Published by
Dell Publishing
a division of
The Bantam Doubleday Dell Publishing Group, Inc.
666 Fifth Avenue
New York, NY 10103

ISBN: 0-440-20009-1

Printed in the United States of America

Published simultaneously in Canada

August 1988

10 9 8 7 6 5 4 3 2 1

KRI

To the nearly 60,000 who didn't make it.
We scratched our grief onto a wall.
And it looks just like your names.

INTRODUCTION
The LRRPs:
Tricks and Tactics

Long Range Reconnaissance Patrol.

Pronounce it "lurp," and when you do, think about a figure half-seen, crouched in the elephant grass or the jungle underbrush, aiming the camouflage-taped muzzle of a weapon at you, and know that somewhere close—very close—there are more like him, doing the same thing.

That was the last thing hundreds of North Vietnamese regulars or Vietcong guerrillas knew, realizing their mistake too late.

The LRRPs were not to be confused with a regular recon outfit. We were specifically designed for missions deep inside enemy-held territory, trained to operate alone, beyond artillery or radio range.

It was easy to confuse us with the Special Forces or the Special Operations Group, but the LRRPs were mostly volunteers from line infantry companies, men compensating for lack of elite training by substituting experience, natural skill, and sheer nerve to get the job done.

We had the World War II OSS "long range penetration" teams as an ancestor, and found our name when the U.S. Rangers worked in Korea, creating the "LRRP" designation.

The term LRRP was part of the U.S. Army from that time, but was almost lost when the Rangers were disbanded.

The Airborne gets most credit for keeping the LRRP concept alive by establishing the Recondo (Recon-Commando) School, an institution that would be carried to Vietnam and manned by Special Forces cadre, training potential LRRP volunteers for the long-range patrol units the army quickly established as the war in Asia heated up.

Early in the war, in the middle sixties, most LRRP units were platoon-size and created on a "provisional" basis. The long-range patrol manual (FM 31–18) gave no authorization for LRRP units to exist below Army Corps level, and then only as a company. The LRRP manual was written for a European war where hiding on mountaintops and spying on road junctions was possible, and the intelligence the LRRPs gathered was owed strictly to Army Corps headquarters.

In Vietnam, brigades and battalions desperately needed information in their local sectors, and the Corps HQ, unable to provide it, allowed brigade commanders to organize their own LRRPs, providing they were not on the books, didn't cost anything, and did not hinder the efficiency of the overall unit from which the personnel had to come.

The army did not like "special" or elite units. The Special Forces were tolerated because President Kennedy himself had given them his stamp of approval.

The Rangers of World War II and Korean fame had been broken up as a unit and sprinkled back into the conventional units. It was considered bad for the morale of regular troops, the military management said, to have elite units in the same army.

The army did not want the LRRPs even though we were badly needed, and began to work to make us more like the dogfaces in the hard-bitten line companies.

In the beginning our provisional LRRP platoons were a ragtag lot, existing on what people and equipment the regular units could spare or be begged out of. There was no set number or procedure for anything.

LRRP platoons could contain ten men or thirty. We usually lived in donated tents near the brigade headquarters, and the outfits from which our volunteers came were responsible for our pay, administrative paperwork, promotions, leave, etc. Our weapons and equipment were what we brought from our parent units, and our rations were provided by falsifying brigade or division mess-hall reports.

The field commanders asked their headquarters sections what they needed to know, and their S2 (Intelligence) officers asked the LRRPs. We went out and got the information any way possible.

There was no one of any rank to interfere with our work since the highest-ranking man on any given patrol was likely to be a buck sergeant.

LRRP tactics evolved around whatever worked. Small teams, four men being almost the perfect number, could operate quietly with the tightest team unity.

The average team consisted of the point man, the team leader, the radioman, and the tailgunner.

Silence was the LRRPs' greatest ally. We modified our weapons and equipment to eliminate potential noises; taping web-gear suspender straps together, tying loose clothing down firmly to keep the cloth from rustling or pocket items from thumping together. Even our metal spoons were padded by tape around the handles to prevent telltale clinking while stirring in the canteen cup. Weapon slings (before the days of the "silent" nylon slings) were removed and sling swivels taped down.

Hand signals were used for communication, and any talking was done mouth-to-ear. Since radios required talking, something not always possible while near enemy positions, prearranged signals with the radio monitoring stations were established that the LRRPs could use by simply keying the handset push-to-talk buttons.

Silent movement through the jungle was performed by having the point man advance ahead of the team a few meters, stop, crouch and listen, then wave for the team to follow. Once all the men were moved up into their new positions and crouched down out of sight, the point moved on.

It was a slow process, and a team could only hope to progress one to two thousand meters a day, but stealth was absolutely necessary in order to survive in enemy territory.

While on the move, the point would watch his front and both sides. The team leader, five meters behind him, would watch over the point's head for tree platforms (a favorite VC-NVA watchpost) or snipers, while keeping the compass azimuth and marking a pace count so distance could be determined.

The RTO (radiotelephone operator) watched both flanks to make sure the team was not approached from the side, and the tailgun watched over his shoulder as he walked, then turned and faced the rear when the team was stopped.

The only way to stay alive was to see the enemy first —and at that the LRRPs excelled. We kept our weapons loaded, rounds chambered, and fingers on the trigger. Surprise encounters with enemy soldiers were almost always ended in the LRRPs' favor, since the Communist, as wily a jungle fighter as he was made out to be, had the fatal habit of carrying his own weapon slung or even unloaded while in a "safe" area.

Since one R of LRRP stands for reconnaissance, the basic mission of the LRRP teams was to get close to the enemy and find out as much about him as possible. Enemy contact, even accidental and possibly resulting in enemy casualties, was a sign of failure on a pure recon mission.

The law is set. Recon teams do not, and I say again, do *not* get caught!

If they do, they have screwed up, and to screw up usually means dying to pay for the sin. Teams doing their job would find the enemy first, shadow them through the jungle and swamps, and either call in artillery, air strikes, or airmobile infantry.

Sometimes a team followed and reported on the enemy for days before the situation allowed an attack. This was risky for one's health since Vietcong and North Vietnamese units rarely traveled alone. Mortar platoons had infantry nearby, and small infantry units had larger units within communication distance . . . usually a day away by foot.

The gathering of real field intelligence was a skill best learned on the job. Chipped bark at shoulder level on the trees alongside a trail indicated the men who had passed were carrying crew-served weapons on their shoulders. Enemy soldiers seen without their rucksacks were not far from their basecamp. Full canteens and packs hung heavily on the backs of those wearing them, advertising they were on the march.

Even the NVA had routines and procedures. A campfire was manned by one cook who fed a given number of men. Latrines in the base-camp areas had the same significant numerical clue.

The enemy ate at certain times, marched at certain times and in certain orders, and even fell victim to habit when it came to the use of trails, roads, and river or stream crossings.

It was the habits of the enemy that cost them the most men. The LRRPs quickly saw how to exploit the weaknesses we had observed. Pure recon missions gave way to patrols that went out to do battle . . . hunter-killer teams.

Ambushes were set where trails crossed water, knowing that the VC would pause to rest or fill their canteens. Long-range artillery was prezeroed on good campsite areas, and LRRPs hid on hilltops to wait for the dawn wisps of smoke from passing enemy units to blend with the mist rising off the jungle and then call the wrath of distant eight-inch howitzers on them.

Trails that showed evidence of recent movement were staked out and mined with Claymore broadsides, mini M-14 shoe mines dotted on all the approach points, and week-long vigils were established in the cane or brush thickets nearby.

Getting an LRRP team into an area was the first problem to be solved, so the method of delivery was carefully considered. Teams could (1) be flown in by helicopter (most common), and then walk into the AO (area of operations), (2) be delivered by water from a boat or sampan, or (3) simply stay behind, after having blended with a large conventional unit. Parachute insertion, while tried, proved to be impractical for the majority of LRRP missions.

Helicopter insertion made a lot of noise, but since there were helicopters in the air over Vietnam all the time, the enemy could not physically man and watch every usable clearing.

A typical insertion by chopper involved the picking of the least likely landing zone, one that did not tempt the enemy to post guards nearby. Such an LZ was usually waist-high or deeper in foliage, stumps, or rocks. Next, the helicopter carrying the team would try to spend the least amount of time near the ground. Actually hovering over the LZ was dangerous, so the team had to jump from a moving helicopter at the lowest/slowest point in the pass the pilot would make.

By having the helicopter speed through its pass, the distinctive sound of a hovering machine was eliminated, and if there were support ships, such as gunships, along with the "slick" carrying the team, they could help add to the ruse by slowing down also, then joining the escaping slick, creating the impression that the whole flight had gone over without a pause.

Two other good tricks the LRRPs used were fake insertions to divert the attention of the enemy and the "DX" (direct exchange) of a team by dropping off one team and picking up another at the same point.

The enemy, if they were aware there was a team in the area, would normally think the team had been extracted and not expect a fresh team to be there to continue the mission.

Team security, be it on an ambush, raid, or recon mission, was still top priority. Men could not toss and turn or talk in their sleep. If they talked in their sleep, we gagged them. Smoking was usually impossible. Even eating depended on having the time and place for it, and in an excitement-charged pursuit, or a recon so close a team could often get involved inside an enemy perimeter, eating and sleeping had to wait.

Guard shifts were established every night, all the men within touching distance of one another, and plans made as to what to do in various types of emergencies. Equipment was kept packed and ready. Most LRRPs never even took off more than one boot at a time, and only then if we had to inspect our feet, not for sleeping or comfort.

To prevent the enemy from possibly tracking a team into its overnight position, it was policy to wait in one place until almost dark, then to change locations quietly, so a night attack would come where the team had been, not where it was relocated.

Keeping in radio contact with headquarters was irregular. The common issue PRC-25 radio was used by most LRRP teams, but with the tall whip antenna instead of the short metal combat antenna that limited the range of the set to about five miles on a good day.

By setting up on high ground, out of the dense forest (the water in the jungle foliage bounces radio waves), and by using the fifteen-foot assembled whip antenna, a LRRP team could talk with radio relay stations prepared for them on mountaintops ten or even fifteen miles out, or wait for a prearranged time to make contact with an aircraft that could monitor their signal.

Situation reports were made on a routine basis in this manner, but emergency radio contact was usually out of the question since the communication conditions had to be right. A team in trouble could not rely on calling for aid. We had to fight, escape, and then make the time and opportunity to tell HQ we were in trouble.

The LRRPs were getting attention from higher headquarters because we were getting results. Some provisional long-range patrol platoons were scoring higher body counts than a few line infantry companies, and most of the

enemy the LRRPs killed were an accident since enemy
contact was not usually the object.

Division headquarters units for the 4th, the 9th, the
25th, etc., soon formed their official, authorized TO&E (table of operations and equipment) LRRP platoons with
MACV* approval. Provisional brigade LRRPs continued
to function, but without the amenities afforded the division
units.

Recondo School, adopted from the Airborne and established by the 5th Special Forces Group in Nha Trang,
South Vietnam, became the finishing school for LRRP
team members.

Recondo was short for Recon-Commando. It was the
army's best school for men who were going to be engaged
in small team action, alone and unsupported, against the
North Vietnamese or Vietcong.

It took three weeks to get a Recondo patch in Nha
Trang, and it was the only school in the army that featured
a real combat patrol as a finishing touch.

The subjects taught at Recondo School were highly
specialized, suited only for LRRP operations. The students
learned advanced land navigation, field medicine taught by
doctors and aimed at teams forced to keep a wounded or
injured man alive for extended periods of time, survival,
photography, rappelling from helicopters, resupply techniques for long-range patrols in the field, and enemy weapons.

Some LRRPs were also sniper-trained. The HALO
parachute (high-altitude low-opening) school at Clark Air
Force Base in the Philippines trained LRRPs along with
Special Forces, SEALs, and Force Recon marines. The
Royal Malasian Tracker School was open to LRRP team
people.

The famous Military Assistance Command, Vietnam,
Special Operations Group (MACV-SOG), operating their
own teams inside Vietnam, Laos, and Cambodia, began to

* Military Assistance Command, Vietnam

use a few carefully selected LRRP platoons in conjunction
with their own missions, particularly in Cambodia.

The official status of the LRRP units brought
changes. Soon, the "Reconnaissance" designation was
dropped, and the role of the "LRP" teams changed.

Seeing how effective the long-range patrols were at
killing enemy troops, ranking commanders began to assign
more and more combat and raid missions to us. Battalion
commanders, realizing how valuable it could be to them to
have the use of a LRP team in their own sector, used their
influence with higher headquarters to "borrow" a LRP
team for a week and conduct local reconnaissance (a function of their own recon units) to help them locate the enemy. Going "opcon" (operational control) to an infantry
battalion commander was risky for a LRP team. The infantry commander wanted to be in constant touch with the
team and move and direct them as he would his own people.

Since stealth, not speed, was one of the reasons LRPs
were survivors, teams that obeyed were taking incredible
chances to satisfy the officer.

LRPs also began to fill gaps in security for division
and brigade headquarters. While special "reaction" teams
were normally organized and held ready for emergencies
like downed choppers near base camps or quick reinforce-
ment of outposts, LRPs were often also given these tasks.

Listening-post work, strongpoints beyond some forward operations base (FOB) wire, local ambush patrols—
even guarding the perimeter began to take away more and
more of the LRP platoon's time.

The army was demonstrating its intolerance for elite
units again, forcing the LRPs back into conventional roles,
and in 1969, the ax fell.

The designation LRRP or LRP was dropped altogether officially and the term "Ranger" was substituted.
The Rangers were going to exist again as TO&E units,
instantly staffed by the LRPs.

While appearing to be a move by the military to hon-
orably restore one of its finest traditions, that of the

Ranger battalions, back to active service, this was in fact the legalization of all the misuse the LRP teams had undergone.

"Rangers" were now assigned to individual infantry companies to walk point for them, perform local recons, night security, and other infantry duties.

Long-range patrols continued to be sent out, but official SOP (standard operating procedure) on the number of men per patrol, weapons, and so forth, prevailed now, and the quality of the leadership was a gamble. Once teams had developed their own leaders, but now it was a matter of chance assignment.

Like the rest of the American effort in the Vietnam War, the Rangers were being wound down. The U.S. had no intention of winning the war, or even of stalemating it, only of getting out.

Author's Note—

This book is as true as I could make it, based on my notes and letters home, and of course on my memory. War is a confusing subject at best, so I apologize in advance for any error.

This is a day-by-day journal, a story of names, dates, and places. Some parents and wives will find their sons and husbands mentioned here. This is one of the reasons I have tried to be so accurate.

Only a few identities in this book have been altered, and for these certain men, it is for their privacy. Of course, the conversations throughout this book are approximations of what was originally said.

FRANK CAMPER

Long-Range Reconnaissance Patrol

25 February 1967: The Insertion

It was very cold in the helicopter this high and this early in the morning. I couldn't recognize specific landmarks, but the area was familiar. I was back in the mountain country along the Cambodian border.

For this mission, it was again Steve Steffens and Payne who rode with Mott and me, toward the new 1st of the 12th firebase.

This was my first extended mission with the LRRPs, and the anticipation of it lay in my stomach like a brick. I had to do well now.

After freezing in our thin shirts for fifteen minutes, I saw the LZ far below us, partially obscured by the mist evaporating from the forest in the sun's first rays. It was a brown scab of earth on a green mountain, as isolated as an island at sea.

I got a better look as we circled down. Great portions of the land around it were burned off black by napalm strikes, pitted by clusters of bomb craters, evidence of the recent battle to establish this miserable, dusty outpost.

Our Huey touched down only long enough for us to jump off, the area still too dangerous for such a good target as a chopper to tarry. We were left standing in the debris of several helicopters that had never gotten off the ground again.

Around us, work details were repairing the defenses shot up just three days ago. We made our way through the activity to the HQ bunker, which was shaded by a cleverly hung cargo parachute.

Mott reported to the operations officer, and went down into the command bunker while we waited outside and stayed out of the workers' way. This firebase was a busy place.

Mott returned a few minutes later. "I got the briefing," he said. "Let's go find a place to talk." We moved near the perimeter and dropped our gear, sitting in a semicircle around our map.

He used his knife as a pointer. "Here we are," he began, touching the tip of the blade to a spot by the edge of the sheet. "It's almost three thousand meters from this firebase to Cambodia."

He moved the knife up slightly. "To our northeast another three klicks, the old Red Warrior LZ. This is where the 1st of the 12th lost so many people last year. It's supposed to be watched by the NVA now. With this LZ so close, they think we might drop another CA [combat assault] in there."

A Chinook hovered in and dropped a sling of 105mm artillery ammo, the turbulence drowning us in dust. Mott waited, allowed the distraction to fly away, and continued.

"Our primary mission will be to check out that area. If we can do that, and we have time, S3 wants us to take a look into Cambodia and see where the dinks have their base camp."

I could see I wasn't going to be disappointed for my first long mission. "How bad are the dinks around here?" I asked Mott. He breathed deeply, seemingly reluctant to answer.

"An ambush patrol hit a squad of them three hundred meters out last night. Two days ago they almost overran this firebase. They're out there."

"Fire in the hole!" a voice bellowed from the headquarters bunker, and all around us, men dived for cover. We didn't know what was happening, but joined them unquestioningly.

An explosion rocked the hill so sharply I thought the entire firebase might have moved over two feet to the west. My head hurt as I looked up. A pillar of smoke and dust dwarfed our position. "What was that?" Steffens choked.

An infantryman lying on his belly close-by laughed. "They just blew a five-hundred-pounder outside the wire. We had a couple of dud bombs after the air strikes." I sat up, brushing dirt out of my hair. "Were you here in the air assault?" I asked the trooper.

"Second wave," he said. "You guys are with brigade recon, right?" Payne nodded affirmatively. "Shit," the soldier exclaimed. "I wouldn't set foot outside the perimeter for a million dollars. Charlie is all over the place out there."

"We heard. How bad was the battle?" I asked, getting back to my original question.

"Bad enough," the dusty trooper replied. "It was bad enough."

The sun was getting hot fast as soon as it rose above the trees. We tied up a poncho liner as shelter, and rested, taking in the sights.

The work parties dug out the bunkers along the perimeter, and increased the fields of fire. A mass grave for the Vietnamese had already been filled outside the perimeter, and the more recent finds of body parts were dragged to the place and buried in a shallow ditch.

"We're pulling listening post tonight," Mott said, "and going on our mission from there. We won't come back in the firebase."

We ate chow with the firebase, served out of their sandbagged kitchen, waiting for the night.

At dark, we put on all our equipment and reported to the perimeter for the listening-post duty.

"Be careful out there," a sergeant warned us. "There's

still butterfly bombs and unexploded CBUs* the engineers
didn't get, and plenty of chopped-up barbed wire."

The wire could snag us, causing unnecessary noise,
but the bombs were killers. We climbed out over the wire
and tiptoed single file into the dark.

Payne led us, heading for a spot we'd been told was
marked by the remains of a burned Huey helicopter. I
stepped on a bomb not twenty meters away from the
firebase. It was partially buried in the soil. "Stop," I managed to say between clenched teeth.

Steffens moved very close. "What is it?" he whispered.

"Bomb . . . my foot . . ." I answered. Steve
kneeled, running his hand down my leg, to my boot, then
onto the bomb.

I couldn't breathe. Then Steffens stood, muffling a
chuckle. "It's a flare canister," he said. I moved on, cha-
grin and relief canceling each other out.

We found the spot where they wanted us. The helicopter was a disintegrated pile of mechanical oddments and
melted aluminum. Tiny white triangles of paper littered
the ground, the corners of a burned manual from the ship.

The area smelled like death. I gagged in the odor. Did
they leave bodies in the chopper? No, it must be some dink
corpse no one has tripped over yet, I thought.

I fully expected our LP to turn into a blind midnight
shoot-out, but the hours dragged by without bother. We
swapped guard, actually able to sleep after worry was replaced with boredom.

The dawn arrived cold and foggy. Mott gave the signal and we came to our feet and entered the ghostly forest,
the mist smothering our footfalls.

For an hour there was no noise to disturb the unreal
quality of the morning as we trod softly through the dew-
soaked bushes. My trouser legs and boots became as chilly
and damp as if we'd forded a stream.

You move with care and caution when your life de-
pends on it. We lifted our feet high as we walked, setting

* cluster bomb units

them down slowly, toeing twigs and roots out of the way, pausing every few meters to kneel and listen.

When blue sky finally shone through the treetops, and we stopped to rest, we found a trail and made radio contact with the firebase. I had counted a thousand meters we'd traveled, a third of the way to our objective.

No small infantry patrols had been sent into this area, for fear of losing them. Three companies operating out of the firebase were working east from us, in hopes they might drive the NVA this way, west toward Cambodia.

I covered tailgun, Steffens watched the flanks, and Payne and Mott held the center. Mott had a long conversation with the firebase over the radio, his map before him, weapon and hat laid aside.

Mott marked the location of the trail on the map, while the rest of us guarded both approaches. "We'll go north as long as this trail holds out," he said. "You take point."

I resolved to shoot first and ask questions later, switching to full automatic and proceeding up the path. This was baiting the tiger and we all knew it. One of the laws of jungle warfare is that if you want enemy contact, get on a trail.

I began to sweat from nervous tension, finding myself frequently holding my breath rather than risk the noise of inhaling or exhaling.

The team followed me, imitating my every move, watching my reactions, stepping where I stepped. The suspense was numbing.

In many places the overhead was so dense the sunlight couldn't penetrate. The trail was dim, beset by shadows, the rightful province of the ambusher.

The trail had a destination. I spied the first bunker far enough in advance so that I could blend down into the shrubbery gracefully. The team behind me went to earth so quickly it seemed a breeze had blown and, like smoke, they had disappeared.

Something was wrong. We were too close to the bunkers not to be dead already if the NVA were alert. I took a good look around. The bunkers seemed to be deserted. Soil had sunk between the logs and the firing ports were covered with withered camouflage.

I signaled for the team to stay down, and I checked out the nearest hole by creeping over to it. I was right. These were all old fortifications. I gave an all-clear whistle, and the team came out.

"Looks like a company or more dug in here," Mott said, surveying the positions. He took out his notebook and began to make a diagram of the bunkers.

We began to recover from the exertion of the day, muscles unknotting, fatigues drying out, stomachs growling for food. I pulled a chicken-and-rice from my rucksack, boiling a canteen cup of water to reconstitute it, and sat back to wait.

I hadn't eaten all day, and I was starving. The ration slowly absorbed the water, swelling the packet. I had twenty minutes to wait for the dehydrated ration to reconstitute, but it seemed like an hour to my empty stomach.

To top off a hard day, a plague of sweat bees descended on us. They buzzed and lit everywhere, coming right back after being swatted off, trying to crawl into the corners of my eyes and into my mouth. I draped a handkerchief over my face.

I made a mistake then. My attention wandered for just an instant. I heard a slight sound near where I sat, and looked swiftly around to see what it was.

I found myself looking straight into the eyes of an NVA. He had come out of nowhere! I was sitting nearly out of his line of vision as he glanced in my direction. He acted as if he had not seen me. I was too stunned to move. He continued to look around, seemingly oblivious to my presence.

Then he casually turned to my left and walked out of sight. I couldn't function. Had he seen me? We had looked each other in the eye! I snap-rolled into a depression in the earth against some roots, flicking the safety off my CAR. I detected no sound. He had to be still out there. Probably just a short distance away, crouched in the underbrush.

I looked back and saw Payne as he repacked the radio equipment. I waved at him. He didn't look up. I motioned frantically, Payne totally not noticing me for what seemed to be one eternity.

When Payne finally saw me, he reacted by tapping Mott and going down into the thicket. We waited. Disaster on the first day? Maybe not. My heart knocked against my ribs so loudly I wasn't sure I could hear anything else.

Payne inched up to me. I indicated. *One dink, moving that way,* in a sign language. Payne pointed to himself, and to the right flank, then to me and to the left, motioning we should go out and get our visitor.

We tried the impromptu pincers movement, but only found each other and the trail on which the man had made his escape. "This is how he got up on me without making any noise," I whispered to Payne. The trail was well used and wide.

We crawled back to the old bunkers to wait and listen.

I reached over and pulled my ration package to me, still hungry despite the circumstances. I found I was shaking so badly trying to eat, I was spilling half the rice off my spoon. When we had finished trying to eat, Mott told us to prepare to move, pointing to the trail.

The trail passed on through the bunkers and went for higher ground. I walked forward a few meters and found another trail branching off ours.

"We'll go north as long as the trails do," Mott said. "I believe they'll take us right to the Red Warrior LZ. And start looking for a good place to spend the night. I want to find a good one before it gets too late."

I agreed. This place was too damn active for us to be stumbling around in the dark. I searched carefully as we advanced, turning down any place that didn't afford maximum protection. It was easy to stay on our compass course. All I had to do was move from one trail to another. We were in a network.

It was hours before I came across some good high ground, and I led us up into it. It was so steep it was hard for us to climb. That was fine. Anyone trying to do it at night would make a hell of a lot of noise.

I pulled up from tree to tree, resting in place occasionally. I reached the top dripping with sweat and bleeding from thorn pricks and grass slices, but I didn't just barge in. I hugged the hillside below the crest, listening, calculating how fast I could jump backward and get away if the hill was already claimed for the night.

I peeked over a fallen log and scanned the hilltop. Safe so far. Loping in a crouch, I covered the distance across the small knoll and took cover behind a tree, looking down the opposite slope.

It wasn't as steep on the far side, being part of a ridge. I waved the team up, and we secured the hill for the night, spreading out. I chose the lower part of the slope, the team assuming its usual defensive position: team leader and RTO in the center, point and tailgun at the far ends.

A stick thrown by Mott hit me in the back while I waited. I turned and felt my heart sink as he gave me the *Be quiet* sign. Payne had his M-16 ready, his attention on something near us.

I picked up my weapon, moving nothing but my arm, believing we were about to be attacked. Mott and Payne sneaked into the foliage, moving with absolute silence. Then I heard it for myself.

A short distance away people were walking by, the scuffing of sandals on packed dirt very clear, voices in Vietnamese conversing without fear of detection.

They walked away. I had edged downward until I was absolutely flat against the ground. I realized we'd camped right beside another trail. Mott looked up at me, the whites of his eyes showing all around his pupils.

We dared not try to leave the hill—they would catch us for sure—but if we stayed here, all it would take was for one of them to get lucky and step off the trail, and zap, instant catastrophe.

When it became fully dark, we pulled in together. Payne made the last radio report of the day by only keying the handset and saying nothing aloud. We just couldn't afford it. We didn't unpack anything, lying with our rucksacks beside us.

Later, lights began to flash in the sky toward the firebase we had left. No one was asleep, so we raised our heads, hearing the sound of gunfire drift in on the wind. They were getting hit again.

The firebase responded with its artillery, firing out rounds in all directions and ranges. Flares went up, and tracers arced over the jungle, red for ours, green for theirs. A burning parachute flare fell into the treetops near us and took away our night, until it sputtered out.

Several stray artillery shells sailed in and hit our ridgeline, sounding much louder at night, the blasts echoing into the valley. Even a marker-round canister or two came whistling down and smashed into the trees, all too near for us.

And we soon had company again. A North Vietnamese squad rushed by us on the hidden trail, equipment bumping, heading for the action.

The night and the battle progressed. More NVA went past us, all involved in their own problems, none even guessing we were in pissing distance.

Then a roar greater than the fight below us vibrated through the valley. I glanced up and saw what appeared to be a million red tracers plunging out of the night sky.

Puff! The old C-47 cargo plane with the electric Gatling guns! Puff belched another terrific volley, an unbelievable column of pure bullets that soaked the forest below like a deadly rain.

That was the end to the fighting. No army could stand up to Puff. The dragonship's engines droned lazily overhead, occasionally spraying around the firebase with a breath more deadly than anything imagined in King Arthur's day.

Then it started coming our way! We had no arrangement for radioing anybody to get Puff away from us, the miniguns drowned out everything, and I expected the fire to nail us to the hill. I had heard of men being killed accidentally by Puff, hundreds of meters from the "beaten zone."

All things considered, it was a long night. The NVA retreated on our trail until dawn, trickling by, disorganized, carrying their wounded and dragging heavy loads.

As soon as it was light enough to see, we were ready to leave. Payne made the radio report, having to repeat himself to be understood, he spoke so low into the mike.

We needed speed, and got off the ridge the fast way, via last night's highway. It was a fresh trail, leading into the hills.

Once we were on low ground and headed for the old Red Warrior LZ, we ducked off the trail and took to the woods again. Evidence of enemy movement was everywhere we looked.

The layer of leaves on the ground had been trodden down in many places by men walking in single file. The dampness of the morning dew betrayed them. The untouched leaves glistened damply. The disturbed leaves were dull. It was easy to see the winding routes Vietnamese patrols had taken only hours before.

We covered the distance to the LZ before noon and without incident, being very careful. I had point again, and saw the first of the NVA fortifications that circled the old LZ.

We stealthily slipped into the old bunker line, the clearing visible ahead of us. The team lay back as I advanced to scout the LZ. I parted the high grass and peered into a vast open field. In the center, like a target, was the landing zone itself, the scars of the battle only now being reclaimed by nature. The pitifully shallow fighting holes had begun to vanish under patches of grass and shrubs.

The line of fire from the NVA position to the LZ was absolutely clear. No wonder they got their butts kicked, I thought dismally. It was so easy to imagine the horror out there, exposed from all sides, the helicopters being shot down, no place to run.

It took time, but we walked completely around the LZ, charting the positions and marveling at them. It was very slow work, checking for booby traps, pacing off yardage, guarding and watching.

Every bunker was firmly roofed over, the mortar pits looked like wells, and trenches connected all the heavy weapons positions. Antiaircraft guns had been set in between the recoilless rifle and mortar emplacements, so a chopper flying across the LZ would be like a clay pigeon launched before a crowd of skeet shooters.

It was nearly dark when we had finished the recon job and had eaten. We sent a long radio report back, describing the patrol up to this point. But as Payne signed us off and packed his mike and antenna, Steffens reached down to his feet and pulled up a strand of buried wire.

"Commo wire!" he exclaimed in a loud whisper. It was gray Chinese issue, not the black U.S. Army wire. "Follow it," Mott ordered.

Steffens ripped the line out of the earth until he came to a tree. It joined a terminal there, spliced into another line. Steffens held up the fistful of wire.

The splice was insulated by paper, and the paper was still fresh. We looked it over closely. They had recently wired this place, expecting to use it again. That answered all our questions for this mission.

Mott pointed to the slight rise toward the west. "Let's get into those thickets," he said, "and take cover for the night. Steve, lead out."

Steffens led us to an entanglement of dried bamboo and vines, and we crawled in like rabbits into a warren. After dark, we moved a hundred meters away on our hands and knees before we slept, to confuse any NVA that might have spotted us earlier.

The stars came out brilliantly and we rested, secure in the dense underbrush, wondering what the NVA were doing tonight. My apprehension was subdued, but it did not go away. We had enjoyed incredible luck so far. It could not continue.

We stayed late in our haven, eating our LRRP rations and making coffee, organizing our gear and watching the

LZ through a hole in the foliage. The sun was high by the time Mott announced our next move.

"We're taking a straight 270 degrees west," he told me, "right to the border. We have enough rations to stay out two more days."

I was given the point again, and I kept a steady pace, pausing only long enough to examine a bit of evidence here or there that the enemy had also been this way.

It was as hot as two hells by noon. The forest had become lush jungle, enmeshed in swampy lowland and thick, green mossbeds along the streams. We ran out of energy pushing through the mass of it, sweat pouring off us, a direct sun cooking us unmercifully.

We found a slight clearing and fell into it, throwing our gear down and gasping for breath. Payne wiped the sweat from his neck with his flop hat. "Where the fuck are we?" he asked, his voice weak from the exertion.

Mott slipped his map from his thigh pocket. "About right here, I think," he said, indicating a place on the border. So this was Cambodia. It didn't look a bit different from Vietnam.

"We need to get an exact fix on where we are," Payne insisted. Steve looked around. All we could see was swamp and rain forest infested with vines. "Can't tell anything from here," he stated.

"I'll climb that tree," Payne volunteered, gazing at a tall stand of trees about a hundred meters away. Steve picked up his rifle. "I'll pull security for you," he said. Payne stripped off his shirt and boots, and slung a pair of binoculars over his neck.

He came back down skinned up a bit, but loaded with information. "I'd put us right on the border," he said as he dressed. "I could orient my map and get those mountains and these streams lined up just right."

Mott considered that briefly, then stood and pulled on his rucksack. "Okay. We're on our way home now. Camper, take the point. Back azimuth 90 degrees, let's go."

I aimed my compass, the arrow pointing our way

back. We slopped through the swamp, trying to keep on the more solid ground as the humidity made the air itself dense and oppressive. Sweat ran in my eyes, and my uniform was chafing and binding, as wet after ten minutes' walking as if I'd dived into the stream.

As I walked through the grass and water, watching where I put my feet, I saw the footprint. It was a tire-tread sandal print, freshly made in the sandy soil alongside the water.

I felt a shock race straight up my spinal cord. They were here, close. Mott looked at the print. "Turn around, go the other way!" he whispered.

I hurried past the team and retraced our steps. The guy who had made that print was only a few minutes ahead of us. I damned the circumstances that had put us here.

I was cautious, measuring my progress in minutes of life and not meters of ground. Mott whistled. I looked around and he motioned for me to hurry, by pumping his fist up and down like a drill instructor ordering doubletime.

I signaled an unmistakable refusal. Mott waved me aside and took point himself. I let him go by and fell in behind. He began to move fast, without caring how much noise he made.

We got out of the swamp and climbed a bombed-out hillside, finding ourselves in a morass of dying elephant grass. Mott hadn't slowed down at all. I wondered if he was giving any thought to where he was taking us.

A semipath through the grass attracted Mott. It had been pushed down before. We tromped on through the grass, chasing Mott, getting more lost by the meter.

Suddenly Mott seemed to fall in a most awkward way, his hat and rifle flying. I thought he'd tripped over a vine. I stopped, and sidestepped off the trail, squatting down, expecting Mott to get back to his feet.

Mott was scrambling to free his rifle from the vines. "Sarge," I whispered, "what's wrong?" Mott looked back at me, his face a mask of terror. Something was very wrong. "Dinks?" I asked. Mott could see something I couldn't.

"Shoot!" I said.

He did nothing. "Goddammit, if you're not going to fire, I am!" I threatened, unsure of the situation. I lifted my weapon and was flipping it off safe when a shot exploded from in front of me, blowing the grass back in my face. My ears rang.

I pulled the trigger instinctively, but my CAR fired just once. I almost had heart failure. I glanced down and saw the selector was only on semi.

I didn't take the time to flip it to full auto. I blasted out the whole magazine in a sweeping fan, my trigger finger moving like lightning.

The shit hit the fan for real then. A deafening cascade of small-arms fire erupted from in front of us. I saw Mott twitching, and thought he was being shot. Bullets hit all around him. I changed magazines, though I wouldn't realize I had done so until I found the empty mag in my shirt later.

Leaves flew off their branches around us and dirt hit my face as near misses bracketed me. I cringed, waiting for the impact of the rounds in my body.

I changed to automatic, somehow making my hand obey, as a Vietnamese jumped up surprisingly close, his AK-47 smoking from muzzle to magazine well, trying to see if he had hit Mott.

I was already pressing the trigger again as he exposed himself, and it was only by chance he was in my line of fire. He never saw me. I swung a burst across his chest and he disappeared, arms flung wide, his weapon spinning through the air.

Unhurt, Mott launched himself off the ground and passed me screaming, *"Go! Go! Go!"* I needed no urging. I was right behind Mott, running as I'd never run before.

It sounded like a firing range behind us. What had Mott done, stumbled into a platoon? I raced through the woods, dodging trees, breaking down vines, losing sight of

Mott. My hat was knocked off. Where were Payne and
Steffens? The NVA were shooting at me with every jump.

I ran into the clearing we'd passed earlier. It was six
inches deep in napalm ashes, and I saw Mott ahead of me,
leaving a wake of dust behind him like a whirlwind.

I caught up with him when he tried to leap through a
forked tree stump and became stuck. I grabbed him by the
seat of the pants and lifted as I passed, literally flipping
him over the fork; he regained his feet and outran me.

The swamp was straight ahead, and I caught sight of
Payne and Steffens waiting there for us. Mott and I dived
into the swamp, totally out of breath. The gunfire had
ceased.

Mott grabbed for the radio handset from Payne, getting me caught in the middle and tangled in the cord. I
accidentally burned myself on my weapon, the short barrel
and flash suppressor as hot as a furnace. "I got one, I got
one . . ." I heard myself saying.

"My map, I think I lost it," Mott croaked. In my own
semistupor of exhaustion I heard that statement. A map
was gold to the NVA, especially one of ours marked with
patrol routes and coordinate codes.

Steffens watched the grass. "We gotta get the hell out
of here, I think they're coming after us!" he warned. Mott
radioed battalion again. "Three-Three, I am changing to
another location, wait out," he said, and began to slog out
of the damp. "Let's go," Mott said nervously.

We trotted to higher ground, so tense an insect
couldn't have moved without catching our eye. We found a
break in the trees and laid out an aircraft marker panel;
Payne hastily set up the radio and Steffens and I staked out
the security.

Steffens cursed; his weapon was malfunctioning. He
discovered it wouldn't change to automatic and had to be
pried off safe with his knife. Payne swapped weapons with
Steve while Mott called in our position.

We could see two helicopters in the air about five
klicks away, and I hoped the firebase would relay our situation to them. But the minutes ticked past and the chop-

pers flew on. "FAC's coming," Mott said excitedly, "get that panel out where he can see it!"

Talk about service. The small green spotter plane was on our radio frequency before Payne could move the panel. Mott keyed the handset and FAC rode the beam in. Payne stood and held the orange panel up like a big bedsheet, what a target.

"He's got us!" Mott said. Payne gratefully dropped the panel. "He says there's a bomb crater six hundred meters west of here, and to get to it!" Mott said.

The two helicopters had caught FAC's call and banked back toward us. Help at last! We ran to the crater, the drumming of the rotor blades getting closer.

I was the first man on the top. It must have been a hell of a bomb that had cleared this hill; it was as bare as a baby's butt. Only one tree was left standing, and it had no bark or limbs.

I saw the crater, the only cover anywhere, and made for it as fast as my rapidly expiring legs would take me. Two helicopters were approaching us in the sky from the east. We'd have transport in a matter of minutes.

But surprise! The NVA had beaten us to the hill. I saw one hiding in a bush, looking the other way. His khaki uniform gave him away.

"Steve, there's one!" I yelled to Steffens, who was close behind me, firing a full magazine at the bush. The man wasn't there anymore when I hit empty. Steffens saw another dink at the far end of the hilltop and blasted him at fifty meters, from the hip.

I saw the man scream and go down. I reached the bomb crater, and the team piled in on me. The NVA ambush was sprung, and its fire was unleashed on us, kicking dirt up all around our hole.

It was a small crater, and the whole team with rucksacks crowded it badly. The first helicopter came in low, trying to find a place to pick us up. Ground fire drove it away.

We threw red smoke toward the trees and Mott called the spotter plane for support. The second Huey was a gunship. He radioed Mott, asking for an azimuth to the enemy from the smoke. Mott quickly supplied that information.

The gunnie made a firing pass, quad M-60s stuttering, hot brass cartridge cases pelting us. The trees in the fire swayed in the onslaught, grass and brush disintegrating in billows of dust.

I crammed another magazine in my weapon and hammered it out in one pull of the trigger, putting out suppressive fire to our left flank. Steve emptied magazines off to the right, and Mott and Payne peppered the front.

"Get down! Rockets!" Mott shouted in the din, and we pressed into the soft earth of the bomb crater. The Huey barreled in like a fighter plane, rocket pods flaring, streaks of fire roaring over our hole, and the tree line exploded into a deafening storm of roots and flying splinters.

"He's coming back!" Mott said, his voice sounding distant to my numb eardrums. The chopper cleared out his rocket racks, dumping everything. The projectiles went by just a few meters over our heads, but one caught our lone tree.

It was a white-phosphorus missile. It hit the very tip of the only standing obstruction on the hilltop and went off, showering us with a thousand arcing bits of incandescent particles. If there had been somewhere to go, we'd have unassed that crater then.

Incoming fire halted completely after the last rocket run. The gunship chose a new direction to rip up the trees from, and blazed down, machine guns running wild. We added as much of our fire at the tree line as we could, our hole filling with expended cartridge cases.

The smoke from the burning trees covered the hill thickly. We lost our visibility and had to stop shooting as Mott announced, "Slick coming in, cease fire!"

The rotor wash from the Huey blew the smoke down and outward as it hovered in carefully. I stepped on Payne's shoulder as I jumped out of the hole, and Mott scrambled out and outran me again as we dashed for the helicopter.

Mott had so much speed built up, he ran all the way

around the ship and came in through the opposite door. Payne made it out of the hole and ran at the helicopter, but something was wrong with his balance. I didn't realize it then, but all during the firefight my CAR-15 muzzle had been inches from his ear, and the firing had temporarily upset his equilibrium. Payne slammed into the doorgunner's machine-gun mount, and had to be pulled bodily into the helicopter.

I was third, as I had slowed down to cover Payne, raking the trees with one of my last magazines, and as I ran for the doorway, firing at the enemy with just one hand holding my CAR-15, my last two or three rounds punctured the tail boom of our own helicopter.

Now we were all in but Steve. He had remained in the crater and continued to fire, dutifully covering his team, performing his tailgun job to the last. He rose and made the dash, the strain showing on his face. His Starlight scope fell from under his rucksack flap.

He knew it fell. He stopped, his eyes still on us, and turned, going back after the instrument.

The rotors were spinning at takeoff speed, and our skids were off the ground. Payne was lying nearly unconscious on the deck, and the smoke was still obscuring the trees.

Steffens got to us just as the pilot propelled us upward. Mott and I desperately grappled at Steve's pack straps, hoisting him in, his feet dangling out during the fast, high climb.

I took one breath and collapsed against the bulkhead, watching the burning hill get smaller in the distance. My Lord, we were out of it.

21 July 1966: The Infantry Business

Fort Lewis, Washington, was near Seattle and close to its port facilities. It was a natural debarking point for troops being shipped to Asia.

American soldiers had left Seattle in troopships bound for combat with the Imperial Japanese forces in the Pacific, with the North Koreans and Red Chinese in Korea, and now it was being used to send us to fight the Vietcong and North Vietnamese in Vietnam.

Troopships and combat vessels had carried my father and uncles to war from the U.S. Pacific coast. Now, at nineteen years of age, as a private in an infantry brigade's headquarters company, it was my turn.

Riding trucks and buses, the 2nd Brigade, 4th Infantry Division, had moved from Fort Lewis to the docks on the 21st of July, to board the U.S.S. *Walker,* an aging troopship with rust streaks on her hull and the distinction of having been twice sunk and raised.

We laboriously filed up the gangplanks, wearing fully packed rucksacks, carrying heavy duffel bags and new M-16 rifles, sweating in the summer heat under our steel helmets.

Getting everybody to a compartment in the pack of humanity was slow, with much pushing, doubling back, swearing, and banging of rifles and heads into plumbing and low hatchways.

We struggled with our packs and cumbersome, weighty duffel bags in confined spaces, often clashing with another column of infantry trying to move in the opposite direction.

Work gangs of soldiers manhandled large crates and boxes down hatches into the holds, performing amazing balancing acts and displays of strength probably not seen since the pyramids were built—or the last troopship had been loaded.

I stuffed my duffel bag into a niche near the bunks in the Head and Head Company compartment, and stuck my rifle and rucksack onto the taut canvas hammock precisely at the top of the five bunks (the navy called them "racks") that stretched from overhead to deck.

We were below the waterline, near the bow, and the hull actually tapered in on us. I climbed up onto my rack, pushing the ruck and M-16 aside, and gasped in the heat

and lack of oxygen. Almost touching my nose was an array
of pipes all bolted to the overhead. I grabbed them to help
lift my body up so I could shift positions, and let go in
pain. The pipes were carrying hot water.

While we fought for places to exist belowdecks, the
Walker crew lifted the gangplanks, and tossed off the haw-
ser lines to the dock.

Tugs nosed in and pushed us away from the pier, only
the men still on deck able to see the activity. I knew we
were under way when I felt the engines vibrating through
the hull of the ship.

I wanted one last look at America, and leaving my
equipment, I went up the stairs and ladders to the hatch,
and climbed onto deck.

The long shoreline of Washington State was getting
smaller in the distance, the docks busy with shipping and
the movement of small and large boats and ships.

There had been no band, no farewells, no ceremony.
Once the *Walker* was out of the way, the *Gordon* would
move in to take on our heavier equipment like trucks,
jeeps, helicopters, and artillery pieces, sailing a day or two
behind us.

I would have liked to wait and watch until I couldn't
see land anymore, but I had to get back below, because I
knew our section leaders would be trying to check personnel lists, and we still had a lot of work to do.

Like a cartridge in the chamber of a rifle, our destiny
was set.

---

2 August 1966: Naha, Okinawa

Twelve long, hot days passed with the special monot-
ony that only slowly crossing the ocean can create.

At first, our officers attempted to keep us busy with
make-work details and training classes on deck, but even

that melted away in the lethargy. The Pacific Ocean was picture-postcard blue, and the weather calm.

The ship had two galleys, one fore and one aft, and they fed around the clock. Each compartment had a chow schedule that required the troops to report three times each twenty-four hours, but not necessarily at normal meal times.

I worked with the brigade operations staff, plotting our course each day on naval charts, and sorting and reviewing orders, reports, and other paperwork.

We passed the islands in the Iwo chain as we approached Okinawa, including Iwo Jima itself, where Japanese and American armies had fought so bitterly twenty years before.

Now we saw Japanese merchant ships passing us on the trade lanes, and were glad to catch a glimpse of other people. Yesterday's enemy was today's friend, and it caused me to wonder at what point in the future we would be working with the North Vietnamese, and fighting an ally we had today.

We were to dock overnight in Naha, take on fuel and drop off mail, and leave early in the morning. The officers were allowed to visit the island, but not the enlisted men.

A diversion from the voyage was the announcement of a talent show. The ship had some drums and electric guitars and amplifiers as part of its equipment, and after a few days of organization, the show was ready.

I was with a group using the instruments to do the 1950s hit "Love Potion No. 9." I didn't play, but I was the only one who knew all the words.

The show was held in the open on the foredeck, using one of the big cargo hatches as a stage. The troops crowded around it, yelling, cheering, encouraging act after act. I was surprised at how good some of the acts were.

When it was time for our song, Naha harbor came into sight. We had been seeing the island all morning. It was a clear, sunny day, and we were singing on the bow, the beat of the drums and the driving notes of the electric guitars making the *Walker* sound like a floating jukebox.

I realized the show had been timed. We were supposed to come into Naha singing and cheering. The army wanted to show how carefree we were, how good our morale was.

That was how we sailed into Naha, looking like happy fanatics, just one big party. I felt like a fool.

Tuy Hoa, our intended destination, was canceled. We were to be diverted to a location far inland in the central highlands of Vietnam, near a city named Pleiku. That was a large change, because Tuy Hoa was on the south central coast, and Pleiku was 125 miles into the country.

Furthermore, the *Gordon*, our sister ship, had suffered a breakdown, and had to dock in Hawaii. We were told we would not have our heavy equipment, vehicles, supplies, and ammunition for our landing. This was a disaster, making us dependent on what we could beg, borrow, or steal from other infantry units in Vietnam until we could be resupplied.

In company formations on deck, we were ordered to give up all of our U.S. dollars and exchange them for military payment certificates (MPC), a scrip that replaced genuine currency for us in Vietnam, to prevent dollars from going into the black markets and on to help the enemy in his war effort.

6 August 1966: Vietnam

I took a few moments off my work detail to get to a porthole and look out. It was early Saturday morning, and the sun was just up.

I saw a coast of green hills and jungles. I was transfixed by it, knowing this was the turning point of my life. Vietnam was the dragon sleeping placid in the dawn, but I had to go into the mouth of the dragon.

* * *

I pulled on my helmet and combat equipment, shouldered my rucksack, grabbed my M-16, and joined the groups of milling soldiers on deck as we boarded the landing craft.

U.S. Navy warships protected us, their guns and rocket racks aimed ashore, and we climbed down into bargelike landing craft–infantry (LCI), not using ropes, but through hatches low in the hull of our ship.

We did not have ammunition for our rifles or food in our packs. This was not a beach assault, it was just a movement ashore so we could organize and prepare to move again.

We were near the coastal city of Qui Nhon, and transport to the airstrip there was waiting, so we could be flown to Pleiku.

My LCI steered us past the sampans to the beach. I couldn't see anything from where I stood except worried faces and steel helmets, until the LCI's engines reversed, and we bumped a sandbar and lurched to a halt, and the LCI's ramp fell.

We struggled through the surf and soft sand, helping each other. Beachmasters barked orders, and directed us through the palm trees to clearings beyond.

Trucks stood ready to take us immediately to the Qui Nhon airstrip. I climbed into a dump truck, squeezing between other soldiers; the driver clashed the gears and we bounced away, landing craft still coming ashore behind us.

We drove through the city of Qui Nhon, and I saw South Vietnamese soldiers carrying old U.S. World War II carbines, M-1 Garands, and Browning automatic rifles. There were sandbag bunkers on every street corner, and barbed wire strung along the sides of roads and across the tops of walls of the low stucco and brick buildings.

As we jumped off our trucks at the airstrip, air force personnel handed us several boxes each of ammunition for our M-16s, but there was no time to load rifle magazines. We were assembled and quickly loaded into big, camouflage-painted, four-engined C-130 transport planes for the flight to Pleiku.

We filled the C-130s, sitting anywhere we could. The tailgate of our aircraft closed as we taxied down the strip and lifted off into the air, gaining altitude, but I couldn't get to a window to look out or down.

I tore open my cartridge boxes like everyone else, and clipped ammunition into my magazines.

We soon landed at New Pleiku Airport; more trucks waited for us there. We left our C-130s and boarded the trucks, gawking at the remote airstrip with its aluminum huts and buildings, rows of cargo and combat aircraft, heavily-armed perimeter defense bunkers, and barbed wire.

The sky had been clear over Qui Nhon. Pleiku was overcast, and it began to rain on us as we drove in convoy along isolated dirt roads into the countryside.

Machine-gun jeeps and M-113 armored personnel carriers of the 25th Infantry Division escorted us. The 3rd Brigade of the 25th Division had a base camp several miles from where we would establish our own. There were also some elements of the 1st Air Cavalry Division near for our security, invisibly located out in the field.

It was the beginning of monsoon season in the Central Highlands, and rain began pouring down on us, making visibility impossible; the road turned into serious mud. I saw our big, all-wheel-drive trucks sliding and swaying over the road, some of them sticking in ditches, left to be pulled out by following vehicles.

When we finally reached the end of the trip, we seemed to be in the classical middle of nowhere.

Before us lay a vast, grassy plateau. Off to the immediate west was a small mountain that rose out of the flatland, and the first thing I noticed about it was the complete tail section of a cargo plane sticking out of the trees on the mountainside—remains of an accident that should have been removed. It was bad for morale—at least my morale.

On the plateau were a few GP medium tents such as I had lived in back at Fort Jackson. It was our advance party from brigade, existing out in the grass like settlers on a wide plain in the American west.

We dismounted the trucks and slogged through standing water, trying to locate our premarked areas (there were wooden stakes in the earth with our unit designations written on them) and drop our equipment. The rain had not stopped, but it had slackened, and, dripping wet, we began to form into lines so we could pair off and set up our shelter halves.

---

8 August 1966: Base Camp

One of the men in the 1/22, my old outfit, was killed when his buddy accidentally shot him in the head with a .45 pistol. It was the 4th Division's first casualty.

I was soaking wet and tired. We worked all day to unpack the trucks that made it through the mud to the plateau, and lay in water all night either trying to sleep or trying to guard.

We ate cold C rations, and drank only the water brought to us from water trailers, and even that was in short supply. Trying to erect the big GP medium tents in the rain and mud was exhausting. The support poles sank, it was difficult to make the ropes tight, and most of our tents looked as if they had been set up by drunks.

Incredibly, it was cold and foggy. We had to wear our field jackets. I had never considered that a tropical country could be as chilly as a cold day in the States.

The fog usually lifted before noon, but the cold and wet stayed. I shivered in my soggy, clammy cotton fatigues, realizing there was a lot about this place we had to learn.

There was firing all night from distant places beyond our perimeter, which was a crude barbed-wire circle around a rain-saturated dump of supplies and frustrated men. Sometimes our own perimeter would open fire at noises and have to be brought under control.

Several mortar rounds sailed in and exploded inside our perimeter, but we didn't know if they were theirs—and therefore intentional—or ours, and just the result of a unit out there getting their coordinates wrong.

---

10 August 1966: Jungle Boots

A big Skycrane helicopter crashed down in the night two miles away from us, but we didn't know it until one of the crew staggered in the next morning. He was badly injured.

One of our Head and Head Company officers was almost killed when a heavy CONEX container fell on him as it was being unloaded from a truckbed. He was evacuated to Japan with crushed ribs.

Fighting southwest of us broke out between the Vietcong and a unit of the 1st Cav. Many of our trucks from Qui Nhon, with most of our equipment and men, still had not arrived, but the afternoon of the tenth we got a treat.

We were each issued two pairs of jungle boots off the back of a truck. The boots had deeply cleated soles and canvas uppers so they could dry more quickly than the leather combat boots we wore in the States.

As I stood in the line behind the boot truck, a patrol from the 1st Cav walked past, all of the infantrymen in it muddy and loaded with ammunition and equipment.

A tall black soldier turned to us, looking at me as I reached for my boots.

"Get 'em big, man, so they don't hurt your feet," he said.

Our trucks were at a standstill. Only helicopters were bringing in food and supplies to us within the perimeter. The rain was perpetual. We finally got the brigade tactical-operations tent up, and equipped the way we had it in Fort Lewis, but this place was another world from Fort Lewis.

The fighting holes we had scraped out of the mud

were full of water. If we'd have had to take cover in them, we'd have drowned.

One wet morning as I trudged through the mud between the headquarters bunker to the briefing tent, to post the latest position reports on the warboard, I saw an M-60 tank swimming and plowing along one of the mud-river "roads" between the tents. It was heading for a spot where at least two other tanks had gotten stuck before and had been pulled out by bulldozers. Each tank had left the hole deeper.

Right before my eyes the M-60 submerged. The crew scrambled out of it, bubbling brown water rushing in their hatches. They stood on top of the turret. If it had not been for the cannon muzzle and antennas sticking up out of the mud, no one would know there was a tank there.

During the worst of our mud, the trucks could not move, the tanks and armored personnel carriers could not move, and finally the D7 dozers were stuck. The only vehicles able to travel anywhere were the huge trucklike "Goers," with massive flotation tires and boatlike cargo beds. The mud had our modern army stuck like a fly in shit.

The mud almost got me killed. Division headquarters had arrived, and was being set up a few hundred meters from brigade, but division had nice new prefab buildings and house trailers that had been flown and placed intact by Skycrane helicopters.

Until the arrival of division, the 2nd Brigade had been the commanding presence. It was obvious the loss of status was felt at my headquarters.

We had to send documents to division every day, and this was done by messenger, with much difficulty because of the seas of mud and general flooding.

When I was told to take some papers to division, I left with my rifle and helmet, and stepped out of the briefing tent into the rain. I was up to my knees in muddy water in no time, and I began to track toward a path that might get me to my destination.

Some places were over my head in mud and water. I

had to make it from island to island on high ground, holding onto barbed wire, posts, anything.

I could see the division area ahead, uphill slightly and
out of the sargasso morass I fought through. My major
obstacle was a road, or more accurately a rutted canyon
about eight feet deep in places and running with sluice
water.

Crossing it was necessary. I found a place and slipped
down the mud sides to the water, splashing along and
looking for a way out. Then I heard the rumble of a diesel
engine.

I looked right and saw the blade of a bulldozer coming my way, collapsing the mud, grading it into something
usable. The operator of the machine was high above me. I
could see his face, but he wasn't looking down.

I ran from the dozer, my feet sticking in the mud. The
jellylike walls of the ruts were trembling with the vibration
of the cleated tracks of the big machine. I knew I could
shoot the driver if I had to, or I thought I could, but I had
to do it quickly. I could hear talk about me tomorrow: "He
was only going to division, and he just vanished."

The dozer was going to plow me under six feet of
base-camp mud. I saw a spot along the mud wall I guessed
would support me and I hit it with all fours, digging like a
cat. I went up the wall and onto the surface as the dozer
passed. The driver never looked my way.

I washed off in a pool of rainwater to make myself
more presentable before I handed the documents to division.

---

20 August 1966: The Skull

An infantry patrol brought in pieces of a human skele-
ton in a cardboard box. They had found the remains while
scouting the tree line far from the base-camp perimeter.

The skull had two bullet holes in it, but perfect teeth.

I adopted it as an ornament for my drafting desk in the
rear of the briefing tent. No one objected.

I met one of the Vietnamese interpreters assigned to
us. His name was Tri, he was twenty-two years old, and he
had a wife and baby daughter in Saigon. He admired my
bowie knife and I gave it to him. He was so short that
when he put the bowie on his belt, the tip of the sheath
touched his knee.

I was detailed one night to perimeter defense guard,
and crawled into a cesspool of a sandbag bunker with another unfortunate trooper who had drawn the same duty.

Sometime early in the morning before dawn, we were
probed, and this time we had genuine movement in the
wire. My partner opened fire, and so did I, and in a few
moments, several of the nearby bunkers were also shooting.

The next morning, blood and scraps of clothing
caught in the barbed wire were found. We had hit at least
one of the group that had tried to penetrate the wire.

I wondered if I had killed anybody.

It seemed that daily one of our men was killed in an
accident. There were deaths from gunfire, vehicle accidents, explosions of mines or grenades, and even the occa-
sional drunken gunfight.

We were three thousand young men, most not long
out of high school, confined in a barbed-wire cage with
almost any instrument of death you'd care to name and
every opportunity to handle them, and we were killing ourselves.

28 August 1966: The Rain

In the late afternoon a rain like nothing I had ever
seen hit us. It was so fierce it forced down tents, the drainage ditches overflowed, and small footbridges built over
the ditches washed away.

Our "roads" flooded out, the meter-deep ruts filling, then overflowing, and the roads vanished underwater altogether.

Trucks on the road were hopelessly trapped.

The newly established brigade field kitchen was ready to serve hot evening chow, but the squall drowned it out, turning the food into soup, then into water after it had washed out of the insulated cans.

I received word that one of the men with whom I had gone through Basic had been killed on patrol outside our perimeter. A grenade on his belt had exploded accidentally, under the body armor vest he was wearing. None of the other men on the patrol were harmed; the boy's vest protected them.

A post exchange was established in a GP medium tent at base camp, selling Coca-Cola, candy, beer, writing paper, envelopes, and cigarettes in exchange for our replacement MPC scrip, but with a limited ration per man.

Rumor had it there was a South Vietnamese government–operated whorehouse in Pleiku. The rest of the rumor claimed that if you engaged the services of one of the women there, you had best wear two condoms, because their venereal disease would eat through the outer one.

When our trash trucks made their garbage runs to the dump outside the wire, the villagers literally stormed them, plowing through our refuse as if they were searching for gold. What they found was much edible food, salable items for the markets in town, and wearable clothing.

The American Army was very rich, and our garbage was rich. I once rode out to the dump on one truck to act as security for the driver and saw the crowds as they mobbed us and the trucks ahead of us.

I was embarrassed for the Vietnamese and for myself.

A helicopter assault was being prepared by the infantry battalions living in base camp. Brigade headquarters needed an officer and radioman to accompany the assault, to coordinate orders, and maintain communications, so I volunteered.

I drew a PRC-25 field radio from supply and went with one of our captains (we had as many officers in HHC as we did enlisted men) on the mission.

The ride out to the target area in the UH-1D (Huey) helicopters took about fifteen minutes. Our helicopter landed in a rough clearing, other Hueys touching down around us as the infantrymen jumped off them, and the officer and I began to relay information back about how the flights of helicopters were doing as they approached, landed, and lifted off again.

The LZ got crowded with all of the helicopters. Another radioman near me had his antenna cut off, the whirling rotor blades of a Huey chopping it as the helicopter passed over the kneeling man.

I kept low, and only suffered one near-fatal accident, when another helicopter banked coming by and the rotor blades sliced the air just above my helmet. With the passing of the blades, the air cracked like a slap in the face.

Once all of the infantry was inserted, the captain and I took one of the Hueys back to base camp. Most of the time it had been so loud from the beating of the rotor blades I could not talk or hear over my radio.

There was little enemy contact on the assault, just a few sniper rounds fired. We were to discover that this was going to become routine.

The enemy would not stand and fight unless he was ready, and he was ready, we would learn, when he had every advantage.

1 September 1966: Operation Sewerd

The monsoons were still with us, but most of our infantry and artillery was committed to Operation Sewerd, meaning they were scattered across the Central Highlands in the rain, living off resupply from helicopters that could not fly most of the time in the storms.

I had the new-issue jungle fatigues, lightweight tropical uniforms with more pockets and better features for jungle warfare than the heavy cotton issue we had for Europe and the United States.

We were actively in the war now, and our Brigade Tactical Operations Center (BTOC) functioned day and night.

My job was to keep the warboard plotted with movements of both our own and enemy troops, indicate locations of enemy contact, and help process and analyze the mass of radio reports from commanders in the field in order to stay abreast of any developing situation.

I also kept charts on enemy and friendly casualties, our sick and wounded, incoming convoys and stockpiled supplies of food and ammunition, and assisted in the command briefings of visiting officers.

This sort of record-keeping made sense except for how we accounted for the casualties. We began with the number of overall casualties and then slotted them into separate categories, like *killed in action, killed as a result of hostile action,* and *killed but not as a result of hostile action.*

There were more, of course. This method of categorizing did not really lie, but it obscured the truth. A briefing officer could quote with confidence a given figure of GIs killed on any one day, or week, since he only used numbers from one or two of the first categories, those literally shot down dead.

Accidents, or men who died later in Japan or in the United States in the hospital, were not included.

There are many names not on the wall of black stone in Washington, D.C. They are not in the right category.

4 September 1966: Attack

Our flares fell, wasted in the rainy mist and low clouds, as the mortars or artillery tried to fire illumination at night.

It was like that on the night of 4 September, as I watched green tracers from a Communist light machine gun arc over our heads and plunge into base camp.

The gun was somewhere on a ridge of high ground just outside base camp, protected by more enemy soldiers, and it swept us with steady automatic fire.

Our artillery finally hit the ridge, and drove the enemy away, the night so dark and the fog so heavy I could hear the explosions but not see them.

As the radio man for the brigade reaction force, I was out with our platoon, lying in shallow water away from our tents and flooded bunkers, expecting the night to get worse.

11 September 1966: Mildew

My leather boots mildewed into a curled crust and I threw them away. All my heavy cotton uniforms from Fort Lewis rotted in my duffel bag. Writing paper absorbed the moisture and shredded if touched by a pen.

Uniforms hung up overnight to dry in our tents were still damp the next morning. The rains pelted us, then subsided, but there was no sun.

Drinking water was still precious. We were issued two canteens per man, per day. We trapped rainwater in empty fuel drums in which to wash ourselves and our clothes.

I had come to the conclusion the war in Vietnam was going to last a while, at least through the term of my one-year tour. On the map, Vietnam seemed to be a small country, but on the ground, looking at the plains and the distant mountains, the actual size of it became a reality.

24 September 1966: Operation John Paul Jones III

Brigade headquarters was active. We were packing again, forming up the "jump" command post we had planned for at Fort Lewis. I was part of the jump CP.

The 3rd Brigade of the 25th Infantry Division was in combat near the border of Cambodia, as part of Operation John Paul Jones III, chasing North Vietnamese soldiers through the mountains and valleys there. The 2nd Brigade, 4th Division, was going to join them.

As part of its Public Relations effort the United States had begun naming its large-scale combat operations with patriotic names instead of using warlike, military titles.

25 September 1966: Jump Command Post

Sweltering, I rode the whole day down Highway 19 toward Cambodia in the back of one of the Brigade communications trucks. It was less than fifty kilometers from our base camp near Pleiku to the Cambodian border. Our orders were to move twenty kilometers, then set up our command post. There were over seventy heavy and light trucks, jeeps, tanks, and armored personnel carriers in the convoy.

We had waited for the worst of the monsoon rains to end before going on the offensive. Now, with the skies clearing, we were moving into the areas where the North Vietnamese had believed themselves safe, their hospital, resupply, and base-camp country.

The road had turned from mud to red dust, and it billowed under our tires and choked us.

Our destination was a spot called The Oasis, which was an old military position that had been used by the French and South Vietnamese before us, and most recently by the 1st Air Cavalry, so it had a history.

We dug a good amount of old rusty munitions, mines,

and other types of explosives out of the ground at The
Oasis. I personally discovered a complete, fused 105mm
artillery shell in the earth.

We erected our brigade tents, built sandbag bunkers,
and unloaded our trucks and trailers. In less than two
days, we had a functioning brigade tactical operations center.

An organized security perimeter had been built
around The Oasis. We became a miniature version of base
camp, with our own infantry, artillery, and transportation
areas.

Our infantry battalions moved from base camp on toward the border, inserted by helicopter assault, and began
search operations to locate the enemy. The Oasis became
the functioning brigade headquarters, relaying orders to
the field battalions and controlling the resupply and support for them.

The Oasis was in the mountains, far away from the
flat plateau of base camp. We could look down below on a
South Vietnamese artillery firebase and a village, or up at
mountain peaks that rose to our north and northwest—
where our infantry was now.

I fell into the routine of the tactical operations center,
arranging for the briefings of the personnel, intelligence,
operations, and supply sections each day, and the special
meetings held in the briefing tent for visiting officers or
other Very Important Persons.

SNELL

The afternoon was hot, the sides of my tent were
rolled up and I sat idly watching the MP on duty at the
opening in the wire that led from brigade headquarters to
the road and the helicopter landing zone. He was only
about twenty meters from where I sat.

I knew the man. His name was Snell, and it was his
duty to make everyone coming into the perimeter unload
their weapons. The wooden sign beside him, propped

against a small sandbag bunker, read *2nd Bde BTOC. CLEAR YOUR WEAPON.*

A jeep stopped in a cloud of dust outside the wire, and three officers jumped out of it. The first man past Snell had a pump shotgun. He racked the slide back and Snell nodded. The second officer had an M-16. He opened the bolt and Snell nodded. The last officer had a .45 pistol. He went to demonstrate that it was unloaded, and with it pointed at Snell's groin, I heard a shot.

For an instant, Snell did not move. I thought he was okay. I had always been told people hit with .45s went down on the spot. Then, Snell collapsed, his knees buckling under him.

I jumped and ran toward him. Our medic passed me, bag in hand. Colonel Miller and other officers were pouring out of the BTOC. I moved back out of the way. Someone took the smoking pistol from the stunned lieutenant and led him into the headquarters.

Snell was carried away to the aid station quickly, and soon only the medic and I were standing there beside Snell's blood on the dirt. The medic had the actual bullet in his hand, fresh rifling marks engraved in it.

"Where did he get hit?" I asked.

"Inside of the thigh," the medic said. "It went all the way through."

Jesus, I thought. A direct hit and Snell had not wavered. The bullet still looked like new. It was not even mushroomed. The facts conflicted with every .45 knock-'em-down story I had ever heard. I realized then they were mostly myths.

I went back to my tent thinking it would be better to leave people's weapons alone as they went about their business. The more we fooled with them, the more accidents we would have.

Snell was back three months later, his leg healed. He was lucky.

I was slowly becoming accustomed to Vietnam now, and working in headquarters was beginning to disagree with me. I felt guilty seeing the infantry officers coming in from the field, or posting the brigade's daily kills and casualties on our charts. I wanted to get out to the fighting.

FLAMETHROWERS

An H-13, one of the light, two-seat observation helicopters, landed early. I was just beginning to sort through the notes on my desk when the pilot entered the operations tent.

The brigade officers were drinking coffee and preparing to begin the day. The pilot threw a stack of black-and-white 8 × 10 glossy photographs on my desk. "Look at these," he said. His mood was curt. "Just had them developed."

A small crowd gathered as I spread the photos. "The NVA had told the Montagnards if they cooperated with us, they'd get hurt," the pilot said, "and son of a bitch if they didn't keep their word."

I was looking at what seemed to be long, even groups of black circles filled with heaped ash. In the middle of each were humped human shapes, their arms entwined.

"The NVA came in the middle of the night and ran all the people into their huts, then they burned them down with *flamethrowers.*" His voice broke on the word. "Flamethrowers," he said again.

As I looked at the photographs, I understood terrorism for the first time.

---

10 October 1966: The Oasis

The small grease-pencil-drawn flag on the plastic flap over the warboard contained a cryptic set of initials. "LRRP." I noticed it was different in several respects from the regular unit markers.

There was no identifying unit code or size indication. The S3 sergeant major walked up behind me as I plotted the rest of the units. "Hey," I asked as I worked, "what does this L-R-R-P stand for?"

He glanced at the map. "That's a long-range reconnaissance patrol. The one you have there is a 1st Cav outfit. We don't have any yet."

"What size are they?" I asked. The sergeant major was already on his way out of the briefing tent. "Only four or five men, I believe," he said, and ducked out under the tent flap.

I stood alone in the big briefing tent, staring at the warboard. Many carefully assembled map sheets under an acetate flap made up the map that was our area of operations. The plastic sheet over it was dotted with units in the field, each one properly and clearly marked in rectangular flags.

Infantry. Artillery. Transport. Armor. Firebases, Forward operations bases, Special Forces camps, base camp, all in place and identifiable. One unit supporting another.

But this tiny unit was just barely on the map. Four men! And so far out! There were no friendly troops anywhere near. What did this LRRP do if they got into trouble?

I finished drawing the changes on the acetate and picked up my clipboard to leave. I looked back at the LRRP flag once more. It fascinated me. Who would want to do that type of work? How did you go about joining them? I had never even heard of LRRP before.

I walked into the next tent and found old Master Sergeant Jones of the intelligence shop. "Hi," I said, sitting down on a packing crate. "How do you go about joining one of those long-range patrol outfits?"

Jones looked at me and smiled. "You don't want any of that, son. Those people are out there asking to get killed."

I liked Sergeant Jones. He was a career man who had fought in the World War II and Korea. As far as I was concerned, he knew all there was worth knowing about the army.

"Are they Special Forces?" I asked. Jones leaned back

in his chair. "No, I don't think so. Seems to me it's all volunteers. Look in that file cabinet by the door and hand me the brigade personnel unit's breakdown."

I found the file, a thick one, and passed it to him.

"Yep. Just like I thought. We're authorized a LRRP platoon. It's only provisional though, because there's no T.O.&E on it yet."

My curiosity was at the maximum. "Sarge, what do you have to do to qualify for it?"

Jones read for a moment. "No special requirements. There's a school planned in Nha Trang the Special Forces will be running to train volunteers."

"What if I want to go?"

"If you'll wait, we'll have our own LRRP platoon right here as soon as we get organized, but you better get that idea out of your head and be thankful you work for the brigade."

I stood up and looked out the tent doorway to the mountains. They were green and far away. Somewhere out there was a patrol of only four men, entirely on their own.

As I went back into the briefing tent I looked again at the LRRP flag on the map. I knew I wanted to join. I'd find out as much as I could about it first. Being in the brigade operations shop I'd have access to the information.

I started laying my plans then to become part of LRRP.

15 October 1966: Pleiku City

I took my first opportunity to go "downtown" and visit Pleiku. All of us from HHC had been working steadily since we arrived, and none of us had even gone to town on an errand or work detail.

Once we had permission to go, a group of us took a light truck back down Highway 19, past base camp, and into town.

Pleiku was a frontier town, lost in the mountains. It

had become an armed camp, with bunkers and fortifications on the approach roads, and many South Vietnamese
soldiers stationed on the street corners.

There were too many things about Pleiku for me to
comprehend at once. The stench of garbage, open sewers,
stagnating water, and decaying market fish and vegetables
at first seemed to be overpowering.

The poverty of the people was heartbreaking, and I
was met everywhere I walked by Vietnamese with open
hands, their clothes ragged, no shoes on their feet, brown
skin taut across their rib cages.

Many children begged, both in groups and alone, al-
ternating between crying to the street vendors with their
black-market cigarettes and C rations to pleading with us,
tugging at our sleeves and trouser legs.

Any building that could be changed into a bar for the
Americans had been converted, selling bottled Vietnamese
beer, canned American beer, and black-market bonded
whisky.

Along with the bars came the prostitutes. They were
young Vietnamese girls who might have farmed in the rice
paddies or worked as laborers, but as whores sought to
make more money for themselves or their families.

They were mostly illiterate, undernourished, and
dressed in the types of clothes they believed were worn by
Western women.

Visiting Pleiku was depressing. The South Vietnamese
soldiers, who lived with it, stood at their posts, impassive
amid the squalor and suffering.

On the black market, we could buy any uniform items
we couldn't get issued from our supply, and could also get
special raincoats, hats, and insignia sewn by the many tai-
lor shops.

I knew that most of the merchandise I saw on the
sidewalks had been stolen, probably at the unloading
docks, or was sold to the Vietnamese by crooked supply
officers or sergeants in either the South Vietnamese or
American armies.

When the time came in the afternoon for us to report back to our truck to leave, I was there early. Pleiku would take some getting used to.

21 October 1966: 75th EVAC

I rode on a supply truck with a few other soldiers out of base camp to The Oasis, settled in with the cargo in the back; the driver was going fast.

We had just driven past the Cateka Tea Plantation between base camp and The Oasis. Cateka was a dangerous place; we often took sniper fire from there. Then we hit a mine.

It was not a big road mine, as mines go, and was probably command detonated (meaning someone was waiting off the road with the detonator), because we were just past it when it exploded. It made a column of gray smoke and showered rocks down on us, but did no damage.

Our driver never stopped. We just kept flying.

My left arm had been hooked over the edge of the truck bed, the wooden railing directly under my armpit, and I realized even though I had changed positions, my arm still felt as if it were asleep.

I went to the medic—the same one who had bandaged Snell—and he told me I probably had a pinched nerve. He sent me to the 75th Evac hospital in Pleiku.

The 75th Evac was a large compound of metal buildings, with concrete sidewalks, drainage pipes, and runoff ditches. I could hear the steady throb of generators and the hum of air conditioners as I walked through the double doors of the incoming-patient building.

The staff, men and women, wore fatigues and white lab coats. I was processed in, x-rayed, and told to go back to the entrance hall and wait. My arm was numb, but what I was seeing made me self-conscious to be there with such a minor complaint.

Wounded were being brought in constantly. I looked down one hall and saw a pile of jungle boots, all muddy, some bloodstained, that was almost up to my chest. They had been cut off, not unlaced.

A shout from behind jerked me out of my stupor. Able men were needed outside to carry in wounded. I could hear a lot of helicopters beating down, sounding like they were right on the roof of our building.

I had one arm that worked, so I ran out with the others, and met the Hueys just now touching down. There were over a dozen wounded on the ships, and I noticed with horror that some of them appeared to be smoking, as if smoldering from a fire.

We carried the limp wounded, their blood still fresh, inside the first building where I had been waiting, placing them on stretchers set up on sawhorses.

I got out of the way as orderlies and nurses swarmed on the row of litter cases, snipping off boots and web gear with sharp, heavy-duty scissors, and peeling off the bloody, ripped uniforms on the men.

Small stainless-steel buckets were placed between the stretchers, and I heard the distinct clink of metal the scissors pulled out of the men as it was tossed into the buckets. There were so many fragments in them some were sticking out of their faces and arms.

The scissors also cut away some ruined flesh, and that hit the buckets with a liquid splat.

One of the wounded who was not as bad as the others began to talk to us. The steel splinters in the men were from 20mm cannon, he said.

"We were just walking over the hill," he said. "The planes hit us so fast we didn't know what happened. The lieutenant was on the radio, screaming at them to stop. They got half my platoon in the first pass."

Our own jets had done it, by accident. The smoke from the wounded would have been residue of the tracer ammunition fanned to life by the helicopter flight.

The worst of the men were being hustled to surgery. I

went into the front hall and was told I was okay, and to report back to my unit.

Years later, the television show *M*A*S*H* would depict a field hospital as a comic affair, but there were no jokes, no zany characters, at the 75th EVAC.

There was just blood, boots in piles too high, and halls of desperate victims.

Alan Alda, if you only knew.

---

22 October 1966: Promotion

My promotion to E4 came through, and with it an increase in pay. I was now designated a "Specialist." The counterpart rank to Specialist E4 was Corporal, but Corporal was not a rank much given any longer.

To make Corporal, you had to first make Sergeant E5 and then get demoted one grade, from three stripes to two.

---

25 October 1966: Roy and Dale

The famous western singing, movie, and television husband-and-wife team, Roy Rogers and Dale Evans, came to The Oasis. We had a stage built for them so the troops could watch. Being in Headquarters Company, I was part of the welcoming committee, and carried Dale's handbag for her off their helicopter to the stage.

Roy and Dale sang songs and told stories about themselves and their cowboy movies, giving the men a good show and some time away from their responsibilities and worries. When it was over, Roy and Dale reboarded their helicopter, and flew back over the mountains to another camp, seeing Vietnam for themselves rather than hearing about it on the news.

I had seen their movies and watched their television shows as a child. I appreciated their effort.

* * *

The 4th Aviation was having a barbecue party, with a jeep-trailer-load of iced beer and soft drinks. They were well into it, and making a lot of noise.

I walked by, and noticed a single Vietnamese man squatting in the hard, hot sun, forced into the position by the barbed wire that surrounded him. He was in "detention," until he could be questioned. There was a woman sitting outside the wire, only a few inches from him.

She had laid a thin handkerchief across the top of the wire to attempt to shade him. It was ridiculous, but it was all she had. Neither of them were speaking. They just sat, while beside them the 4th Aviation ate their just-off-the-grill steaks and punched holes in the tops of the iced beer cans.

I didn't know anyone in the 4th Aviation, or why the two Vietnamese were there, but I didn't like it.

"Hey! Hey! Don't mess with those people!" an officer said to me. I followed my orders and walked away.

---

27 October 1966: Jump Command Post—Again

We received the order to quickly break camp at The Oasis and move deeper on into the war zone our infantry troops were establishing.

It had taken us over a month to dig in, sandbag, string barbed wire, and get The Oasis functioning smoothly. It took thirty-six hours to strike the tents, repack them and all of our equipment, destroy our fortifications, and leave in convoy.

We drove over seventy kilometers into the mountains of southern Kontum Province, our trucks heavily overloaded with tent flooring, equipment crates, and baggage.

The dusty trek ended in a huge, abandoned rubber plantation, the rubber trees planted in long, even rows as far around as we could see. We took machetes, axes, picks, and shovels, and cut places in the jungle to set up the new brigade command post. Everyone worked hard, and soon our big GP medium tents were rising out of the underbrush and bamboo.

As we worked, a warning was radioed for us to abandon the new camp, leave the tents in place, and move back to higher ground and link up with infantry units. The North Vietnamese Army was in contact with our infantry battalions, and the fighting was coming our way.

We climbed aboard our trucks and moved into the hills, where a temporary barbed-wire perimeter had been established.

It rained on us that night, the 29th of October, and while we huddled inside our trucks, in the valleys around us our infantry battalions were attacked viciously by determined North Vietnamese Army units. I could see the tracers and aerial flares from my truck, and realized the fighting was getting closer to us.

The enemy had also spotted us as we had begun to set up the headquarters, and mortar shells began to drop down the hill where we had been working.

At first light, I put on my wet boots, and jumped down off my truck. Headquarters Company's top sergeant came running down the column of parked vehicles, shouting for us to get ready, grab our weapons, and move back to the rubber plantation.

The jungle was still thick with morning mist and dripping with dew. We drove the trucks down into the plantation, being the only troops in the entire area, and dismounted, forming into squads and fire teams to sweep through the area.

I could feel my stomach contract and anticipation rise in my throat. We searched the tents we had left erected the afternoon before, wary of booby traps or snipers hiding in the greenery of the rubber trees, but as the sun broke clearly over the hills, the tension subsided.

The helicopters began flights out to the infantry units near us, to pick up casualties. It took us many hours to calculate the number of dead, both theirs and ours.

Setting up the BTOC took the rest of that day and

part of the next, all that before we could take the time to prepare our own living quarters. We had become efficient in command-post moves now, and our engineers had built us a shower tent near a stream, with pumps taking the water, filtering it, and spraying it through shower heads onto slat-board floors. We all managed to get a turn in the shower tent. The water was cold but it was wonderful. We had eaten little and rested less for the last few days, and any comfort was welcome. The 29 October battle made the news.

NEWS ITEM: 30 October 1966
'GREENHORNS' STAND FAST
SAIGON (UPI) Veteran North Vietnamese troops Saturday charged repeatedly in human-wave attacks against "greenhorn" American infantrymen in the Central Highlands near the Cambodian border.

The hard-hit GIs held their ground and killed 52 while suffering "moderate" losses.

Three U.S. Army helicopters flying to the aid of the besieged Americans were shot down by Communist groundfire. One of the aircraft crashed in flames, with "heavy casualties" to the crew.

A U.S. spokesman said the Communists apparently threw a reinforced North Vietnamese battalion against inexperienced troopers from units of the 4th Infantry Division that arrived in Vietnam only two months ago.

The Americans, in their heavy combat debut, absorbed some of the worst punishment troops of the crack North Vietnamese 610th Division could deliver during the attacks.

A spokesman for the 4th Infantry said the American defenders from the 2nd and 3rd Brigades of the 4th Division suffered "moderate" casualties during the fight— meaning they were hard hit.

Familiarity and experience had brought something else to headquarters. Our officers had discovered they could take the enlisted men and use us for personal labor. I was once ordered to wash the muddy boots of a lieutenant with my rationed drinking water, while the officer stood there wearing them.

We did all the labor to erect and sandbag the officers' tents, and we had to dig and fortify the officers' bunkers before we could make our own.

If any of the brigade officers wanted our tents or bunkers for their own, or wanted us to break down and relocate their personal sleeping tents, we had to do so.

Enlisted men were kept from buying soft drinks or beer off the mobile PX truck, but the officers had that privilege.

To top it off, our brigade maintained an officers' mess with wooden floors, tables with white linen, china and silverware, and its own ice-cream-and-ice-cube-making machine.

I was assigned KP duty there one day, and at breakfast, the officers' special cook would not let me serve the pancake syrup until he was sure it had been properly heated and poured for each officer into individual bowls.

Brigade headquarter's officers tried to live like royalty, while the rest of the men—and officers—in the infantry units and support units scratched out an existence in the field.

---

31 October 1966: The Rubber Plantation

Mail arrived; I received a Polaroid camera from home, and began taking photographs to show what our camp looked like.

I didn't know what to call our new camp. It did not yet have a name, just the code 3 Golf.

The captured enemy weapons coming from the field were all Chinese-made rifles and light machine guns. Most of them seemed to me to be in poor condition, usually rusty, with parts missing or broken. I was surprised they would fire, but they obviously did.

Prisoners our infantrymen took were also sent to us. They were young Vietnamese men, all scared, starved, and willing to talk.

I suffered an illness that severely weakened me, but it passed in twenty-four hours. I vomited until I had the dry heaves, and broke out in a raging fever. I was terribly thirsty, but promptly threw up whatever I tried to drink. For the next two days, I couldn't eat, and the least exertion caused nausea.

I did not know it at the time, but it was a malaria attack. Fortunately, the daily pills we took to prevent malaria would also keep it suppressed, except at the very beginning.

1 November 1966: Transfer

I made formal application to leave HHC and go to an infantry unit. The LRRP platoon was not yet in operation, and I didn't want to wait for it, plus I realized I needed field experience.

8 November 1966: Limbo

As the result of my request for transfer, I was moved out of headquarters and placed in the reaction platoon, which was actually a labor platoon. We did garbage removal, guard, kitchen labor, and helped improve the bunkers and trenches. One of the details I worked was riding to native villages as guard with my M-16 and picking up laborers to bring back to clear fields and fill thousands of sandbags.

The natives were not Vietnamese, but Montagnards (French for "Mountain People") of the Rhadé and other tribes. They were dark-skinned and of a different race than the oriental Vietnamese.

The Montagnards were primitive. They lived in grass

huts, pierced and distorted their earlobes, wore almost nothing but loincloths, and most of them were infected with diseases.

We paid them rice and salt for their work. They needed the nutrient iodine in our salt. Without it, they suffered a more rapid breakdown of their health.

Their skin was commonly thick, wrinkled, and spotted with infections and sores.

Despite all this, they were a proud and able people, and they worked honestly without begging, which was more than I could say for the Vietnamese.

10 November 1966: Orders

I was told to pack and prepare to leave. My orders for the infantry had come, assigning me to Company C, 2nd Battalion, 8th Infantry. I was through with the petty kings at Headquarters and Headquarters Company. I also felt I could respect myself now. I was trained to fight, and I was in a war. I belonged in the field.

My friends in brigade acted as if receiving orders for an infantry company were the same as a death sentence.

I rode in a convoy from the rubber plantation back to base camp, getting off at the C Company 2/8 headquarters filthy with road dust.

The 2/8 Battalion area was almost deserted; all of the men except a small staff were out in the field. I was told by clerks in the orderly tent to find a tent and rest until they arranged for me to be issued my equipment and sent to the field.

I located a GP medium tent, dropped off my equipment, and washed, water being plentiful from the tank trailers parked around the area.

Base camp was bigger now, and incredibly organized. The mud roads of the monsoon were packed and paved with gravel, some permanent buildings were going up, engineer teams worked in every direction, and cranes littered the skyline of tent roofs.

They were building a city where there had been a tent slum. Drainage ditches were fitted with concrete pipes, and signs identifying units and directions had been erected.

Base camp was large enough now to need signs. Months ago, those of us inside knew where everybody was.

Alone in my tent, I lay on a cot, glad to be where I was, and went to sleep.

---

14 November 1966: Firebase

I rode out to the war in a Huey, wearing my steel helmet, canteens, ammunition pouches, rucksack, and carrying a used M-16 the supply sergeant at base camp had given me.

The helicopter ride was high and long, giving me my best look yet of the mountains and jungles of the Central Highlands.

Once we landed at a Special Forces camp, to drop off a passenger, and I saw one of the Green Berets there carrying a very early model of a weapon we'd had in the test group in Fort Jackson, a short version of the M-16 rifle called the Colt Commando. I wished I had one. With its telescoping buttstock and short barrel, it was a handy weapon.

Finally, we reached a hilltop only eight kilometers from Cambodia. The skies were gray and it was raining. I got a view of the camp from the air as we circled for landing. It was all logs and sandbags, with shirtless, laboring men carrying artillery shells to the battery of 105mm howitzers dug into emplacements inside the barbed-wire perimeter.

When we landed, I was sent to report to the 2nd Platoon, and there I met Lieutenant Tossher, who would be my platoon leader, and the men in my squad.

We were isolated on that hilltop, with nothing but jungle around us as far as I could see.

Routine for our platoon was to stand guard at night, and stand guard in the daytime. In between, we filled sandbags, worked on the bunkers, or helped improve the perimeter defenses. I was not going to complain. I wanted to improve anything that might save our lives.

The artillery batteries fired night and day, making sleep while not on guard something very elusive. They were firing support for infantry companies out in the jungle on search operations, if they needed artillery to blast suspected enemy positions or had to hammer North Vietnamese trying to attack them.

NOBEL'S KNOB

My new company had been blooded in the late October battles, and I heard the men talking of what they called the "Battle of Nobel's Knob," named after Captain Nobel, our company commander.

Captain Nobel and C Company had held a hill one night against a much larger Communist force, and survived. The battle began one afternoon when C Company found a recently abandoned village and, after discovering evidence of NVA occupation, burned down most of the huts and killed all the pigs and chickens they found. They even broke the crockery in the cupboards. The village had been supporting and aiding the enemy.

After that, a soldier named Matty was killed by a sniper, and Captain Nobel called in his patrolling platoons back to the overnight hilltop position he had picked near the village.

The NVA hit them that night, probably expecting only one platoon to be on the hill rather than three. The battle went on into the night, the rushes by the NVA cut down by C Company, but at a cost in American lives. I was told some of the wounded GIs died the next day because they could not be evacuated.

Although description of the battle differed with the memory and opinion of each teller, to a man they were united on one point: Captain Nobel had kept them together, and had done everything he should have done that night as the enemy tried to overrun them.

We lived on C rations, and I began to memorize the code numbers the manufacturers used to indicate what type of food was in what C-ration box. We had B1, B2, and B3 units. It was important to learn which had candy, which had fruit, and which had my favorite main meals. I learned how to heat the rations, or boil water for coffee, with small pinches of highly flammable C4 plastic explosive.

We were issued two meals of C rations a day. We traded a lot of our canned food with each other, and experimented with mixing or spicing the food to get different tastes.

16 November 1966: Battle

I was put on listening post with Kircher, one of my squad members, our position far enough outside the perimeter of the firebase for us to give warning if we were about to be attacked by the NVA. What this meant in reality was that the enemy would make noise killing us, and the camp would be alerted.

We sat in silence, guarding each other's back, watching the forest, when shooting began, sounding to us like it was somewhere down the hill from the firebase. We decided there was a platoon taking weapons practice.

The shooting became more intense, with more weapons involved. It didn't sound like a practice anymore. I asked Kircher what we should do. He said we had to sit and wait until we were relieved of duty.

Soon artillery shells began to fall, and now we could determine they were hitting the hill beside us. That hill was higher, and steeper.

The rifles and machine gun were now an unending din. A serious battle was going on just out of our line of sight, and we were nervous.

"They must be hitting the firebase," Kircher said. "They might try coming up this way, too." We lay down, aiming our weapons into the jungle, expecting to see the uniforms and faces of North Vietnamese any moment. I had my M-16, Kircher his M-79.

"Why don't they send our relief out?" I asked, when the hour for our guard to change came and passed.

"Because they're busy as hell. We just have to stay put," Kircher said.

Now propeller-driven A1-E Skyraider fighter-bombers circled the firebase, and I could see them through the treetops. They began to dive and bomb the nearby hilltop just across the deep valley from us.

"Hell, I know what's going on," Kircher said. "That's A Company up there! They were going up to check out that hill. One of our patrols said they thought they saw an NVA patrol up there yesterday!"

Kircher was right. I had overheard the ambush patrol that had returned early that morning, just as Kircher and I were getting ready to leave, telling how they had seen a small squad of enemy soldiers quietly moving across the hilltop.

A Company (one of the line companies that made the 2nd of the 8th Infantry Battalion) had just come into our firebase last night, returning from a company-sized sweep. Since C Company had "palace guard," the battalion commander would have sent A Company up the hill.

Now it sounded as if A Company was in trouble. The thunder of the battle echoed down the valley and off the hillsides, and even from our listening post, Kircher and I could see the smoke rising above the trees from the bombs and artillery.

We waited until late in the afternoon, and decided we should return to the firebase, orders or no orders. We had been forgotten. When we reentered the perimeter, we did it with loud, clear shouts to the guards that we were American soldiers coming in.

Everyone in the firebase that could be was below-ground, taking cover in the bunkers. Pale, grim faces watched the hilltop across the valley. It was not far away, perhaps three hundred meters.

"A Company's getting their ass kicked up there," one of the men in my squad said as Kircher and I dropped into the bunker beside him.

Now that I could look directly at the hilltop, it was a terrifying sight, not for what I could see, but for what I knew was happening. The radio reports coming back to us from the A Company commander said they were pinned down, caught in a crossfire between camouflaged machine-gun bunkers, and they had casualties they could not save.

He called the artillery directly in on the enemy bunkers, which was where he and his men lay also, and talked the Skyraiders through their strafing and bombing runs.

"Better get ready," Gemmel, our other M-79 grenade-launcher man said. "They'll be sending us up next to reinforce A Company."

Sunset finally came, and C Company was not ordered up the hill. Instead, A Company managed to break off the action, saved by the coming darkness.

The men of A Company did not come back to the firebase as a unit. They straggled back in small groups, climbing up the hill to us from different sides, indicating they'd had to escape from the battle any way they could.

Some of them had lost their helmets, some their canteens and ammunition pouches. They were muddy and sweat-drenched, and they clutched dirty, burned-out weapons. Some of them were crying. Some of them were just staring into space.

By talking to the ones who would explain, we learned they had indeed gone up the hill shortly after dawn, looking for signs of the squad our ambush patrol had seen.

They walked into an interlocking bunker network, machine guns in each one, and when their point man had been killed in the first burst from the enemy, he had fallen on top of an enemy bunker.

Several men had been killed trying to reach him before the battle developed into a no-win situation for either side, the North Vietnamese trapped in their bunkers, still firing their machine guns, the American infantry trapped in hollows and behind trees, with the artillery and bombs falling on them both.

Three American bodies were left on the hill. The next day, A Company would go back up the hill to get them, refusing help from us.

One of the infantrymen from A Company had brought a captured Communist light machine gun off the hill with him, and he set it on top of a bunker, in plain sight of the hill.

"I want them to see it," he said. "I just want the bastards to see it."

19 November 1966: Near Miss

As I slept on the ground outside our squad bunker, well before dawn, a single mortar shell, whistling through the air as it fell, hit a few meters from where I lay.

It failed to explode, and buried itself over a meter into the ground. I had heard the shell coming down, and dived into my bunker as it hit.

The entire firebase went into a frenzy of action, the men grabbing their helmets as they awakened, going for cover as I did.

Not another mortar shell followed, but we lost the remainder of the night's sleep.

20 November 1966: Night Ambush

After dark, my platoon deployed on an ambush, and I lay in tension all night, listening to the nocturnal sounds of the jungle. I tried to sleep when it was my turn, but I was too uncomfortable wearing my helmet, ammunition pouches, and canteens. Ambush is an art. I wanted to learn it, since killing the enemy before he knows you're there is the best way to do it. Survival does not always allow for heroism.

When we returned from the ambush, our orders were to prepare to "saddle up," slang meaning to get our equipment ready to move out on operations. We were going to leave the relative haven of the firebase and go out in search and pursuit of the enemy.

I collected all my rifle magazines. I had sixteen in all, and I inspected and loaded them carefully.

Each man was issued several meals of C rations, and two small blocks of TNT high explosive, so we could blow down trees to clear out helicopter landing zones.

The platoon sergeant made me fire-team leader of Bravo Fire Team in our squad, my first designation of responsibility.

22 November 1966: Corpses

We started early in the morning on our push, walking out of the firebase and down into the valley, then up the hill where A Company had been mauled.

I carried one of the extra two-hundred-round boxes of M-60 machine-gun ammunition. Each squad had the responsibility of carrying two boxes to help feed the gun in case we needed it.

At the top of the hill, we discovered the shallow grave of an enemy soldier killed on the 16th. The man had been buried by his own people, and when we pulled him out of the ground with wires attached to his belt and suspenders, his head broke off and rolled to my feet. It looked like a mudball.

I kept my handkerchief over my nose as I waited by his grave, and finally we moved on. The smell of the dead was constant around the hilltop. There were corpses we were not finding.

---

23 November 1966: Walking

We did not stop until nightfall. The jungle had been incredibly thick, and our point team often chopped a path through with machetes.

We had searched an area earlier in the day that had been blasted by a B-52 bomb run. The damage was unbelievable, and it was difficult to imagine anyone living through the destruction we saw. There were bomb craters so deep a truck could be swallowed in them, and trees over a meter thick were splintered and snapped off at their roots.

Some of our men fainted from the heat. We walked loaded down like pack animals, carrying almost as much equipment and ammunition as we had body weight.

Leeches, a problem I had never had in headquarters, were plentiful. They attached themselves to our necks and arms, and had to be cut or burned off. Sometimes, if they were hidden under our clothing, they stayed on until they became so full of blood they burst, making large splotches of blood on our fatigues that resembled wounds.

We stopped to dig in and clear an LZ for resupply. We had been out of water all afternoon. I scooped out a shallow prone trench shelter, and was dry-shaving while the other men worked at their digging.

I heard the shell falling, at first faint, then louder. It seemed to be coming right into our perimeter. It was not uncommon to hear shells go over, that happened frequently, but this one was coming *down*. I looked at my friends. They were oblivious to the warning.

"Incoming!" I said, and threw myself on the ground. The men around me stopped digging, looking at me as if I were joking.

The shell was real, and hit us with a tremendous explosion. I felt the heat and the concussion. A tree fell. Men were shouting and screaming.

Our camp was dimmed with a haze of smoke and dirt in the air. The smell of the explosive was bitter. Then, nothing, not another sound, followed.

The screaming stopped. It had been some soldiers trapped under the fallen tree. When they were pulled out, we discovered no one in camp was dead or even injured, and we began to laugh about it.

"Damn, you got good ears," one of my squad told me.

We received an explanation a few minutes later. It was one of our own 4.2-inch mortar rounds that had fallen short. The mortar battery responsible for it apologized.

We had come close to being one of brigade's convoluted statistics.

Helicopters brought hot Thanksgiving dinner out to the field to us in insulated cans. The food was wonderful. We set up a regular serving line and ate everything they sent us.

26 November 1966: Enemy Contact

We walked right into the enemy that morning. My platoon led the company, and Lieutenant Tossher was up front with his radioman, on the heels of the point. I was a squad back, just putting one foot in front of the other, one more GI in a long line, wishing I were somewhere else.

A wild flurry of gunfire exploded from the point, and I dived for cover. I realized my M-16 was useless under me, and I jerked it out, trying to look forward under the rim of my helmet, but could see nothing but the roots of the tree I was behind and the jungle-boot soles of the man ahead of me.

The firing continued, our left and right flankers firing now, and I knew we had hit something big. I was trying to make sense of the situation in all the gunfire. I heard a cry for medic, knowing someone was down, and a voice up front began yelling, "Bring up the Ninety! Bring up the Ninety!"

That scared me. The "Ninety" was our 90mm shoulder-fired recoilless rifle. If we needed that, we were in trouble.

Then, as quickly as the firefight began, it ended. I was still confused. A few of the men around me spoke in hushed tones in the sudden silence. I stayed where I was, behind the tree.

"All right, all right," said our platoon sergeant loudly as he walked past us from the rear of the column, "you can get up now, let's go." He was a stout Hawaiian, his rifle slung over one shoulder, and he appeared nonchalant. His actions and words made it seem as if we had no worries, and should be ashamed to be on our noses in the dirt.

We got to our feet quickly. The column began to move forward again. We passed a dead North Vietnamese soldier lying in the leaves, his head distended and bloody, hair and bone bulging over his ear.

He wore khaki fatigues and had ammunition pouches slung bandolier-style over his chest. A steel shovel protruded from under his packstraps, and there were new bullet holes in the blade.

Lieutenant Tossher had killed him. Later I found out what happened. We had met an NVA unit of unknown size literally head-on. Tossher had seen their point man first, the man who now lay dead on the leaves, and opened fire with an entire magazine from his M-16.

Our flankers had encountered their flankers at the same time, but with more distance separating them, and they had begun to fire on each other. During all this, one of our sergeants had been hit in the shoulder, but wasn't hurt too badly.

The dead man was wearing all his equipment, meaning his unit was on the march, like us. They had not been ready to fight, and they ran. Tossher had the dead man's SKS rifle. Incredibly, the Vietnamese had been walking with his weapon slung.

We moved on and left the body in the jungle.

We linked up with B Company on top of a hill and dug in for the night. B Company had gotten to the hill before we did.

An ambush was waiting for them there. As the B Company's point man walked up the hill, he was shot.

Return fire from B Company drove the ambushers off before we reached them. I saw the wounded point man leaning against a tree, doped on morphine, while the medics took care of him.

He had been shot in the arm with an M-16. Several of the B Company troopers who had been near him said it was probably one of the weapons A Company had lost on top of the hill the day they were ambushed there, before we left the firebase.

The boy's arm was wrapped in bandages, but I could tell most of the flesh and muscle from his upper arm had been shot off. It was evidence of the destructive power of the 5.56 mm bullet, just like the technicians had told us at Fort Jackson.

The wound was there for me to see for myself, on a soldier who should have been in high school, bagging groceries for extra money and taking his girlfriend to the movies.

It began raining again in the mountains, and we were wet and cold. Resupply in the rain was risky and the helicopters were grounded, so we had to go without food until the storm cleared. We did not see the sun for two days.

* * *

I lightened my load by throwing away everything I
did not absolutely need, but the weight I carried was still
too much.

Our company carried M-72 light antitank weapons
(LAWs), which were single-shot rockets with disposable
launchers, an M67 90mm recoilless rifle and ammunition,
and the captain increased the two boxes of machine-gun
ammunition to three per squad.

The 90mm rifle was really useless to us in the jungle,
even though we had antipersonnel rockets for it that contained hundreds of steel fragments.

The leeches, ants, and mosquitoes were eating us
alive.

My squad, already short four men, went down to
seven after Harris, one of our riflemen, severely chopped
himself in the leg with a machete as we were clearing fields
of fire. We evacuated him by helicopter.

---

29 November 1966: Squad Leader

I was appointed squad leader after the platoon sergeant and the previous squad leader got into an argument.

The authorized strength of a rifle company was over
two hundred men; a platoon over forty, and a squad was
twelve.

My squad was down to a fire team, just five, our platoon wasn't thirty men, and our whole company less than
a hundred.

Illness and injuries had reduced us to half strength.
Our feet were rotting inside our boots from being constantly wet. Cuts infected quickly. We all suffered from
heat rash, and we itched badly, but still, each morning we
put on our equipment, picked up our weapons, and moved
on, looking for the enemy.

No one would carry trip flares, smoke grenades, or
extra rifle ammunition. It was simply too heavy.

It continued to rain, and when we were wet, we shivered in the chill. If the sun came out, the heat of the day became blistering.

The weather and the jungle were killing C Company.

SHOOT/DON'T SHOOT

Many times we were confronted with the choice of firing or not. This is a problem common to all soldiers in war, but it was a special problem to us. We were under orders not to fire on unarmed personnel, and for that reason, many of the Vietcong and North Vietnamese used the ploy of unarmed scouts or point men to temporarily confuse us.

The trick was used on us at the end of November.

We had found a trail by accident shortly after dawn. It was twenty feet wide and so well-traveled it was worn down to the sand. Trees sheltered it from observation by air.

Early that morning, with mist still hanging low, and the gray dawn blocked by the high mountains, we waited around the edge of that massive trail, all of us apprehensive and silent, while a small patrol quietly walked the sand to scout ahead, and our company commander decided what to do with our discovery.

"This is sure a big son of a bitch," Kravitski whispered to me, peering down one approach of the trail through the cold gloom. He let the muzzle of his M-16 brush the dew-wet leaves as he crouched into a more comfortable position.

"Keep it quiet, Ski," I replied, watching our helmeted soldiers on the other side of the trail, hidden in the foliage, their faces pale against the early shadows.

The patrol returned with the report that the trail was clear for at least a hundred meters, and just as wide and spooky. No doubt about it, we had something. The captain had notified battalion by radio of the situation, and we soon had an order to follow the trail.

"Second platoon, take the point," the captain said,

and we began to assemble. A machine-gun crew came up from the weapons platoon to walk with the point. The gunner carried his M-60 casually in the crook of his arm, muzzle down, a fifty-round belt laid over his shoulder, and his assistant followed closely with enough ammunition to keep him in action until we could shed the hundred-round boxes we all carried and get them to the gun.

I had a full two-hundred-round box, one of the two my squad carried, and I lugged it in my left hand, my M-16 in my right.

My squad was spread out along the sides of the trail, all walking slowly, the sand crunching under our jungle boots, rifles up and eyes straining to see into the shadows under the huge trees.

At times we halted, when paths off the trail were encountered. The morning wore on, our tendency to move quietly relaxed, and our patrols checked the trail forks with less caution.

Near noon, it was hot, and the weight of my ammo box seemed more real than the threat of an ambush. "Hey, Camp," Ski said, relieved to be able to speak after the enforced silence of the morning, "is this one of them elephant trails? Looks like a regular highway."

"Yeah," I said. "They carry rockets and heavy stuff on elephants, but this trail hasn't been used in a while, lots of it's still covered with dry leaves that have been here since the monsoon."

"They probably gave it up as a supply route when we started patrolling up here in the mountains," Kircher said, his expression strained from the heavy bag of 40mm grenades hung across his shoulders. "Remember those empty hospitals and base camps we found before Nobel's Knob, Ski?"

"Hey, yeah, Camp," Kravitski said, "you shoulda seen that. They had regular bomb shelters, man, it woulda took a direct hit from a B-52 to blow those dinks out."

"I'd just as soon get off these mountains," Kircher said. "One of these days, we're gonna walk up on one of those things with people in it, and we're gonna be so deep in shit . . ."

"They shouldn't let a company go out on its own," Gemmel swore from the rear of the squad. "Only battalions or more."

Up front, the point had found a clearing, and as the company filed into it, we split into squads to make a perimeter. That was good. We could rest, and maybe eat.

The clearing was small, about fifty meters across, and waist-deep in dry grass. The trail narrowed to a path and centered straight across the clearing and into the trees on the other side.

"Camper," the platoon sergeant called, "put your squad on the trail up front with the gun."

I looked at the trail and the trees beyond. The machine gunners came up and took a position just off the trail near me. The three-man crew added badly needed people to my five-man squad. "Kirch—you and Gemmel take that side of the trail, me and Ski'll be over here. Gutierez, you get with the gun crew."

Ski and I found a comfortable place in the grass and lay down facing the tree line. In a few minutes the perimeter was secure, and weariness brought quiet as the infantrymen napped or opened canned rations.

I laid the box of machine-gun ammo near my rucksack, felt around in my pockets until I found a lump of C4 plastic explosive. In my pack I still had a day's rations or better. I took out a B3 can of cookies, canned jam and cocoa, and ran my P38 opener around the top, leaving the lid partly attached for a handle, and dumped the cookies out into my hand to catch the crumbs.

I ate the crumbs and stashed the small jam can back inside my pack. The cookies I balanced on the outside of my pack to keep them off the ground and I tore open the cocoa packet.

As I set fire to the small lump of plastic explosive to boil the stream water I had carefully poured from my canteen into the cookie can, I kept watching out toward the trees, my rifle near at hand. Kravitski slept, leaning on his pack in the grass close to me.

I was tired and would have liked to rest as well; the calm of the halt took its toll on my vigilance.

The crew played cards over the M-60, their sergeant dozing in the sun. Possibly the most alert people were in our two-man listening post out beyond the perimeter.

Suddenly, one of the machine gunners glanced down the trail and saw an unarmed Vietnamese soldier strolling straight toward our company, obviously ignorant of the fact we were all hidden in the grass. The man wore a dark blue sweatshirt and khaki trousers, and had a faded green flop hat pulled down over his military haircut.

The gunner dropped his cards and snapped the M-60 up to a firing position as his assistant gunner grabbed for more belted ammunition, and four more soldiers, in North Viet khaki, armed with AK-47 assault rifles and wearing ammunition pouches and canteens, came into sight right behind their point man. It was an NVA recon team, probably trying to locate our company. Our sudden stop in the clearing probably had confused them. I would have been confused too, if I had lost track of a big, noisy infantry company.

But the M-60 gunner did not fire. The weapons-platoon sergeant, in shock at the unexpected situation, forgot if he had a cartridge in the chamber of his M-16 rifle and pumped his bolt. The sound of that bolt slamming forward was as loud as a hammer striking steel in the tranquil noon.

I was drinking cocoa when I heard the bolt, and the sound carried such an urgency that I dumped my cocoa, snatched up my rifle, and went down to a prone position. Before I had my rifle to my shoulder, other bolts had clanged open and shut, and it scared the hell out of me.

For an instant the perimeter was a flurry of clattering rifle bolts. It was a panic that fed on itself, as men took that extra step of life insurance to make positive their weapons were loaded.

I held my breath, my eyes fixed on the high grass and

the trees, heart working overtime, expecting any second for the shooting to break out.

I picked up my box of machine-gun ammo and crawled to the gun. "What happened?" I asked.

" 'Bout five dinks came down the trail," the weapons sergeant exclaimed. "We had those bastards cold! Why in the hell didn't you fire, Gig?"

"Shit! I didn't want to hit our LPs out there!" the machine gunner said.

Talk about shock. Think about that NVA patrol, hearing a hundred rifle bolts slamming right in front of them. They're probably still on the run.

I was too nervous to even worry about the loss of my cocoa. I packed my gear and waited for the word to move out.

---

6 December 1966: Mercy

Unexpectedly, we received orders over our radio to gather the company because we were going to be airlifted back to one of the forward operations bases. This was incredibly good news. We were tired, sick, and frustrated from fruitlessly searching for an enemy who had proved he would not stand and fight until he was ready.

Helicopters carried us back, the cool air at high altitude making us shiver as we had in the rain, but this time we smiled about it.

WESTY

The choppers put us down at the remote end of the long dirt landing strip at 3 Golf, the forward operations base established by brigade in October while I was with them.

As we unloaded, our platoon sergeants ran up and down the strip yelling for us to get into the bunkers and stay there, except for one man on guard on the bunker roof.

We filled the bunker line, but we were confused. We were low on water, out of food in most cases, and many of the men needed medical treatment for infections and illness. We had been sixteen days straight on the sweep, and we needed showers, hot food, cold drinks, and rest.

In my bunker, we were getting angry. There was no explanation for this harassment. Finally, a light truck drove down the bunker line and passed out dry, bread-and-bologna sandwiches, but no water.

"I know the guys in brigade," I told my squad. "I'm going up there and find out what's happening." I slipped across the airstrip to the supply dumps, then through unit areas until I found brigade.

The men there were glad to see me. I felt self-conscious because of my dirty fatigues and welts and scratches, but I was proud of myself.

"Look," I said to a brigade S3 captain, "my company is down at the far end of the landing strip, with no food or water. Some of the guys are sick. Nobody will let us come in! I've got to get some supplies down there, we've got to do something about it."

"Your people will have to stay there until the inspection is over," he told me.

"Inspection?" I asked.

"Yeah, Westmoreland's here. He don't like to see dirty troops, and your people are filthy. It looks unmilitary."

"Filthy!" I blurted, almost a shout.

"Sorry," said the captain. "He won't be here long. You better get back with your unit."

I walked back to the airstrip in a condition of shock. We were being hidden because we were *unpresentable* to General Westmoreland. I was so frustrated and angry I wanted to cry.

I damned the war, the army, and Westmoreland. I hope to God he reads this.

Our infantry company was assigned to provide security around a new area that brigade wanted to use as another field headquarters.

We trucked to a group of old buildings atop a broad hilltop. The main structure was a large church, and around it was a grouping of small barracks and convent-like buildings, but there was not a door left in a doorway or a pane of glass in any of the windows.

The walls were bullet-scarred and there were years of debris and rubble in the corners. We discovered tunnels leading from some of the buildings to others, and investigation into them was abandoned because of the smells of old death our searchers encountered. It was better to leave well enough alone.

We were given the story a unit of French soldiers had used this church as a fort in 1952, and the Vietminh, as they were known then, had attacked and killed most of them here.

As we watched the brigade troops move into the church to set up the new brigade tactical operations center, and as sandbags and other fortifications began to be erected in the windows, I thought of how the old church resembled the Alamo, where that small band of American rebels had made a stand against the army of Mexico in 1836.

I knew the story of the battle well. I hoped we were not going to make a last stand here.

Winning wars, not being gloriously defeated, was my concept.

13 December 1966: Volunteer

A call for volunteers was sent out by brigade to all infantry units asking for men to join the new long-range reconnaissance patrol platoon. I had been waiting just for that, and promptly let my platoon leader know I wanted to go to the LRRPs.

We volunteers were sent to 3 Golf, 218th operations area to rest, take over the perimeter guard, KP, and work details, so other men could be turned loose to go back into the jungle.

Harris, my squad member who had accidentally cleaved into his leg with a machete in late November, rejoined us at 3 Golf. His leg had healed, and we were glad to get him back.

He had become a good friend of mine in the infantry. He was quiet, capable, and had an interest in what I had told him about the LRRPs. He said he wanted to join with me.

17 December 1966: LRRP Training

Harris and I were given leave from C Company to go to the LRRP School.

A permanent Recondo School was being established in Nha Trang, on the coast of Vietnam, but it was not yet ready to begin steady training cycles.

The Special Forces in Pleiku were holding training for LRRP personnel, giving lessons on enemy weapons, advanced first-aid techniques, map reading, survival, and other related skills a small recon team would need to know to perform in the field.

We attended the Special Forces course, and absorbed everything they taught. I knew maps well, better than anyone in my class, and had no trouble with even the most

complicated techniques of triangulation, declination, side
elevations, and scaling.

We learned those methods of radio communications
we would need as small teams operating beyond normal
radio range, and the basics of photography so we could
bring back better evidence of our sightings than just description.

We also learned ground-to-air signaling, and how to
use the new, top-secret Starlight night-vision scopes.

I enjoyed the training, and graduated near the top of
my class. I had wanted to be a LRRP since I had first
known what it was. This was my chance.

My infantry friends seemed to think going into the
LRRPs was the same as a death wish, believing in safety in
numbers. I thought being with a small team in the field
was far safer than being with a large unit, because a large
unit was looking for a fight, and a small team was just
doing its reconnaissance job.

I didn't want to join the brigade LRRPs. I wanted to
go to the MACV LRRP and special-operations group, and
put my name in for the new Nha Trang Recondo School.

SIN CITY AND THE SYPHILIS BAR

Outside base camp a frontier-type collection of huts,
shacks, and other buildings had grown up. It was called
Sin City by the soldiers, and it dealt in the basics—liquor
and women.

The 4th Medical actually sent inspection teams to Sin
City to inoculate the prostitutes and issue them updated
identification cards. No inoculations, no ID card, and that
translated to no business, so the 4th Med always had a
long waiting line of women at their trucks.

I wanted to see Sin City for myself, so Harris and I
went out through the base-camp wire, cutting across the
minefields and kill zones. We could have gone the long
way, out the front gate, but we had no passes, and we were
cocky and figured we could get away with it. Some of the

perimeter guards yelled at us, but we just went on our way and waved back at them.

There were board sidewalks from establishment to establishment, a civilized touch. I saw right away most of the soldiers visiting Sin City were base-camp types—"clerks and jerks," we called them. They filled the bars, or staggered down the street, feeling their beer.

A few combat infantry were there, too. Telling the grunts from the clerks wasn't hard. The base-camp commandos knew the bar girls by name, knew all the prices of drinks and sex, and knew where to go for the best bargains. They also wore uniforms marked with proper insignia and rank.

The line troopers wore ill-fitting fatigues without insignia or rank, clothes taken out of a pile at their rear-area supply tent, clothes washed clean of blood, clothes that might have been on a dead man last week.

They also wore scuffed jungle boots washed free of mud and perhaps daubed with a little polish in an effort to satisfy a base-camp officer. With their fresh-scrubbed faces and gaunt appearances, they looked like a military version of a poor relative from the sticks.

Harris and I went into a wooden bar with a front sitting room and plenty of windows, taking a table in the corner. We ordered drinks from the little bar boy, and when our whiskey cokes were delivered without ice, the smiling Vietnamese bartender apologized in English and sent the boy away for ice with a curt command and a sharp clap of his hands.

Two of the whores, just girls really, came from out of the back room to sit with us. They were smiling and smoking cigarettes, trying to talk to us in broken English.

I noticed with a start that one of them had a portion of her nostril eaten away by syphilis. Outside of photographs, it was the first time I had seen it. She had tried to cover it with makeup, but the thinned, brownish, decayed-leaf appearance of the spot was already eaten all the way through; the 4th Med penicillin wouldn't cure that.

There was a tug of sympathy in my heart for the girl, but a cold knot of caution was in my throat.

I waited in the front room, drinking slowly at my whiskey cokes as Harris got drunk, got laid; then I steered him back to camp that afternoon, going in through the wire again.

19 December 1966: The Bob Hope Show

I watched Bob Hope's traveling entertainment show at base camp. It was ironic, base camp had grown so much it had engulfed the small ridge off which we had taken so much machine-gun fire one night during our first weeks in Vietnam, in the monsoon. Bob Hope's stage had been built against that ridge. It was hard for me not to think of it as outside the wire, in enemy territory, but despite my feelings I enjoyed the show.

Bob Hope had started touring and entertaining American and Allied soldiers in World War II, and his shows had become a holiday tradition.

One platoon of C Company, 2nd of the 8th Infantry, had been chosen to be flown back out of the field and see the Bob Hope Show.

It was 1st Platoon, whose leader was Lieutenant Braun. It was fortunate for them in a way, because fate had marked the entire platoon. Most of them did not have long to live.

22 December 1966: The Dawnbuster Show

There was an Armed Forces Radio station for Vietnam, and it had, among its features, the *Dawnbuster Show.* It followed a civilian rock-and-roll format, but started each day with a rousing, "Good morning, Vietnam!"

Some of us laughed at it, some of us hated it. I had not heard it until I came back to base camp. I personally thought the show was insane.

25 December 1966: Christmas

I stayed in the 2nd of the 8th Battalion's area in base camp for Christmas. I discovered it was no longer just "base camp," now the new troops were calling it Dragon Mountain Base Camp.

Armed Forces Radio broadcast quiet, traditional Christmas music, and the battalion mess hall made a large dinner for us that was served all afternoon.

I checked the battalion-orderly tent and was told I was on orders for the official Recondo School course at Nha Trang, and would report there on 7 January, 1967. I also learned my assigned date to return to the United States was 6 June, 1967.

One of the brigade officers traded me a .45 government-issue pistol, and a couple of magazines for it, for an air force survival knife I had gotten during my LRRP training. I thought the .45 might come in handy, and hooked its leather holster to my web belt. I planned to use it as a backup weapon on patrols.

1 January 1967: Airmobile Assault

At the stroke of midnight, it seemed every weapon on the perimeter opened up. The men on the perimeter security at base camp were celebrating the New Year with the fireworks they had available to them . . . M-16 rifles, .45 pistols, and M-60 machine guns.

After sunup, Harris and I were ordered to rejoin my infantry company, because of a major air assault the battalion was about to make. My orders for Nha Trang were postponed.

By dark on New Year's Day, I was sitting with my company near the old Oasis location, packing for the assault.

The next morning, we all loaded into big, twin-rotor Chinook cargo helicopters and flew back to the Cambodian border.

The Chinooks put us down on grassy hilltops, and we quickly assembled and moved into the jungle, and bad luck caught me almost from the instant I came off the helicopter.

I lost my C rations in the rush to get into the grass and establish a security perimeter, trying to carry a wooden crate of mortar ammunition with another soldier.

We were carrying 81mm mortars with us this time, so we had to carry the shells for it as well.

I had a reserve Vietnamese long-range patrol ration packet, which was food packaged just for the Oriental soldier. It was rice and dried fish—minnows, I decided, little dried heads, tails, and eyeballs.

I volunteered for the water run so I'd be sure I got full canteens, and walked over a kilometer with a small patrol from the platoon to a stream we had passed earlier in the day, and I carried twenty full canteens back for my squad.

We saw an enemy soldier on our way back, but he was a long distance away, and for a few moments stood still in a group of dead trees, his arms at his sides, causing us to doubt if we were looking at a man or not. When we decided we did have a North Vietnamese in sight, and one of the patrol aimed his rifle in that direction, the man dropped and ran. He was too far away to chase, so we walked back to the company night defensive position.

Peace was the name of a black soldier in my squad. One afternoon as we were digging in and clearing fields of fire, there came a shout from the bottom of the hill, and I turned to see what was happening.

Peace was springing up the hill like a kangaroo, his pants around his ankles, one hand holding his helmet on his head, the other, even with his rifle in it, trying to pull up his trousers.

Bare-assed and wide-eyed, he was yelling "Git! Git!" at the top of his lungs.

We literally had to tackle him to slow him down. It took a few minutes for him to get enough composure to speak, and then was still on the verge of panic.

He said he had walked downhill to take a dump, and when he squatted down, he realized he was just a few feet away from a hidden NVA recon soldier who was watching him.

Peace had slapped at the safety of his M-16, but could not develop the presence of mind to move it, so he did the next thing that came to mind. He began to shout "Git!" as loudly as he could, and tried to run for safety.

"Who were you telling to git, the NVA?" I asked.

"I don't know, man," Peace muttered. "As long as one of us could git, it was all right."

Our company encountered a fresh road cut out of the jungle by our own engineers, and we were ordered to provide security for them as they rammed and ripped the forest with their heavy bulldozers. We had not been recently resupplied, so the engineers gave us C rations. The sight of the front-end loaders, bulldozers, dump trucks, and road graders out in the jungle was amazing. I wondered how they managed to get them this far into the mountains. No roads led to the border area where they worked.

Skycrane helicopters, perhaps?

5 January 1967: Delay

My commanding officer, Captain Nobel, said I could not be released to go on to Nha Trang for the new Recondo School. There were actually four of us scheduled —Jones, Harris, Magnum, and myself—and we were all denied.

I realized our CO did not want us to leave the company, because they would still be responsible for us even though we were serving with another unit. It meant they would have to carry us on the company roster, handling our pay, mail, leaves, and other administrative details. We would be four men the company could not replace, because we would technically still be part of them.

Understanding this made me decide to volunteer for the brigade LRRP platoon. Brigade had requested any and all volunteers to fill up the platoon, and no unit commander could keep a man from going. The four of us made the official request to our platoon leaders.

---

6 January 1967: LRRP Team

Lieutenant Tossher came back from his talk with the captain and asked Harris and me if we would volunteer to go on a long-range patrol the next day. The battalion wanted to send a LRRP team on ahead down the valley to scout the way for the infantry. The mission would take six days. It was a ploy to keep us.

Harris and I both said we would be glad to go. The six-man team was assembled out of the company. Only Harris and I had any special training; the rest of the team were infantrymen.

We were given the mission briefing, stocked up on rations, and walked into the jungle away from the company, our friends watching us go, sure we had lost our minds. We left our helmets with them and wore soft caps.

We had a specific distance to walk each day. It was really too far for a long-range patrol, where silence was vital to survival, but the planning for our mission was made from an infantry officer's viewpoint. We were being controlled like an infantry patrol, but we were fewer and much farther away than any common patrol.

I knew we were in trouble when our point man tried to use his machete to cut the trail. Harris and I stopped him. The hacking of the machete was too loud. With an infantry company behind you, it might be okay to hack with a machete, but with a team of only six men, it was suicide.

The infantrymen wanted to dig in at night and build cover out of logs, the same way they would have done back with the platoon. I argued them out of that as well.

We were required to stay in radio contact constantly with battalion headquarters, the same way a company on the march would, and it required we carry many extra radio batteries.

Our patrol continued down the valley, the battalion several days behind us, and while we found many old signs of the enemy having lived and moved through the area, we had no evidence of anything recent.

This caused battalion to order us to "get busy and find something," as if irritated we had not located intelligence of vital importance or had not killed any enemy soldiers. This was how the officers of the higher command talked to field-grade officers, goading them into "success," and after a few days of nervous, careful patrolling, even the infantrymen on my team were upset with the infantry mentality.

As I watched my feet, aware of the possibility of mines, or of the arming lever or wire of a booby trap, I saw a bit of canvas protruding through the sandy soil.

I held up my hand to stop the team, and bent to examine my find. It was the edge of a Chinese-made AK-47 ammunition pouch, the type worn across the chest. I poked at the hard-packed sand around the canvas, but it was hard, like limestone, and would not easily move.

Harris crawled up to me on his hands and knees, and asked me what I had found.

"Ammo pouch," I whispered.

"Might be a body," he said.

I scraped at the soil with my knife, digging around the canvas, and struck something harder than the pebbles. It was a human rib bone, and as I removed more dirt, I could see it was charred. I pulled part of the ammo pouch out of the ground. It too had been burned. My guess was napalm.

"Think we ought to dig him up?" I asked Harris.

"No, let's just report the body and the location. He was probably killed by the 1st Cav last year. They can add it to their count."

I agreed. I didn't want to start robbing graves. We left the bones in the earth and wrote down the position in the team leader's notebook.

I brushed the dirt off my hands and kept moving.

During one rest break, a large snake crawled into our camp. It slithered under Harris's low-slung hammock, causing him to quickly jump up. I was half-asleep at the time, and, due to his sudden movement, almost shot him.

We temporarily lost radio communications for a day with battalion, but thought we had been located when a light spotter aircraft flew over us. We moved into a clearing and waved at him. He responded by calling in artillery fire on us, the first shell hitting in front and the next behind, getting us in a good bracket. The pilot was mistaking us for enemy forces, because we were in a small group. We ran like hell and hid from the plane.

I could see this would be a problem on any long-range patrol. Americans were expected—by other Americans—to be with large forces.

When we later made radio contact (we were at the range limit of the short combat antenna on our PRC-25 radio), and reported a wide but old enemy trail, our battalion commander ordered us to walk it for a distance of eight hundred meters and then come back. It was a dangerous assignment, but we did it.

Stepping lightly and slowly, expecting at any moment to see a fully equipped NVA company ahead, I walked point.

It happened with no warning. I caught a sudden image of motion from the corner of my eye as something—no, *someone,* because I saw arms and legs—fell out of the tree beside me and crashed into the bushes.

I spun to fire, and came face to face not with a man,

but an ape. He had apparently been in the tree, watching
me, and somehow had fallen right off his perch. He was
stunned and I was terrified.

The ape raced away, leaving me to sink down and
take a deep breath.

"What was that?" the team leader asked me, himself
down and ready for trouble.

"A goddamn monkey," I said, and with my heart
coming back under some control, I motioned us up, and
we went on.

The commander was thinking of us as a unit to be
ordered around the same way he would have controlled
one of his field companies.

We lost radio communications again once we were in
the lower country, and regained it a day later, still moving
toward our predetermined pickup point.

13 January 1967: Pickup

We located a sandbar beside the river for the helicopter to extract us from, but when it arrived, the pilot did not
land. He hovered the Huey just above the water, and our
team scrambled aboard. I was tailgun and stayed on the
sandbar with my M-16 pointed at the trees.

When it was time for me to board, I turned to the
hovering chopper, but it was drifting away from the sandbar, out over the water. I chased it, splashing up to my
knees and then my waist. The helicopter kept moving
away.

The team was lying on the cargo deck, hands out-
stretched to me. I threw them my rifle, and jumped at the
skid, and missed. I was up to my chest now in the river.

Hueys don't hover well over water. I jumped up again
and got my hands on the skid, and hands grasped my rucksack and arms. As I hung out the door, water pouring off
me, we gained altitude and flew away.

We had been on patrol since the 7th, and had made no

enemy contact, and had discovered little about the enemy.
Battalion headquarters was not pleased.

What I had learned personally was that trying to perform long-range patrols in the infantry fashion, or under
the control of an infantry officer who simply issued orders
to us over a radio, was asking for the kind of trouble you
don't live to tell about.

The helicopter flew us to 3 Church, the newly established base where the old abandoned church was located.
For two days we had been hungry, our rations insufficient
for the length of the patrol. We found one of the infantry
chow lines. Dirty, camouflaged, and wearing soft hats instead of helmets, we slipped into the serving line to get
something to eat.

A fat sergeant major, spotting us easily among the
cleaner, helmeted infantrymen, stormed up to us.

"Who are you goddamn people with?" he demanded.

"The army," I said, mystified by his question.

"Whose goddamn army?" he shouted.

"The U.S. Army," I said.

"Well, you get the hell out of my goddamn chow line!
If you don't belong to this outfit, you don't eat with this
goddamn outfit!"

The six of us looked at each other. We were not ready
for anything like that. "Sergeant, we've been out on the
Cambodian border for the last week, on a long-range patrol—" our ranking man said.

"Don't give me that shit!" said the sergeant major.
"We got rules around here! You ain't got no steel pot! Everybody that eats here has to have on his helmet to go
through this chow line!"

"We don't have helmets—" I said.

"Everybody in the whole goddamn U.S. Army has a
helmet!" the sergeant major shouted. "Now get out of my
chow line, or I'll call the MPs!" With that, he stomped
away.

Some of the infantry nearby took off their helmets and

offered them to us, trying to apologize for the sergeant major.

I could tell by the sergeant major's weight he was no field soldier. He had a base-camp job. I hated the fat man with all the energy I had left.

We thanked the soldiers there, refusing their helmets, and walked behind the mess tent, where one of the cooks was waving to us.

The cook was embarrassed. He handed us several boxes of C rations, and told us to sit down out of sight and eat while he went to get us some iced tea from the vat on the serving line.

Our team was debriefed by the battalion-operations officer at 3 Church. I learned the name "Church" was going to be replaced by "3 Tango," since "Church" wasn't part of the NATO phonetic alphabet.

We were then flown back to our company, which as usual was deep in the jungle near the border. They still had our helmets, and we rejoined the infantry.

17 January 1967: Road Security

C Company was assigned to pull security for the engineers who were still building the jungle road.

The road now had an artillery firebase as an anchor point on it, from where support fire could be delivered against any attacks on the engineers—or the security forces.

21 January 1967: Infantry Actions

Harris and I were interviewed by Lieutenant Lapollo, the brigade LRRP platoon commander, and accepted. Lieutenant Tossher told us we could go as soon as Captain

Nobel, our company commander, came back from his leave.

The new firebase was on top of a steep hill at the southern end of a rugged chain of hills. To our west about three kilometers was the river, and to our east about three kilometers was a higher and even rougher mountain ridge-line.

Just to the immediate south of our landing zone and the firebase itself, down in the low ground, was a large abandoned enemy position composed of trenches, fighting holes, bunkers, and tunnels.

Each day, one patrol had to be sent to search the riverbanks for signs of enemy activity. Another patrol had to walk to the ridgeline and do the same thing.

Another platoon was given road-security detail, and the last platoon, Weapons Platoon, stayed in the firebase to man the mortars and guard the perimeter. That accounted for all four platoons, the complete strength of C Company.

Second Platoon—us—took the daily patrol up to the ridgeline, and while we were walking the ridge and trying to recover from the exertion of climbing it, we saw movement in the underbrush.

We spread out, and approached it carefully; suddenly several Montagnards wearing rough-woven blankets leaped out of the foliage and raced away, not stopping even as we yelled at them to halt.

One of our men discovered a child they had left behind. She was about ten years old, starved, and had more sores and skin infections than I had seen before on one human being.

Her friends had left her, and their baskets, blankets, and curved Montagnard machetes. When we radioed back the information to battalion about what had happened, we were ordered to return her to the firebase as soon as we could. The battalion commander decided her family or friends might have been a scavenging party sent out by the North Vietnamese.

We turned around, and walked her off the mountain and back to the firebase, a trek that took hours. Climbing

up the hill toward the firebase, we were caught in demolition blasting by the engineers who were clearing trees
around the perimeter, and barely escaped having several of
our men, including myself, killed.

The little girl told an interpreter who was flown specially to the firebase that one of our men stole her bracelets. That was true, and our platoon sergeant who had
taken them was made to give the bracelets back to her.

Then she said her family had indeed been working for
the NVA, but had been released because there had not been
enough food to feed them. They had been starving.

The next morning, the whole company was ordered
back to the ridgeline. Second Platoon was not very popular
with the rest of the men because of the extra work we had
caused.

The push up to the ridge was treacherous, plowing
through spiked plants, thorned vines, and meshed, interwoven jungle so thick in places we had to beat it down
with rifles and machetes. I took point position on the way
up, and it seemed as if I lost a quart of blood from cuts. I
looked like a pair of sadists had beaten me with whips.

Just as we sat to rest in the early afternoon, trying to
open some C rations and eat, Lieutenant Tossher smelled
something dead. We stopped eating, and began to search
for the body.

A group of our men a short distance up the hill from
me found the source of the stench. I walked up to them.
They were picking at something in the hollow of a tree.

It was a dead baby, wrapped in an army mosquito net,
"buried" with an old baseball cap and two empty tin cans.
I knew something about Montagnard burials, having visited their villages when I was security for the brigade labor
trucks.

They used a totem pole at the head of their graves,
very much like the carved medicine poles of the Indians of
the American West. The pole was the way to heaven.

The tree would have sufficed for the pole.

They also buried precious objects with their dead, as
gifts for the next life. This starved, displaced family obvi-

ously did not have anything precious, so they had buried what they had, a baseball cap and two tin cans.

Lieutenant Tossher pulled back some of the mosquito net on the little body with the tip of his bayonet. "About two years old," he said. "Probably died of starvation."

He stood aside while one of our men took an entrenching folding shovel and threw a few spades of dirt into the hollow of the tree.

We left.

On an ambush patrol near the river, our platoon lay in position when we heard movement, then voices. Squad leaders motioned to their men. Hands found mine detonators. Machine guns were shouldered and aimed.

We saw them coming, just hazy figures through the vines. Lieutenant Tossher prepared to give the signal to open fire.

We all realized it at the same time. It was A Company moving up the river, walking slowly, and talking. No one had warned us they would be there. Seeing the outlines of their helmets and hearing their faint voices stopped the ambush at the last moment.

We let them go past, shaking our heads in disbelief. It would have been so easy to have killed them.

We had to be more careful.

DONUT DOLLIES

Out of the sky came a Huey that landed inside our perimeter, and from it bounced three young American girls. They wore the uniform of the Red Cross, cotton dresses printed in gray-and-white pinstripes. They were unofficially called "Donut Dollies," and for this firebase, they were certainly something out of the ordinary.

No one had to call us up to the LZ to see what they were doing there. I watched them set up a chalkboard on an easel, and unload several boxes of what looked to be donuts or cookies. I also noticed the crew of the girls'

Huey kept their equipment on, and stayed near the helicopter. They were ready to extract the girls instantly if anything happened, like a mortar attack, or a riot among the troops.

Their show got under way quickly, and I was astounded. The girls were going to play *games* with us. They had a version of a TV game show, and they pitched into it like professionals, with much showmanship and enthusiasm.

I could not believe it. Here were three young, spunky girls, all of them probably ex-cheerleaders, and they were going to carry on a chalkboard word game on top of a forward fire-support base in a genuine war zone! I wanted to get up and tell them they could get their energetic little tits and asses *shot off* out here.

At first, the girls were having to coach responses from the men, and they told us jokes, and they giggled, sweating now in the direct sun. I began to appreciate them. They knew what they were doing.

Soon the men were shouting answers to the chalked questions as the girls overcame the reservations of the combat veterans, and before long we were all laughing together.

The show lasted an hour. When it was over, the board and easel went back aboard the Huey, and as the pilot cranked the turbine to life, the rotors beginning to spin, the girls opened the boxes and passed out cookies to us. I stood in line and got a handful. They were hard, cheap cookies with a little dollop of frosting, like mothers buy for small children.

When the girls, helicopter, and cookies were gone, and the firebase seemed suddenly quiet, I went back to my bunker.

Cookies and cheerleaders. What a war.

I missed out on one.

Our company split up in the hollow, on the dirt road the engineers had just cut, with my platoon going to the river and the two remaining platoons inspecting an old NVA bunker complex the bulldozers had cut into.

An NVA recon squad had been shadowing us all day, totally unknown to the entire company, but everybody makes mistakes. They got caught.

A fan patrol, passing through the bunkers and trenches, spotted the camouflaged Vietnamese and opened up on them. The dinks dropped into the musty bunkers and the battle was on.

A couple of GIs were lightly wounded, and the captain decided to save the hassle and obliterate the place with artillery. The NVA were pinned down and could not escape.

The artillery blasted away most of the natural concealment around the bunkers, uprooting several trees and caving in a roof or two.

A lieutenant sent in a few men to check out the results. The troopers crept forward, and the Viet assault rifles cracked into life. The probers fell back, and the fight was remounted in earnest.

The M-60s saturated the area, eating up belt after belt as the gun crews shot the bunker faces away. The M-79 men popped in volleys of high explosive with their deadly grenade launchers, trying for direct hits through the bunker view slits.

And then the shouting began. It was in Vietnamese. They called from hole to hole, shrilly screaming at one another. The words "*Chu Hoi*" were recognized. Surrender! They wanted to come out.

Two of them stood, hands high. They were dazed and blackened from the explosions. The entire company lay in silence. Suddenly automatic fire ripped out and the two tumbled, cut down by their own people.

The GIs were enraged. They attacked and swept over the bunkers with speed and weight of numbers. They killed the rest of the recon team. The total body count was seven men.

We arrived in time to see the corpses before they were pushed into a ditch and buried. The story was related to us as it had happened. We all had our opinions, of course, but I was secretly proud of the small squad that had put up such a fight.

A detail covered them with a few spadefuls of dirt and we walked away.

ARC LIGHT

The early highland morning was cold as usual. We awoke on the mountainside firebase, with the sun just beginning to fill the vast valley below. I swallowed the taste of sleep in my mouth and staggered down the hill to the LZ. Two Hueys approached, flying in the shadows.

The company stirred. Hot breakfast was coming in by airmail. Men gathered gear and straightened the clothing they had slept in.

The helicopters touched down on the rocks, like giant eagles roosting, and infantry unloaded the insulated canisters of food.

Organization came quickly to the chow line. No one was in the mood to play. I was one of the first to be served, and walked a short distance away to sit and eat. There was black coffee, watery scrambled eggs, and lots of white bread.

A B-52 strike was scheduled for this morning. Word was passed around to watch the valley. We were going to have a show with our meal.

I ate my egg sandwich and drank the strong, hot coffee, idly gazing down the length of the valley. I wished we had bacon.

We heard the start of it. It was a distant rumble that came rolling out of the valley and up the cliffs to us. There were no individual explosions. It was a steady roar, growing louder.

I looked up into the transparent blue sky for the planes. I saw nothing but some wispy clouds. Not even a contrail.

I felt the ground tremble. We were over a mile away from the strike and the mountain was moving!

Then we saw it. Blink-quick flashes, hundreds of them, fanning through the treetops. And the noise! Lord, what noise!

A fog of water vapor followed the blasts along the valley floor. It was the dew recondensing in the air. For a moment I was awed and a touch of fear fluttered through my chest.

The planes were so high I couldn't see them, and they were doing this! War took on a dimension I had not known it had.

It was over quickly. The echoes remained for a breath, and then, except for the smoke, it was peaceful in the valley again.

I was amazed we could do that. My God! Amazed.

I took a small patrol one kilometer off the firebase to do a check of the jumbled logs and trees the engineers had blown down to clear a better avenue of approach into our landing zone.

We were concerned the enemy might hide commando teams in the thickets, in preparation for easily infiltrating our perimeter at night; they could lay in explosive charges, and blow the barbed wire so attacking infantry could rush through.

I felt we would have a better chance of catching a small group with a small group, and volunteered for the duty.

The downed trees made a broken mass of trunks and branches so interwoven an acrobat would have had a hard time picking a way through.

My team heard voices coming from the branches; we stopped, our hearts racing, all of us ready to fire, but we needed to get closer in order to confirm the target.

Then, like the incident by the river, we recognized the voices as English. I led my team closer, listening, and soon we knew we were near Lieutenant Braun and the 1st Platoon. They were not supposed to be there.

I called out to them, and they dropped, grabbing

weapons and rolling into defensive positions. After challenging us, they allowed our team to enter their enclave.

Braun was sitting against a tree, reading a paperback novel, his feet bare, boots unlaced and set aside. His men were arranged in a loose defensive perimeter, but they were also relaxed, their C-ration cans and light tropical poncho liners spread out where they were resting.

"What are you doing here?" I asked Braun.

He appeared ashamed. "Don't tell anyone you saw us," he begged. "We're supposed to be on patrol down by the river. The men just couldn't take another day of it. I had to give them some time off."

The platoon radio was near Braun. He would have been sending false position reports back to Captain Nobel, making battalion headquarters think his platoon was patrolling the riverbank.

I told Braun I would not reveal what I had seen, and the men on my patrol said the same thing. We had sympathy for any infantry like ourselves. I took my small patrol back up the hillside to the firebase.

If I had reported Braun, perhaps I would have saved the lives of his platoon. They had less than three weeks to live.

---

23 January 1967: Discord

While assigned to string new rolls of concertina wire around the perimeter, an argument broke out between Peace and one of our white sergeants.

It was a hot day and tempers were thin, and the stress of the daily patrols was taking its toll.

When the sergeant ordered Peace to string the wire, he refused. The sergeant cursed him. In a rage, Peace snatched up his M-16 and aimed it at the sergeant's chest, ready to kill.

I was the only man on the platoon-sized work detail not carrying a rifle. I had my .45 pistol in a belt holster.

When the muzzle of Peace's M-16 leveled at the sergeant, one of the sergeant's friends raised his M-16 at Peace. A friend of Peace aimed his weapon at that man, and in a few seconds, almost everybody had a weapon pointed at somebody else.

Everybody but me. My pistol was in my holster. For a long, stunned moment, no one fired. I realized all of them were waiting for an overt act by anyone. I also realized if I unsnapped the holster flap and pulled out my pistol, that might do it. I froze, looking at ready rifle muzzles all around me. At that moment, I learned how foolish a man with a pistol feels among a group of men with assault rifles. I lost any faith or fascination I had ever had with pistols during that incident.

Without warning, a soldier near Peace grabbed the rifle from his hands, and the situation was over.

Because I had a pistol, the sergeant placed me in charge of Peace. I put him under arrest and took him back to the acting company commander.

I ended up keeping Peace under guard at our squad bunker. I didn't want the job.

"What do you think they'll do with me?" he asked.

"I don't know," I said. "You'll go back to base camp. Maybe you'll get a transfer."

"I guess they'll send me to LBJ," he said. LBJ was Long Binh Jail, where soldiers were imprisoned in-country. He was despondent, looking into the jungle.

"You can have my .45," I offered. "I'll tell 'em you took it. Get some C rations too, and head for Cambodia. It's not far away."

Peace looked at me as if considering the offer, then he leaned back again against the bunker. "No," he said, "I'll go to LBJ. At least it'll get me out of the field."

We put him on a helicopter for base camp that afternoon. I never found out what happened to him after that.

25 January 1967: Puff the Magic Dragon

I sat on guard duty on the perimeter of the firebase and watched the awesome streams of tracers falling out of the sky from Puff, who was many kilometers away.

"Puff the Magic Dragon" was an old C-47 twin-engined, propeller-driven cargo aircraft that was fitted with three 7.62mm General Electric Vulcan "miniguns." They were called miniguns because the larger versions of them came chambered for 20mm cannon shells.

Each gun had six barrels powered by electric motors, and could fire up to six thousand rounds per minute. That was one hundred bullets a second from just one gun.

Called to a target, Puff circled it, and fired down with all three miniguns roaring at once, creating a sound like a dragon might, a howling, throaty thunder.

Each time Puff fired a volley, a solid yellow-red hail of tracers plunged to earth. The rate of fire was so high, even with only every sixth cartridge in the belted ammunition a tracer load, it looked like all tracers.

Somewhere out in the jungle along the border, one of the infantry units or a firebase like our own was in contact with the North Vietnamese, and had Puff firing support for them.

Our 105mm howitzers were blasting away, loading and firing methodically, each report so loud it was painful, like being hit in the head with a board.

It was night in Vietnam, and out in the dark, the killing was still going on. I was thankful it was not happening on my hill.

Thorn punctures in my left hand had infected badly, swelling with pus pockets, making it impossible for me to close my fist. I let the infections fester until they burst on their own, and I regained the use of my fingers. I did not want to go on sick call and be accused of trying to get out of duty.

On another patrol by the river, my platoon was glimpsed by one of our own helicopters flying fast, at low level over the water, and fired at by its machine gun. We scrambled and tripped out of the way, bullets from the helicopters striking the trees around us with the sound of carpenters driving nails.

Before we could respond in any fashion, the helicopter was gone.

At dark, we dragged back to the firebase from the patrol and went to see what was left of the chow brought in by helicopter earlier in the day. The food left was cold, and there was little of that.

A 4.2-inch ("four-deuce") mortar nearby was firing a mission for someone far away; we ignored its concussive blasts as we picked up our rations, until one blast differed from the others.

I looked quickly over my shoulder, and saw flames spout from the mortar tube as the propellant that should have fired the shell burned instead of exploded.

I could see the shell itself quite clearly, just exiting the tube, spinning end over end. It was a gray-painted chemical shell.

A 4.2-inch mortar shell is slightly more than 105 millimeters in diameter, which is to say, large enough to blow away most everything on our section of the firebase, and this one was loaded with evil white phosphorus, which would set us on fire.

Those of us who realized what was happening moved with all the speed we could manage. I dropped the paper plate I was using to salvage some food out of the insulated cans, and dived over a sandbag wall into another mortar pit, landing on an 81mm mortar and knocking it over.

The 4.2-inch WP shell came back down near its mortar tube and thudded to the ground, but did not explode, its impact fuse requiring more velocity than the short arcing flight had provided.

We all hugged the ground for a few moments, realizing we were going to live, and went back to our duties. A sergeant for the mortar section ran up and began to curse me for knocking his newly cleaned and oiled mortar into the dirt. M-16 in hand, I told him what I thought of mortar-section people who stayed in camp all day, greedily overate on food sent to be shared with the infantry, and then berated a man for wanting to save his life . . . and I hinted if he didn't go back to his bunker, I might kill him on the spot.

He left my area in a hurry. I was in no mood to tolerate fools.

I took out a five-man overnight ambush patrol that night, and set up on a knoll overlooking the road.

Early in the morning, Kravitski, who was supposed to be on guard and radio watch, fell asleep on duty, and began answering calls in his sleep. He was answering for other stations, saying "Roger" and "Out," and generally raising much consternation on the radio net.

What woke him was when he gave someone a "Roger," and they said loudly, "Don't give me a roger, just do it!"

Kravitski opened his eyes, then woke me up, thrusting the handset in my face, and said, "You talk to them! There's crazy people on the radio!" Then he went back to sleep.

I had been taking him on some of my small-team actions over the last month, and he was usually so scared that when he had to say something, he'd whisper so low I couldn't hear him, causing me to ask again and again what he was saying, until he'd whisper, "Forget it!" and turn away.

Captain Nobel had returned from his leave on the 30th, bringing news that the 2nd of the 8th was going to be changed into an armored unit, and get M-113 armored personnel carriers, vehicles we called "tracks." He offered me the job of track commander. It meant the whole battalion was going to get to stop wearing out jungle boots and start riding.

He did not give permission for Harris and me to go to the brigade LRRP platoon. He said C Company had another important mission coming up, and every man would be needed for it.

I had heard that before.

3 February 1967: Battalion Sweep

All four infantry companies of the 2nd of the 8th packed up and left our firebase, walking toward the Cambodian border in a battalion sweep, trying to force the enemy to run away, fight, or otherwise move and expose himself.

The field routine was back. Wake up in the morning, put on all my equipment, walk all day, fighting through the jungles, picking at leeches, sweating, straining, holding in anger, fear, frustration.

At night, we stopped, dug fighting holes, cut down fields of fire, pulled guard duty, and sent out night ambushes and listening posts.

Sometimes the routine was interrupted by a few moments of terror if we accidentally encountered an enemy soldier, or group of soldiers, them firing at us and us firing back as they ran away.

They did not want to fight. It was not their time, or their choice. They let us walk, using up our strength, patience, and supplies.

They waited.

11 February 1967: Base Camp

Mail had been delivered at our overnight position with boxes of ammunition and cases of C rations. As I read one of my letters, I learned my mother had been in a serious automobile accident in the United States, and had almost lost her foot.

When I took the news to my platoon sergeant, he told Lieutenant Tossher, and I was given permission to return to Dragon Mountain Base Camp and make a telephone call home from the new satellite-relay station that had been built there.

On the flight back to Dragon Mountain, I realized I could go directly to brigade and get my assignment to the LRRPs, taking advantage of getting out of the field. Captain Nobel would not like it, but as long as I was with C Company, on constant field operations, I would never make it to the LRRPs.

I was not satisfied with the infantry anymore, because all I could see us doing was playing the game in exactly the way the North Vietnamese wanted. It was the most classic guerrilla principle in action: "When the enemy attacks, retreat. When he rests, harass. When he retreats, attack."

I was sick of being the fool. In the LRRPs I knew I could take the war to the enemy . . . my way.

---

12 February 1967: Recon Trooper

It was obvious we were wasting time, and blood, with our infantry actions. We deployed platoons, companies, and battalions. They were as obvious in the field as herds of elephants. The enemy simply sidestepped us most of the time.

If there was a fight, it was because the North Vietnamese were ready for it, dug in, supplied, and in position exactly where they wanted to be. When we walked into them the killing began, but it too often was one-sided . . . in their favor.

With recon teams it was different. Small, quiet, and appearing in unexpected places, our Special Forces, special operations, and long-range reconnaissance patrol teams were not only bringing back useful intelligence, they were killing enemy soldiers.

I looked at the infantryman's steel helmet as the symbol of the line trooper, clumsy with ammunition and equipment, scared, soaked with rain and spattered with mud.

Now I could take off my helmet. It was like the infantry, heavy, giving a false sense of security, hard to manage. I replaced my helmet with a soft, narrow-brimmed flop hat.

I was now a recon trooper.

13 February 1967: Tet

The Tet (Lunar New Year) Truce ended on midnight of the 12th. We had a cease-fire agreement with the North Vietnamese during the two weeks of Vietnamese Tet holidays.

Our intelligence from aerial photographs and recon teams revealed the North Vietnamese had used the relief from our bombing and artillery to resupply themselves. More trucks than ever rolled down the Ho Chi Minh Trail that flanked the Cambodian border, unloading food and ammunition for resupply points along the border, where it could be divided into man-packed loads, and infiltrated across into South Vietnam.

As famous as the Ho Chi Minh Trail was with the media, a substantial portion of war supplies for the Vietcong and North Vietnamese came from ships docking at Cambodian harbors, where their cargos were loaded onto trucks and driven across Cambodia to the South Vietnamese border for hand-carried infiltration.

One of the new brigade LRRP teams had encountered a unit of North Vietnamese shortly before the Tet Truce was over, and two members of the recon team were wounded, but they reported they shot four enemy soldiers in the firefight.

Both wounds were nonlethal, one man grazed on the shoulder, the other hit in the side. Both men would get back from the patrol.

Sergeant Littlejohn was the man hit in the side. He was evacuated to Japan for surgery, and left his weapon—a World War II U.S. .30 caliber carbine—with the LRRP platoon supply sergeant.

---

14 February 1967: The LRRP Platoon

After making the overseas telephone call home from Dragon Mountain Base Camp, and settling my mind that everything was going to be all right with my mother's medical treatment, I stopped by the brigade headquarters personnel section, and told them I had come out of the field to join the LRRPs.

They prepared my paperwork there, and gave it to me to personally deliver to Lieutenant Lapollo, the platoon leader.

Now, not even Captain Nobel could make me go back to the infantry.

A convoy was going from Dragon Mountain to 3 Tango. I climbed aboard one of the trucks, and found as comfortable a place among the boxes and baggage as I could for the long hot ride out.

When I jumped off the truck, I noticed how much 3 Tango had improved since I had first stood security over the Montagnard laborers as they chopped back the jungle around the empty church building.

There were now graded roads, barbed-wire fences, and wooden frames for tents. At the rate it was growing, 3 Tango would become another base camp, I thought, sidestepping work parties sweating with giant loads of C rations and ammunition.

I found a military policeman and asked the way to the LRRP platoon. He pointed up the hill toward the church building. "Right there by brigade headquarters," he said.

I walked up the hill. I was out of the infantry.

Two men in tiger fatigues, the green-and-black-striped uniform worn by Special Forces and long-range patrol teams, lounged on top of a low bunker. I approached them, feeling out of place in my infantry equipment.

"Hello," I said, "where do I find Lieutenant Lapollo?"

"What do you want him for?"

"I've just come in from the field to join you guys," I said. "Lapollo's expecting me."

The two men looked warily at me. I could tell the attitude of the LRRP platoon personnel was different from what I had been accustomed to in the infantry.

"Try the radio bunker," one of the men said, pointing toward the squat, sandbagged structure beside us. I nodded thanks and stooped slightly to clear the low doorway, and edged through the blast baffle, an outer chamber that required two changes of direction to enter the main bunker room.

It was cooler inside, and much darker. My eyes adjusted to the difference. Lapollo sat in front of the radios, reading a coverless copy of *Playboy* magazine.

"Well, I'm here," I announced, handing him the assignment papers from brigade.

"Good!" Lapollo said. "Damn, I'm glad you made it today. Everybody is out but one team, and I've got to cover the radio."

"I tried to get here last month, but Captain Nobel wouldn't turn me loose," I said.

"Well, go find a bunk," Lapollo said, "and see me when you get settled."

"Yes, sir," I said, "and thank you, sir."

Three medium tents were the living quarters for the platoon. They were surrounded by low sandbag walls and backed with bunkers just a jump out the doorways. The sides of the tents were rolled down against the sun and dust.

Inside was a jumble of cots, weapons, wooden crates, and duffel bags. An empty cot was pushed into a corner. I lay my rucksack down on it. It would do fine.

A Communist AK-47 assault rifle hung from a tent pole. It was clean and well oiled. It was obviously not a souvenir. It was someone's weapon who lived here.

Olive-drab packets, marked "Ration, Subsistence, Long Range Patrol," cluttered some of the cots.

"What are you doing in here?" a voice asked from behind me. I turned too fast, revealing he had startled me, and saw a man I hadn't noticed was in the tent.

"My name's Camper," I said, unsure of how to begin with him. "I just joined the platoon. The lieutenant told me to bunk in here." He was a young soldier like myself, and he wore faded-out tiger fatigues. I noticed he did not wear boots, but Vietcong sandals.

"What outfit you from?" he asked.

"Second of the Eighth, C Company," I said, but the answer made no impression on him.

"Can I take this bunk?" I asked.

He shrugged. "I guess so. The guy who sleeps there is in the hospital in Japan."

I sat down and opened my rucksack. The soldier in sandals watched me unpack. He looked to me like he might be Spanish, or maybe American Indian.

"Hard to spot somebody when they're holding real still, ain't it?" he asked.

I nodded.

"You seen any combat?" he asked, but it was not a question, it was a challenge.

"Yeah," I said. He seemed satisfied with that.

"It ain't like being with a line company, being out with a team, you know that?" he asked.

"I know that. That's why I'm here," I said. There was silence for a moment.

"My name's Harmon," the soldier finally said, ex-

tending his hand. I took it. He smiled, and I grinned back
in relief. He would later tell me he was an Alaskan Indian.

"Welcome to the LRRPs," he said.

There wasn't much of a routine around the platoon
area. It was more like a transit station. Men off patrol slept
during all hours, teams came and went, and very few people were there at any one time.

The only place you could find someone twenty-four
hours a day was the radio bunker.

I reported back to Lieutenant Lapollo and received
my first on-the-job training in the radio bunker. It was
headquarters for us, and every man was expected to function in it.

We monitored our own teams in the field, which involved arranging air, artillery, or other fire support for
them if necessary, or helicopter extraction if needed. So
radio watch was a very important job indeed.

Lapollo spent the rest of the day with me, showing
how to take situation reports (sitreps) from teams in the
field, and familiarizing me with the unit codes.

I put on the headset, and acknowledged the team Sitreps, copied intelligence reports, studied the map of our
current area of operations, and drank coffee.

I knew how to get artillery or air support from my
experience with brigade and classes at the LRRP school.
There was a posted list of units to call in an emergency
near the mapboard, giving the radio frequency and call
signs of the 4th Aviation (for helicopters), the 4th of the
42nd Artillery, and the forward air control unit at New
Pleiku Air Base.

Late on the night of the 14th, 3 Tango was mortared,
Communist 82mm shells sailing in and exploding across
the airstrip, and among some of the tents and bunkers.

I heard the first few shells detonate, the concussion
from them vibrating my cot, and quickly but calmly
moved to the bunker. There were only a few of us in it, and
we said little.

There were flashes that lit up the trees near the church and outlined the tent roofs by the landing zone as the mortar shells struck. I didn't risk too long a look out the bunker viewslit, worried a round might hit directly outside.

There was nothing to do during a mortar attack except sit it out.

The next morning, I learned there were only light casualties and little real damage. We had been extremely fortunate.

A two-man LRRP team far outside the 3 Tango perimeter had actually been close to the enemy mortar. They came in on the morning of the 15th, telling us about how they would hear the mortar shell leave the tube, then a few moments later, listen to it explode in 3 Tango. One of the team was Speck, a seventeen-year-old, who had kept saying, "Those poor bastards, those poor bastards," over and over as we were mortared.

Without radio watch, I had no duty, so I began to settle in, and after breakfast on the 15th, my first order of business was to draw my special equipment from the LRRP supply tent, which was run by a full-blooded American Indian named Sergeant Snake.

The radio bunker and the living tents formed two sides of a small compound. At the far end was the supply tent. It appeared deserted, but I had learned caution.

"Anybody home?" I asked, leaning over the sandbag wall across the front of the tent and peering into the gloom inside. I could see crates of equipment in there.

"Yeah, just a minute," said Snake, coming from the back. He was heavyset and had an irritated expression.

"I'm new," I said. "I need to get my equipment issue."

He accepted that without further qualification and began to gather equipment, laying it on the sandbags before me.

"One strobe light. One snap-link. One survival knife, sorry I don't have no more sheaths . . . One indigenous rucksack. Four canteens. You got your own weapon?"

"Yeah," I said, "I've got my M-16."

"You plan to keep it?" he asked. That seemed like a strange question to me. I shrugged.

"I've got a couple of AKs in here, and Littlejohn's M-2 carbine," Snake said, "but I'm short of magazines."

"I'll keep my Sixteen for right now," I said, and signed for the equipment.

"Oh yeah," he said. "You can buy your tigers downtown."

I knew tiger fatigues were not issue, so it didn't bother me that I had to get my own. "Sure," I said.

The 2nd Brigade long-range reconnaissance patrol platoon was provisional, and therefore unofficial. Everything going to the LRRP platoon—from ammunition to personnel—had to be begged, borrowed, or stolen.

Only division-level LRRPs were authorized. Since the 4th Division headquarters did not yet have their LRRP company fully organized, for the time being, we were it.

I packed items in the empty wooden mortar-ammunition box under my cot, and decided to visit brigade and see how my friends there were doing. I hadn't seen them since last November.

My first stop was to see Captain Wilson. He lived alone in one of the officers' two-man "pyramid" tents that were pitched behind the church building. I looked in through the tent doorway and saw him lying on his cot.

"Hey, Captain," I asked, "can I come in?"

Wilson looked up at me. He was a muscular man, balding now, and he wore a permanent squint.

He was fifty-three years old, and he would never make major. The army felt he did not have the education. His experience, beginning in World War II, apparently didn't count.

He knew war inside out. This was his second tour in Vietnam, this time as a brigade operations officer. On his first tour, he had commanded an infantry company.

Wilson strained mightily at the rules, taking unauthorized flights out to field units in enemy contact, organizing and training the brigade reaction platoon, and telling the other officers how to run their business. They wanted to get rid of him.

"Where the hell you been?" he asked as I stepped in and sat down on a footlocker.

"I've been in the infantry," I said. "I just joined the LRRPs. I thought I'd come over and see if you'd found a slot with a line company yet."

Wilson swung his feet onto the bamboo mat in front of his cot and sat up. "LRRP? You are a crazy son of a bitch. Let me see that weapon."

I handed him my M-16. He examined it and handed it back.

"Better get yourself a carbine and throw that hunk of shit away," he said, "you'll live longer if you listen to me."

"What's wrong with my Sixteen?" I asked.

"They're breaking down in all the line companies. Jamming all the time." He reached over to his desk and picked up a folding-stock paratrooper carbine with a long thirty-round magazine inserted in it. "The carbine will fire when that toy has given up. It's just a better weapon, son."

I took the carbine. It was slightly heavier than my M-16, but it felt good. It was true many M-16s were jamming. I didn't know why, since we had such good performance out of them in the small-arms-weapons test group.

Mostly, the malfunction in Vietnam was a failure to extract a fired cartridge case out of the chamber, and the only way to get a stuck case out of the weapon was to knock it out with a cleaning rod down the bore. Many of us had taken to carrying an assembled cleaning rod taped to the foregrip of the rifle.

"I can get a carbine," I said, thinking of the one Snake had offered.

"Why did you join the LRRP platoon?" Wilson asked.

"Safer," I boasted. "Too easy to get killed out in the infantry. At least the LRRPs don't go around shooting at each other. They don't make stupid—"

"How old are you?" Wilson demanded.

"Twenty, last October," I said.

"I think the oldest kid in your outfit is twenty-three," he said. "The most experienced of them might have six months in the country. The Vietnamese have been fighting somebody here since the end of World War II. That's over twenty-five years. That's before you were born."

Wilson was angry. It was like I had turned on a switch in him.

"There are some real soldiers out there with the VC, believe me! You are worse than just inexperienced, boy, you're cannon fodder."

I recovered enough to reply. "The LRRPs are good," I said, "they—"

"Good?" Wilson said. "Those are adults out there in the jungle with rifles who want to kill your ass. Good? You better get good! You better goddamn well get perfect!" He snorted in disgust and lay back down on his cot.

"Well . . ." I said, uncertain of what to say.

"Well, hell," Wilson spat.

I stood to leave. "Sorry, Captain," I said.

He looked me straight in the eye. "You take care of yourself," he said.

I almost felt a chill.

I had faith in my decision to join the LRRPs. Tales about their luck and prowess were becoming common. Just before I had joined the platoon, one of the teams had reached a state of legend for an incident that almost got them all killed.

The team leader was a southerner, and instead of an M-16, he carried a commercial, semiautomatic Remington shotgun mailed to him by his father. He had painted the new shotgun with olive-drab enamel from the motor pool, and he kept the long barrel so he could make fifty- and seventy-five-meter shots. "Sawed-offs are for bank jobs, not field combat," he said.

His team had been lying in ambush in the jungle when a North Vietnamese mortar platoon walked by, loaded with mortar tubes, base plates, ammo, and shovels. The

LRRP team fell in behind them at a discreet distance, to see where they were going.

The mortar platoon stopped at nightfall, and the LRRP team moved in closer. Then something like three companies of NVA infantry came out of nowhere and set up a perimeter around the mortars and, of course, the LRRP team.

As long as it was dark, there was no problem, but at dawn, there was sure to be trouble.

The team made a plan. They waited for dawn, and as soon as the first glimmer of gray was visible through the trees, they radioed for a massive artillery-fire mission right on top of the camp. It was a drastic situation.

When the shells began to shriek in and shatter the trees, the team tried to run. The artillery barrage was more fierce than they had expected, and instead of escaping, they were forced back to cover, along with the stunned, disoriented enemy.

"We made it to a kind of shallow, dried-out streambed, and that was it," the team leader later told me. "There were NVA running everywhere, man, it was crazy. It was still too dark to really see, and the damn gooks were trying to jump in the streambed with us. We started shootin' 'em."

He said that in the confusion, the enemy didn't realize where the gunfire was coming from, and didn't know they were leaping into a ditch with Americans.

Finally, both the LRRPs and the North Vietnamese were using the same spot for cover. The team knew they could not stay, and ran again; this time a shell exploded close enough to them to blow the team leader's web gear off him, and he lost his shotgun.

The team got away. The NVA were hurt badly.

When he returned to the platoon, the team leader seemed to mourn the loss of his Remington more than anything else.

I realized I had left the field just in time.

The fighting that had begun as mortaring grew, and by midday every unit of the 2nd Brigade in the field— infantry, firebase, or convoy—was under attack.

An M-113 track and two jeeps hit mines out on the road the engineers were cutting through the jungle on their dawn road-clearing sweep, blowing them to junk, and killing the crews.

The general situation in the highlands since Christmas had been too quiet, and suddenly we had action and it was getting too big for us to handle. We knew the enemy had been working on resupplying himself. Now we knew what for. A full offensive was under way.

I went back to Sergeant Snake and asked him for Littlejohn's carbine. He gave it to me, along with a sack of magazines. I took it to my cot and learned how to disassemble it, adjust the sights, and use the automatic selector switch. I didn't want to trust the M-16 on a LRRP patrol, where, if one weapon failed, it was twenty-five percent of the firepower available.

As I worked on the carbine, I was told I would go on an overnight two-man patrol out near a Montagnard village. My partner, a LRRP named Huebner, was also originally from the Second of the Eighth, and he told me what to bring.

We would not be sleeping, so we would carry no ponchos, and we would not eat, so we would take no food. I was to take nothing but my weapon, magazines, and a fighting knife.

Huebner was carrying an M-16 fitted with a Starlight scope, and wearing a PRC-25 radio so we could keep in contact with the radio bunker.

Our mission was to move after dark to near one of the closest Montagnard villages and set up a sniper position, where we could shoot any people we saw carrying weapons.

Our overnight mission passed without event, but by daybreak, we could tell something was wrong.

There were dozens of Huey helicopters circling 3 Tango.

Huebner and I hurried back to find out what was happening.

---

16 February 1967: Disaster

A twin-rotor Chinook cargo helicopter brought in about thirty dead infantrymen from the 1st of the 22nd. The Hueys landing on the pad up the hill beside the hospital tents were dropping off wounded, and they were landing at the rate of one helicopter every two minutes.

Huebner and I saw the dragged-in wrecks of the jeeps that had hit mines on road-clearing patrol the morning prior. One of them had its frame bent totally back on itself, the rear axle almost touching the engine compartment.

I saw groups of soldiers from the 1st of the 22nd frantically breaking open cardboard boxes of rifle ammunition, loading new magazines, and each time a hundred magazines would be filled, they were bagged in ponchos and carried up to the landing zone to be thrown on an outgoing helicopter.

Word came to the LRRP radio bunker that C Company, 2nd of the 8th, was deeply involved in combat. Two of the platoons, Braun's First and Tossher's Second, were taking heavy casualties. It was my unit.

I sat on my cot in the LRRP platoon area, and looked at the other men waiting with me. They were from infantry companies themselves. Our friends still in those companies were cut off and fighting for their lives.

All of us felt the same way, and began packing our rucksacks and cramming ammunition into our pouches.

Four of us from my tent started up the street toward the
landing zone, rifles in our hands.

A group of MPs stopped us.

"Where the hell do you think you're going?" the MP
sergeant demanded.

"To the field," I said.

"We got orders. Nobody goes up to the LZ without
permission," said the MP.

"Get out of our way!" one of the LRRPs with me
said. "We have to get out to our units!"

"You go to your commanding officer and get his authorization," barked the MP, "nobody goes up there on his
own."

"But we have to go! Those are our buddies getting
killed out there!" the young LRRP beside me said, tears in
his eyes.

"What's going on here?" demanded Lieutenant
Lapollo, coming up from behind us.

"It's my company, they're getting wiped out," sobbed
the young LRRP who had been with the 1st of the 22nd.
"I've got to go out there to them, don't you understand?
They need everybody they can get!"

I was as emotional as the man speaking, my hand
trembling as I held my carbine. I wanted to jump on the
first helicopter out, and get back to the field to take care of
my squad.

"Hold on, you're with the LRRP platoon now,"
Lapollo said, "you're not in the infantry anymore. They
can handle themselves. You've got a job to do here!"

"But my company . . ." said the LRRP.

"We're getting our missions now. We'll be sending out
teams today! You volunteered to do this job, now, damn it,
you're going to stick to it," Lapollo said.

I looked at the others. I had only just joined. I didn't
even know them by name.

"Yes, sir," said the trooper meekly, and walked back
down the street. We hesitated, but Lapollo and the MPs
were resolute.

I went back to my tent and put away my equipment.

Lapollo came into my tent. "If you really want to help," he said softly, "why don't you go up to the aid station and do what you can for the medics? They need it."

I nodded, and Lapollo handed me a signed pass. I walked back to the MPs, showing them my pass, and trotted up to the aid station.

The scene there was hellish.

The landing zone was littered with scraps of aluminum from helicopter rotor blades. It was a small pad, and only one Huey could comfortably set down on it at a time, but the air traffic controllers were trying to land two or three ships at once, and there had been rotor-blade impacts.

Several ships that had sheared their rotors were pushed off to the side.

The line of waiting helicopters fluttered and thundered endlessly up into the sky, each one carrying wounded men who needed emergency medical care.

As a ship landed, soldiers stormed aboard, lifting out the wounded and moving them near the aid tents. The wounded were not on stretchers. The stretchers had all been used hours ago. Now, it was a matter of manhandling limp bodies—or twisting, agonized wounded—and finding a place to lay them.

Piles of ammunition alongside the landing pad being loaded aboard the outgoing helicopters were constantly restocked by infantrymen carrying boxes of machine-gun belts, rifle ammunition in quick-load stripper clips, crates of grenades, and bags of Claymore mines.

The aid tents were long since full, and the areas around them had been covered with wounded. Bodies, some alive and some dead, lay on sandbag walls around the tents, on top of bunkers, and in rows on the company streets between the tents.

I saw one wounded soldier, sitting against a sandbag wall, who kept covering the face of a dead man in front of him each time a helicopter would partially blow the poncho off the corpse.

Wounded men shrieked in pain. Medics among them

worked as fast as they could, injecting morphine, checking casualty tags, and trying to decide who would go next to surgery and who would not.

Those who were obviously dying were left on the ground. Those who had a chance were sent into the tents where doctors and medics worked desperately to save their lives.

Chaplains from the infantry battalions were also there, going on their knees from man to man, trying to give words of hope, getting blood on their hands and Bibles as they touched the boys, looking as pained as the wounded they attended.

Some of the helicopters were wobbling in flight, going around the others, smoking from bullet holes in their engine cowlings, trying to land before they crashed.

A few of the helicopters came in with doorgunners and crew chiefs missing, shot out of the aircraft while trying to rescue wounded from jungle landing zones under heavy fire.

There were also wounded and dead pilots and copilots in some helicopters; whoever was left up front who could still fly brought them back.

Ten-gallon vats of iced Coca-Cola and Pepsi sodas were carried to the wounded. I saw one laborer loading ammunition on the outgoing helicopters try to get a cold Coke out of a vat, but the soldiers giving out the cans pushed him away, shouting the drinks were only for the wounded.

I stopped a medic, and asked him what I should do.

"What outfit you from?" he shouted above the roar of the helicopters. I told him.

"We're getting a lot of wounded back from the 2nd of the 8th," he said, "they're over there," and pointed. I thanked him and ran to them.

I found a group of stunned, bloody, filthy men, some of them still wearing part of their field equipment. All of them seemed to be alive.

I took a double handful of sodas out of the vat, and

stooped in the middle of the survivors, opening cans and thrusting them into their hands.

"What's going on out there?" I asked.

"First Platoon's cut off," grunted one of the men. "They're getting wiped out. Goddamn gooks are all over the place . . ."

A medic looked at me. "You from C Company?" he asked.

"Yeah," I said.

"You want to take a look at these bodies?"

I followed him. He led me to a group of poncho-covered corpses. "They sent these guys in this morning. They were killed yesterday. Do you know any of them?" he asked.

I lifted the poncho over each face. Their hair was matted with dried blood. Dirt stuck to their cheeks and some of them had open shrapnel rips in their skin.

"No," I said. "These guys might be with the engineers. I don't know who they are."

"We're expecting a big load of bodies tonight or tomorrow," said the medic. "We won't start getting them until some of this shit dies down. Got to get the wounded out first."

I worked the rest of the day moving wounded, giving water to those the medics said could take it, separating the ones who died from those who were still alive, and listening to disjointed, incredible tales of death and survival from the stricken soldiers lying on the dirt.

I remember the worst of it came when we ran out of places to put the casualties. Every ledge, bunker roof, street, and alley had been occupied, and still the helicopters kept coming.

Enemy weapons were sent back. There were all types, AK-47s, SKSs, RPD light machine guns, Tokarev pistols, even cans of ammunition and hand grenades.

Many of the weapons were battle-damaged, with bul-

let holes in their stocks and shrapnel scars on the metal.
Some of them were burned by napalm to metal skeletons.

Most of the ammunition was still in new paper packages, evidence of the recent resupply. I realized how crazy
our politicians were to agree to any cease-fire that would
allow the enemy to prepare himself for an offensive like
this. Our leaders had done it simply to try and look good.
For their concern over their public images, we were dying.

I had heard that politicians were ignorant; now I believed it. They were as much my enemy as the North Vietnamese were. To live through Vietnam, I had to survive all
my side and the enemy could throw at me.

When I walked back down the road to the LRRP
platoon, I went directly to the radio bunker and asked for
news of C Company.

All we could learn was from the radio traffic. It
seemed the 1st Platoon had been isolated and was under
siege, with the rest of the company trying to break through
to them.

They were in the area near the road-security firebase.
They had been on patrol going to the river. I knew very
well what the terrain was like. The trees were double canopy, too dense even for smoke grenades to be seen through.

17 February 1967: Casualties

One of the LRRP teams sent out on the 16th quickly
ran into the NVA, killed three of them, and managed to get
extracted by helicopter back here to safety. Struthers, a
black LRRP, was point man for the team. He saw the
enemy first and killed all of them himself. He said they
were on a water run, carrying canteens for their unit.

The second team, with young Speck on it, was flown
out to their target area, but their helicopter hovered too
high, actually over the treetops.

Speck hesitated, realizing they were too high. The

doorgunner pushed him and he fell out of the helicopter, through the branches, and hit the ground, spraining his ankle.

He lay there, looking up at the hole he had made in the tree limbs. The Huey was still hovering, just above the hole. Speck lifted his M-16, and later told me that if the chopper had tried to fly away, "I would have brought the son of a bitch down myself."

In the ship, one of the team grabbed the doorgunner in a headlock, and jumped out, taking the crewman with him, and the rest of the team followed.

The LRRP team carried Speck to a hiding place, pushing the confused, frightened, and weaponless doorgunner along, and they radioed for an extraction at dawn.

The brigade had so many helicopters shot down by the morning of the 17th they were becoming scarce. Resupply missions and Dustoffs (code for pickup of wounded) had priority over everything, which included LRRP team insertions, so I did not go on patrol.

I went to the C Company orderly room/supply tent they maintained at 3 Tango, which was not far from the LRRP platoon area, and asked for news on the 1st Platoon. There were two unwounded survivors from the battle, and one, Dresden, told me the story.

Braun had taken his platoon down out of the firebase toward the river, as all of the platoons had done so often. It was a three-thousand-meter walk, the ground low and damp, grown over with thick vegetation.

He chose a route commonly used by the river patrols because it was easier walking than the other terrain.

They had stopped to take a short break in place, all standing. Braun sent out a scout to the left and right flanks, letting the men relax while they waited.

One scout came back, saying he had seen nothing unusual. The other scout returned at almost the same time, saying he had found evidence of recent chopping and cutting of the jungle foliage.

As the man spoke, the platoon was hit with a barrage

of automatic fire. Dresden said he thought at least fourteen men, half the strength of the 1st Platoon, were hit in a matter of seconds.

Everyone in the platoon dived for cover, and tried to fire back, but they were caught on low ground. Braun ordered the platoon to carry its wounded and try to get to higher ground. Enemy fire came down on them from uphill, where they had walked past camouflaged North Vietnamese ambushers.

The platoon couldn't make it to higher ground, so, trapped where they were, they organized a defense perimeter and tried to hold.

Up at the firebase, Captain Nobel responded to their radio plea for help by recalling the 2nd and 3rd Platoons, which were on patrol in the mountains, and sending them to the aid of the embattled 1st Platoon.

Helicopters had been dispatched to pick up the two platoons, but could not reach them quickly, because there was no place to land.

Artillery and air support, including Puff the Magic Dragon with its triple miniguns, was called to help. The problem was the dense forest, with the trees so close together and so heavily canopied, helicopter overflights could not even see the ground.

Trying to get accurate artillery fire around the 1st Platoon was difficult; shells hit in the tops of the trees and exploded. Puff would not fire too close to the platoon, because of the tremendous spread of his "beaten zone."

By the time 2nd and 3rd Platoons could get aboard helicopters, fly out to a usable landing zone near the battle, and begin to walk toward it, most of the men in the ambushed platoon were already dead.

With tears in his eyes, Dresden told me how withering the enemy fire had been, clipping through the leaves, tearing the brush apart. Wounded men were hit, and then hit again.

He said an M-79 grenadier blinded from a head wound had continued to fire, the man beside him unable to move but acting as his eyes.

"Our perimeter got smaller and smaller," Dresden said. "We kept crawling closer together."

Braun himself had been shot in the foot, and was bleeding badly, but stayed on the radio, pleading with Captain Nobel for help.

Nobel tried to reassure him, telling him he was only eight hundred meters away, then seven hundred, and so on.

Finally, Braun made his last radio call. He said, "I've only got four men left. Put the artillery on my position."

Then, Dresden told me, he pulled the pin on a grenade, held it to his stomach, and contracted into a fetal position, still holding the live grenade.

"Why did he do that?" I asked.

"The dinks were coming through shooting the wounded," Dresden said. "Braun figured when they got to him he might be able to take a few with him."

The artillery began to crash in, blowing down the trees, and forcing the enemy soldiers away. The shelling continued until Captain Nobel stopped it.

"We shot the 2nd Platoon's point man when they broke through to us," Dresden told me. "We were crazy then, we were shooting everything. The captain and his men came running in anyway, trying to throw up a defense perimeter. They found Braun, and got the grenade out of his hand. He had passed out."

I knew many of the men in the 1st platoon. Little Beady, who had carried an M-79 grenade launcher, Batman, Powell, Sergeant Coffey, Sergeant Smith . . . lots of them.

There had only been about twenty-eight men with Braun that morning when he left the firebase. The platoon was that far understrength.

Had the massacre of the platoon been Braun's fault? Were he or his men being careless? I had caught him lax before, lying to the captain. I wished I had reported him, but it was too late.

There was another macabre fact. Over a dozen of the M-16 rifles recovered from Braun's platoon were found jammed, most of them with cartridge cases stuck in their chambers.

The B Company tent was beside C Company, and as I was saying my good-byes, I noticed a largish bear cub waddling past the sandbags.

It was explained to me that was Bravo bear, B Company's mascot. They had killed its mother while on an operation, and, out of guilt, had taken the cub to raise. I could only imagine the surprise of the line trooper who had happened across a mad mother bear, but obviously his M-16 had been enough of a match.

One of the B Company soldiers asked me if I wanted my picture taken with the cub. He had a camera in his hand.

Bravo sat with his back toward us, ignoring everybody.

"Turn him around," said the man with the camera.

I knelt and touched Bravo, who whirled around and had his teeth in my hand so quickly I didn't have the chance to jump back. Bravo was not a dog. He was a *bear,* and he was not playing. His sharp teeth were going into my hand.

I hit the bear with the butt of my rifle, a bit awkward because I was holding it left-handed, and continued to hit him between the ears until he let go.

The soldiers were howling with laughter. I was apparently one more sucker who had fallen for the get-your-picture-taken-with-Bravo trick.

Embarrassed and angry, and still sick about the 1st Platoon, I walked away.

---

17 February 1967: 2300 Hours, 3 Tango LZ

It was almost midnight, and Lieutenant Lapollo and I waited on the landing zone near the aid tents. It was quiet now.

I had a battery-powered lamp in each hand, and

walked forward when we heard the big Chinook helicopter coming. I began to swing the lamps so the pilot would see me.

The Chinook came down, the blast from its twin rotors staggering me as I signaled for the pilot to hover, descend, and touch down.

As the pilot cut the engines, two trucks from graves registration drove in behind the big helicopter, and the Chinook's cargo door lowered. On the trucks were over seventy bodies, each one zipped inside a heavy green vinyl bag, and identified with a graves registration tag.

I held my lamps up so the work party could see to carry the body bags off the trucks and inside the helicopter. Each time they laid a bag down, I could hear the corpse's head hit the deck separately—until one of the infantrymen helping unload threatened the graves crew with their own deaths if they did not show more respect for his friends in the bags.

I had volunteered to come up to the LZ and help with the loading. Most of the men in the bags came from the 2nd of the 8th. I could read their names on the tags as they were carried past me.

I wanted to help my old battalion out just one last time.

NEWS ITEM: 18 February 1967
GI'S ASK FOR FIRE ON OWN POSITION
SAIGON (UPI) A Communist battalion overran a U.S. infantry platoon in South Vietnam's Central Highlands Thursday. The desperate Americans called in artillery fire on their own positions and then fell silent.

Radio contact with the platoon was broken. It was not clear whether the American casualties resulted from artillery fire or from fierce hand-to-hand combat with the 400-man Communist battalion attacking the platoon.

The platoon's parent company watched helplessly a mere 200 yards away, pinned down by Communist gunfire and unable to come to the rescue of the infantrymen.

The action came on the day that it was announced American dead in the Vietnam War went beyond 10,000.

There was a call for all of us not on patrol to go to the brigade briefing tent, and I walked there, wondering what was going on.

We were told to take seats on the benches facing the warboard, the same one I used to keep posted. Colonel Miller, the brigade commander, and several of the headquarters officers waited for us to assemble.

A captain began the talk, speaking about the value of LRRP units, and how we were such an asset to our brigade and division, but he was just the warm-up for Colonel Miller, who took the stage in front of the warboard.

He told us how proud he was of us, what a good reputation his LRRP platoon had, and how we were admired by other units. His praise was welcome, but suspect. Commanding officers rarely get the troops together to brag on them to their faces.

Miller detailed some of the missions that impressed him, naming names, smiling, sometimes walking up to individual soldiers and touching their arms respectfully.

He got a few laughs with easy jokes, and he promised recognition for our good work. Then, still with no specific point made, he dismissed us.

We went back to our tents feeling appreciated and capable, but we wouldn't really know why we had gotten the glad hand until the next day.

---

19 February 1967: Volunteers SOG—5th Special Forces Group

"Hey, we got a formation outside," somebody said as he walked through my tent. I looked up from where I lay on my cot and frowned. Damn, I didn't feel like any interruptions. But the guys were stirring, pulling on shirts and flop hats. I saw them moving through both tent doorways.

Everybody seemed to be gathering on the far side of the tents near the company street. I ducked out under the tent flaps and took a place in the group.

There were only about a dozen or so of us in now. One team was out on patrol, and with R & R, wounded, and schools, that accounted for everybody. We stood quietly, bored with the heat and with the army.

The lieutenant and a stranger wearing clean unmarked fatigues walked in front of our little band of renegades, and I realized there was going to be more to this than a petty ass-chewing.

The attention level of the men perked up when the lieutenant spoke. "We've got an unusual mission we need volunteers for."

Volunteers? We were all volunteers! Nobody was in LRRP because he was forced into it. I thought you just raised your hand once and after that they sent you wherever they wanted.

"This mission is out of artillery, radio, and air-support range. You can only make contact with an aircraft twice daily by radio. There may be no helicopters to get you out."

The lieutenant was serious. He let us consider what he had said for a moment. "All we need now is one team. We can't tell you where you'll be going until the mission briefing. Okay, who'll volunteer?"

There was a pause as we looked at each other, questions in our eyes. Then, as a group, we all raised our hands.

The stranger looked at the lieutenant. The lieutenant smiled. "Okay. Thank you. We'll pick who we want and let you know this afternoon."

We drifted back to our tents, I lay down and went back to sleep.

They only picked unmarried men for that mission.

It was a melodramatic gesture, one that would not be observed anymore as soon as our platoon command became accustomed to these new missions.

We had just begun working with the Special Operations Group, and attached to the 5th Reg.

One of the men I knew on that first over-the-border mission into Cambodia was Holloway. He was black, and one of the best men in the LRRP platoon.

Holloway and his team came back very shortly after an insertion attempt. They had never gotten out of the helicopter.

He said they had flown over the border toward their target area in Cambodia, their mission pure reconnaissance. His Huey had been escorted by two gunships.

Close to the target area, they were fired on with ground-to-air rockets.

The pilots banked the helicopters sharply and raced back to 3 Tango.

I was waiting at the airstrip when they landed. Everybody aboard the helicopters was excited. "You should have seen those missiles!" Holloway said, holding his hands spread apart as far as he could. "They were this big!"

A secondary target area had been plotted, and the team was ordered to reinsert. They did this doubtfully, because having to abort the first attempt had left them with a feeling the mission was unlucky.

The helicopter dropped Holloway and his team into a bomb crater just over the border. It was dusk, and rain was beginning to fall.

Attracted by the sound of the helicopter, North Vietnamese moved in from several directions. Holloway's team saw them coming, and hid themselves in a large bush near the crater.

For hours in the dark, with heavy rain coming down, the NVA searched for that recon team, guessing they were close to the bomb crater.

Holloway and the team stayed in the bush, not moving or speaking, while the enemy walked all around them. Holloway said that just before dawn the NVA left.

When the first chance for a radio contact came, the LRRPs talked to the relay aircraft over their area, requesting emergency extraction. They were picked up out of the same bomb crater, soaking wet, shivering from the cold and near catastrophe.

Our first secret over-the-border mission taught us a lot.

We changed to walk-over missions into Cambodia, not air insertion. Being located as close as we were to Cambodia, it was easy for one of our teams to drop near the border and make a slow, careful penetration by foot, using a weaving motion to cross and recross the border, checking on supply and infiltration routes, or to walk straight into Cambodia and arrange for an air extraction at the end of the mission.

The Special Operations Group (SOG) used as a cover the title "Studies and Observations Group," and was a Central Intelligence Agency function, in conjunction with Military Intelligence.

In 1967, SOG arranged itself into three basic areas of action: Command and Control North, (CCN) for missions into North Vietnam and northern Laos; Command and Control Central, (CCC), for central and southern Laos; and Command and Control South, (CCS), for Cambodia.

Before this Command and Control arrangement, SOG had operated out of forward operations bases given numbers; 1966–67 marked the reorganization period.

Our brigade commander, Colonel Miller, had volunteered the services of his long-range patrol platoon to Special Operations, and needing the manpower, they took us.

Such was the secrecy, even units working with SOG did not know their total missions, and often did not know what other people or units were also with SOG.

Going into joint operations with the Special Operations Group brought changes to our platoon.

Within the next few days, we received several teams of Montagnard mercenaries, new weapons, allocations for our men to receive special training, and an Air Force and CIA liaison.

The weapons were new Colt Commando XM-177E1s, the short version of the M-16 rifle I had fired during the weapons test. They were now issue for Special Forces and Special Operations units.

We were also given rifles based on the standard M-14, equipped with powerful telescopic sights and built specially as sniper rifles.

A Special Operations liaison officer was there helping us to check in our new personnel and equipment. As the Montagnard mercs erected their tents, our LRRP platoon sergeant watched them with some misgivings.

When the liaison man asked him what procedures we would use in employing the mercenaries, he replied, "I don't know. My people have never worked with the NVA before." It was a classic slip of the tongue.

We had fifty of the new Colt Commandos. We called them CAR-15s, a misnomer from an early designation Colt had used for all its new weapons. I knew the actual name of the weapon was Colt Commando, and it was stamped on the receiver, but to all the troops it was the CAR-15.

Each man in the platoon, about twenty of us, were given a CAR-15, but the remainder went to brigade officers and friends of brigade officers.

In the days following this new gift of weapons and men, our status became clear. The Montagnard mercs were to operate as guides and scouts with us. This was their home ground, their tribes living from the highlands of Vietnam to the jungled mountains of Cambodia.

They were short, strong men who smiled a lot and carried carbines. They wore green fatigues and obsolete U.S. web gear, and most had a colorful bandanna knotted loosely around the neck.

Some of our men volunteered to work with the 'Yards, but I had my reservations. I was making decisions concerning my one and only ass, and I told the platoon sergeant I didn't want to go on patrol with the 'Yards until I knew more about their habits.

I was assigned to an all-American team. My team leader was to be a young sergeant E5 named Mott, but he was on a mission and I had to wait to meet him.

I had listened to several of the experienced men in the platoon discussing Sergeant Mott.

Both Clark and Hart, two of the platoon's original members, didn't like Mott, and refused to go on patrol with him. We had the option, in our all-volunteer unit, of refusing to go out with a man we felt unsafe or incapable.

Clark, Hart, and I had been assigned on the 16th to go with Mott until our mission was cancelled, and they had flatly refused.

I reserved judgment on Mott, and waited until I could meet him.

I found Mott reading a map behind the ammo bunker, and sat down beside him. "Hi," I said, "I'm Frank Camper. Lapollo told me I'm on your team."

He looked at me. He had a pale complexion and bland features.

I didn't like his eyes. They seemed to be shielded, making it hard for me to trust him.

I extended my hand, but he ignored it.

"What's your first name, Sarge?" I asked.

"Call me *Sergeant* Mott," he said.

I felt an instant dislike for him.

"I understand you're new at this," Mott said, "so I want you to keep your mouth shut and follow orders. We're going into a hot area, and I can't afford any mistakes."

We were to be Team 4, our mission to try to locate the North Vietnamese headquarters group for the enemy divisions that had been attacking us.

The divisions themselves were pulling back into Cambodia, hurt badly from our airpower and artillery, and our infantry was now on the offensive, pursuing them as they retreated.

Reinforcements were flying into Pleiku from the 25th

Division and the 173rd Airborne to assist the 4th Division. We needed all the help we could get.

"Better be careful," Harmon told me when I returned to my tent to pack. "I heard old Victor Charlie don't like people snooping around out there." I managed a laugh I didn't feel as I placed my new canvas rucksack on the end of my cot. Lightness was important. What would I need?

No spare clothing. Nothing extra that did not contribute directly to my ability to move, shoot, or communicate. I decided to take my new CAR-15 with me instead of the carbine, and counted out 14 twenty-round magazines from my mortar box, checking each one for fresh ammunition.

I had four fragmentation grenades, but went to the supply tent for two smoke grenades, a red for enemy contact and a green for general signaling.

I tucked an international orange marker panel and two hand-held skyrocket flares in with ten packets of long-range patrol rations, the dehydrated original type.

I topped off the rucksack load with a tightly rolled poncho, and tied the flap down securely. In the outside rucksack pockets, I stored three canteens.

Finally, I strapped on my web belt and ammo pouches, shouldered the rucksack, and tested the weight of the entire rig. It was heavy, but it rode well. I picked up my new CAR-15, and felt ready to go.

Then I took off my gear and lay down on my cot fully dressed, trying to sleep. It seemed like hours before I lost track of noises and the men coming and going in my tent, but in actuality, it was only minutes. Then someone shook me out of my sleep. It was predawn, and still dark.

"Let's go," Mott said.

ARC LIGHT

In the chill of the predawn, I rolled out of my bunk, quickly slipped on my equipment, and met Mott and the others on the dark landing zone beside brigade headquarters.

An aircrew was boarding a Huey slick on the LZ. I wished I had some coffee. We trundled into the Huey, its cold metal deck wet with dew. The pilot and copilot flipped switches, and, with a smooth whine, the main rotors began to turn, gathering speed. The crew chief and doorgunner wore nylon flight jackets, not a bad idea for a cold morning.

The pilot watched his gauges, warming up the transmission. The rotors whirled faster now, vibrating the ship, cutting the air with a whistle. In the dark, our running lights seemed unusually bright, reflecting off the rotor blades above us, making pools of light on the ground. The deck rocked, and my stomach sank as we went up, banked, and I could see out the open door the hundreds of tent roofs of The Oasis, and in a few moments, we were in a sky that had gone from night to pearl dawn.

The rising sun was behind us, illuminating the cloud banks with streaks of silver and pink.

With Mott and me were Payne and Steffens. I hadn't been out with any of them. Mott carried an M-16. The rest of us had CAR-15s. We rode with our rucksacks on, our soft hats rolled and stuck inside our shirts because the slipstream would have ripped them off our heads.

After a twenty-minute flight, we banked again, and in the better light saw one of our muddy, miserable, artillery firebases below. The flickers of morning fires around its perimeter were like yellow stars as the infantry heated their C rations.

The pilot dropped us quickly into the perimeter, and we jumped out and ran from under the whirling rotors, which could dip to something like less than six feet at the tips, conditions permitting.

An officer, who looked as haggard as the infantrymen huddled around their bunkers, walked out to meet us. He and Mott shouted at each other in the racket made by the helicopter, trying to make themselves understood. Outgoing mail and a few soldiers boarded the Huey.

The officer waved, and walked back to the command bunker. Mott told us to find a place and get comfortable, that there was no mission for us yet. The Huey lifted off and was gone.

I was disappointed. The drama and effort of the dawn flight, the anticipation, the lightness in my stomach, had been for nothing. We could just as well have slept late, had breakfast, and caught a flight of convenience to this hill. I dropped my ruck, unpacked enough to find my C4 and boil some water in my canteen cup for coffee, and after I drank it, I covered myself with my poncho liner and went to sleep.

Mott didn't get our mission until that afternoon. We were told to wait until dark, then leave the perimeter, moving as a night patrol to the top of another hill several kilometers away, and be in position there by dawn.

From the hill we would have a view of the valley, and we would stay there and observe. The valley was on the Cambodian border, and was used by the North Vietnamese for infiltration.

Except for the night patrol part, it sounded like a good mission.

I studied the infantry as we spent the afternoon resting and talking. With a perspective I had not had before, I saw them as mud-streaked scarecrows in ill-fitting jungle fatigues and heavy, hot helmets. They had the eyes of doomed souls, eyes that showed no hope.

At chow that afternoon I was surprised to see Bessesi, a cook I knew who was injured when his truck hit a mine on a convoy from 3 Tango to The Oasis.

"Hey, Bessesi!" I said, "I thought they sent you home!"

"No," he answered, "all that mine did was knock me out of the truck."

"What are you doing way out here?" I asked.

"Living in a deep hole in the ground," he said. "Come over and see it."

I took my chow and followed him to a bunker entrance. We walked down steps into a miniature cavern. It was ten feet deep, and roofed over with metal and timbers. All of his cooking supplies and equipment were stored there.

"Fancy," I said.

"I'm not taking no more chances," Bessesi said. "You know, I never really believed there was a war going on until I hit that mine."

"Where were you when we got mortared at 3 Tango?" I asked.

"Basecamp. I never saw anything until I hit that mine."

"Well, it's a real war all right," I said.

"No shit," Bessesi said.

As soon as the evening shadows were deep enough, the sun down behind the mountains, our four-man team walked out of the firebase perimeter. The infantry along the bunker line wished us luck.

We moved down the hill in the dark, going into the trees, rustling the bushes as we felt our way forward. Night patrolling was the most dangerous work of all. Under the canopy of trees, it was totally black, and anyone listening nearby could hear us going cross-country through terrain that would have been difficult to penetrate in daylight.

All we could do was go slow, step carefully, and grope ahead of ourselves like blind men.

I had some experience at night movement, and, after a rest break, took point. I held my compass in my left hand and my CAR-15 in my right. Mott counted pace, to keep track of our distance covered. I placed one foot out at a time, shifting my balance, holding still and listening for a moment, then doing it again. I could not see where I was going.

The packstraps of the canvas NVA rucksack I wore rolled into knifelike coils and cut into my shoulders, hurting badly. I had to get a frame for it. My luminous compass dial seemed bright in the almost complete darkness, casting a glow on my hand and face. I kept to my azimuth, hearing heavy breathing and the breaking of brush behind me as the team struggled along. Mott had to keep reaching and touching my pack to stay in contact.

Sometime after midnight, the terrain began to rise, and I knew we were going up our mountain. I climbed onward, forced to sling my weapon, my hands needed to grasp trees and rocks for support. The mountain was rugged and steep. I could hear the noises of uprooted vines and the scattering of pebbles we dislodged dropping down the incline, knowing a fall would mean serious injury.

Mott stopped me on a small, level bit of ground. "It's almost three in the morning," he said, "the top of this motherfucker can't be far. We'll stay here until we can see."

That was fine with me. I eased out of my pack, and lay back on it, my CAR-15 in my lap, and was asleep before the tailgun was over the ledge with us.

It was dim when I opened my eyes again, and I sat up, alert, silent. The mountainside went up above us, but there was a suggestion of sky through the trees. Mott was awake, too, and only had to tap Payne and Steffens to make them ready.

We climbed the rest of the way with the first sun of the morning touching the treetops, and by 0600, we were on the crest. The climb was exhausting, and I was hungry. We fitted a small antenna to the radio. I opened a LRRP ration and began to heat water for it.

The view off the mountaintop was panoramic. Below us, the valleys of Cambodia were still in darkness, but soon we would be able to see.

Payne contacted the firebase and gave the handset to Mott. As I poured the water into my ration, I saw Mott's face go pensive, then sour. He gave the handset back to Payne.

"We've got to get off this hill," he said. "Battalion says there's a mistake. There's going to be an Arc Light here soon."

Arc Light, of course, was code for a B-52 strike.

We were silent for a moment. We had risked our skins

to walk through the night, climb this mountain, only to put ourselves in the way of our own B-52s.

"What?" I asked. "Those idiots should have known about an Arc Light!"

"Eat your chow quick," Mott said, "we're getting out of here."

We were fed, packed, and ready to go in thirty minutes. I had seen the ungodly destruction of earth and trees caused by the massive bombs from the high-flying, invisible B-52s.

I took point. This had to be quick and dirty, because speed and distance mattered now more than anything else. We didn't know at what moment the bombs were going to fall, or exactly where. We could only run. I checked my compass, and took us down the mountain, aiming for the general direction of the firebase.

The team had to keep up with me. It was light now and they could see. I didn't look back often. It took an hour to get all the way down the mountain, all of us stumbling and falling a few times, sometimes rolling until we could grab a tree.

Gasping, but on more level ground now, I took another compass reading and led off, sweat dripping from my cheeks. I used my CAR-15 as a club, striking at limbs and thorns, using my body and equipment weight to smash through bamboo and interwoven clumps of fronds or vines. I knew I sounded like a bull coming through, but the alternative was to go slow and risk a 500-pound bomb on my head.

I resolved if I saw any NVA, I would just yell "B-52! B-52!" and they would run with me.

There was no stopping, no radio contact, no pauses to plan or confer. We ran, we trotted, and we ran some more. At any moment I expected to hear the rolling, all-encompassing thunder of the Arc Light, and I tried to imagine what it would look like. Would I be able to see the flashes of the bombs exploding? Would I see the shock waves? Would it be a violent tidal wave of trees uprooting and flying at us?

We did not halt until midafternoon. Mott finally caught me, breathing hard. We were on the edge of a deep dried-out streambed. It offered cover, so we jumped down into it. I took out a canteen and drank it dry. I was reaching for another when I passed out from exhaustion.

I heard and felt nothing until Mott shook me. He looked as groggy and disoriented as I felt. I noticed the sun was almost down. I had been unconscious, or asleep, for a few hours.

Payne raised battalion headquarters on the radio. The Arc Light had come and gone on target, the infiltration route we had originally gone to watch. We were at least safe now from bombers.

We ate again, watching over the edge of the dry streambed like fugitive doughboys peeking from a trench. After we buried the ration packets, we saddled up and began our creep back to the firebase. This time I went slowly, hunched over my CAR-15, eyes nervously shifting from side to side. Darkness was coming rapidly in the depths of the valley we followed, but we were close now to the firebase, perhaps an hour or less, if we didn't stop again.

I heard the shells coming down.

I dived into the trees, the team behind me doing the same thing, and with great crashes, the 105mm high explosives dug into the hillside near us.

Mott covered his head with his arms. "That's their damn registration fire! They'll hit *us!*" he said. Every evening, American units in the field would call in artillery around their own positions, to get it pre-aimed, or registered, so if they needed artillery support in the middle of the night, it would be on short call.

"Radio!" Mott said, and Payne crawled to him, more rounds impacting, but this time on the other side of us, about a hundred meters away. Payne screwed the short combat antenna to his PRC-25, and Mott began trying to contact battalion headquarters in the firebase.

He couldn't make contact because of our low position in the valley—FM radios transmit poorly from low ground —and crosstalk on the battalion radio net, but he did learn something. We were caught in the overlapping registration fire between the firebase and an infantry company on a nearby hill.

"Break! Break!" Mott kept saying into the radio, trying to get someone's attention, but the shells kept falling all around us, obviously coming from two different directions from different batteries. The valley rocked with concussions and echoing shocks. There was nothing to do but ride it out and hope we didn't get killed.

When the last round had hit, and we had waited for a long time to make sure it was the last round, we grimly began moving forward again. I was disgusted with the mission. It had been incredibly dangerous, and for no gain.

By dark we found the start of the long slope up to the firebase. Ahead the trees ended; the slope was bare earth the last fifty meters to the perimeter.

Getting into the firebase would be tricky. There were trip flares and jumbled, rusty barbed wire on the slope. If we made noise, the perimeter guards, warned about us or not, might fire.

Mott took the radio and told battalion we were on our way in. They asked Mott on what side of the perimeter we would be approaching. Mott told them the south; they ordered us to go on.

I started up the hill with extreme caution, wondering if I would live to see the top. We had only been under way for a few minutes, just approaching the cleared kill zone, when Mott whispered for me to stop.

"They have movement, and they're going to fire an illumination round on it," he said.

"Where's the movement?" I asked.

"North slope," Mott said. We sat still. There could be a patrol, or advance party of an assault force of NVA, coming up the hill just like us.

With a hollow echo the round belched out of the

81mm mortar tube up the hill. Then, like a blazing star, it burst almost directly over our heads.

"That's us!" Mott said into the radio handset, "that's us! Don't fire!"

Mott ripped his map out of his pocket, and under cover of a poncho, frantically examined it with his flashlight. "We're on the wrong slope!" he told battalion. I bit my lip. Mott was the team leader. He had the map. He was supposed to keep up on things like where we were.

The flare would have alerted and frightened the soldiers on the perimeter. Word to watch for us would be passed to the bunker line from battalion, but I knew everyone on guard would not get it. All it took to kill us was one nervous grunt who had just woken up.

"I can get us in," I said. Mott hesitated before he asked me how.

"Let them cool off for a while," I said, "then we'll crawl up out of the tree line. We can move slow and get in between the bunkers. They're too far apart."

"Why wait?" Mott asked. "Let's go now. I just told them we were coming in."

"No," I said, "let 'em get sleepy first."

Mott knew enough about infantry habits and agreed with me. It sounded crazy, but we had a better chance if we simply infiltrated the camp.

It was almost 0300 hours as I parted the last cluster of concertina wire and crawled forward. I was exactly between two of the big sandbagged perimeter bunkers. I lay and listened for noises, for conversation, for footsteps, but there were none near me.

I poked my head over the berm, looking into the quiet, dark firebase. The moon was lost in the clouds. We had night on our side. We had not rattled one can of empty rifle cartridges in the wire, we had not hit one trip wire on a flare.

Handsignaling for Mott, Payne, and Steffens to follow me, I slid into the camp, my cheek to the dirt, then rolled aside as the team elbowed inside. We waited on our stomachs for several minutes.

"I'm going to the command bunker and report in," Mott said. "You guys lay down and get some sleep." Payne and Steffens began to spread their poncho liners, but I was hungry.

"I'm going to the chow bunker," I told them, and dropping my rucksack, I walked to Bessesi's bunker and went down into it.

He was asleep on his cot. I woke him up with a gentle shake on the shoulder. "What you got to eat?" I asked.

"Hey," Bessesi said, "where did you come from?"

"We just infiltrated your wire," I said truthfully. "Most of the guys are asleep on the bunker line."

Bessesi jumped up and put on his helmet. "Stay here!" he said, "I'm going out there and wake those bastards up!" I tried to stop him, but he ran out of the bunker. I could hear him going down the perimeter, rousting everybody, and in spite of my fatigue, I had to laugh.

We had a short debriefing the next morning, and received an alternate mission. A team was needed at another place, and we were to be resupplied and moved out. The helicopter was waiting.

The story of that mission is told in full in the first of this book.

28 February 1967: Second Thoughts

We had been back one day from the mission I opened the book with. I was sitting on my cot, marveling at what had happened, wondering how we had all come out of it alive, and seriously considering what my chances were of living through another enemy contact.

Our team hadn't survived because we were such superior soldiers; we'd had pure luck on our side. How long would that last?

Sergeant Mott walked up behind me, put his hand on my shoulder, and leaned down so he could speak almost directly in my ear.

"If you tell anybody what I did out there, I'll kill you," he whispered.

"What?" I asked, shocked.

"I mean it, *I'll kill you,*" he said, and walked swiftly out of the tent before I could reply.

I was shaken by his threat. For a few moments, I didn't know precisely what he meant, but I figured it out.

I had seen him paralyzed with fear, unable to shoot or make decisions, when we first walked into the enemy. That was no man to have as a team leader.

I didn't know if he was sincere about his threat. I hadn't thought twice about how he performed. I had assumed he was scared, and let it go at that.

Now I had Mott as well as the war to worry about.

---

2 March 1967: Security

We were not allowed to take identification, either identity cards or steel dog tags stamped with our name, rank, and service number, with us on patrol.

While we were in 3 Tango, we could carry personal identification, but before we left for the field, we turned in our wallets to Lieutenant Lapollo.

We had a choice about notification of our next of kin in case we were wounded, captured, or killed. We could have no notification made under any circumstances except death, or we could authorize notification for wounds if we were not conscious to make a decision.

Both choices were for "casualties occurring in Vietnam."

If we were killed over the border in Cambodia, there would be no notification of next of kin except to report us missing in action if our body could not be recovered. It was part of the job, and we accepted it.

So effective was security protecting the Special Operations Group that it would not be until July of 1973 that disclosure of the missions, and the casualties, would be made to the American public.

5 March 1967: Mission

The helicopter dropped our four-man team off on a river sandbar, and flew away. We traveled two kilometers or so, going due north up the river, staying close-by the banks, but thick underbrush and bamboo made it slow going.

I walked point, carrying a spare radio in my rucksack in addition to other equipment. I had tied the canvas North Vietnamese–type rucksack to my GI-issue aluminum rucksack frame, and it carried the weight well.

I wore a genuine North Vietnamese dark blue turtleneck sweatshirt I had taken out of a pile of captured enemy equipment, which, coupled with my faded tiger fatigue trousers and green soft hat, I hoped I might confuse any enemy soldier who might see me for just a fraction of a second, long enough for me to use my CAR-15 on him.

Our mission was to find an NVA headquarters believed to be in this border area, which had been reported by prisoners.

Our only communication—again—was by radio relay to an aircraft. We sent in situation reports four times a day. There was no chance of making radio contact at any other time.

6 March 1967

It rained on us during the night, and I discovered the new Special Forces poncho I carried, lighter in weight, but smaller than the standard ponchos, was no good. I was soaked.

The fire selector/safety switch on my CAR-15 locked up on me, and had to be forced. I took my knife blade, rotated the switch to full automatic, and left it there, knowing I no longer had a safety.

We discovered fresh markings on a trail, probably less than twelve hours old, in the morning as we crept along. We knew then the enemy was in the area, so we circled our trails once, then moved up onto an embankment overlooking one of the streams that ran into the river, and lay in ambush.

By nightfall, we had not seen anyone, so we climbed down off the embankment, and slowly walked toward a dense stand of bamboo to use as an overnight position.

We saw fresh footprints alongside the riverbank, made while we were in ambush. It was an enemy patrol. They had been following us up the river, but when we had circled and moved up to the embankment, they lost us.

Their prints continued north, up the river.

We took defensive positions, and unfolded our map. There was a major stream intersection about a kilometer ahead. People tend to stop at such natural features, such as road intersections, forks in a river, and so on. It is the same human trait that makes a person walk to the only tree in a pasture.

The enemy patrol might stop to rest, or to set an ambush at the intersection ahead. We waited until our radio-relay time came, and called in an artillery barrage on the stream/river intersection, hoping we had caught the North Vietnamese team.

Deep in the bamboo, we ate, and arranged night guard shifts. There were noises from the jungle later that could have been cautious search teams looking for us. We lay under the bamboo and didn't make a sound.

The next morning, we waited until we thought it was safe, and located our pickup zone. The helicopter got us out soon, everything working smoothly. We had been careful, we had evaded the enemy, and maybe we had hurt him. I felt tired as we flew back, but more confident.

To live, we had to get better than good. We had to achieve perfection.

I made "recruitment" handbills that the LRRP platoon could hand out to the rest of the brigade. We needed more people, and the only way to get them was to advertise. The handbills were to be distributed by us to various aviation, artillery, and infantry units.

The handbills were printed by a small print shop in Pleiku. The platoon paid for the job with contributions from all members.

It made me feel slightly odd to recruit in this way, as if the LRRP platoon were an army within an army, but that was not too far from true.

Pleiku City had been temporarily declared off limits, except for four hours a day. The American soldiers were spending too much money there, and inflation had caused prices to rise drastically.

A fair-price list was being agreed upon by the town council and the 4th Division headquarters to get the soldiers back.

A rickshaw ride that had been ten piastres before had jumped to one hundred, because GIs would pay it. The American soldiers were unable to deal with local merchants, not knowing the value of anything, and by virtue of the soldiers using military payment certificates, or Vietnamese currency, cost had no relation to what any service or item was worth in terms of U.S. dollars.

2nd Brigade LRRP recruitment handbill, issued by the 2nd Bde, 4th Inf Div., in May of 1967:

During June and July many of the experienced troops of the 2nd Bde LRRP will be rotating.

To prepare for the personnel changeover, the Bde LRRP is now interviewing and selecting interested volunteers.

Due to the nature of LRRP work—we are looking for good "field troops" who have a practical knowledge of map reading and land navigation.

If you are interested in excitement, responsibility, challenge, and the feeling of really doing something during your tour, try the LRRP.
REQUIREMENTS: 1. Rotation date of 15 Oct. or later. 2. Previous experience in a recon or rifle platoon.

If you are selected and meet certain physical and mental requirements, you will be eligible to attend the Recondo School in Nha Trang.

Further information may be obtained from your Bn S-2, Bde S-2, or any member of the Bde LRRP unit. Don't be afraid to ask!

Walking down the streets of Pleiku I was barraged by the usual challenges, offers, and pleas, all in badly broken English.

"Hey, Joe, you want Number One Baby-San?"

"Buy pot, Joe?"

"Me Number One girl, me no sick!"

"I love you too much."

"No can do!" argues a merchant over a price.

"Hey, Joe, you buy phenuts?" begged children selling small bags of locally grown peanuts.

"You buy watch, my friend?"

"Goddamn you," says a child, smiling and waving.

"Where you work?" asked a bar girl.

"How long you stay Vietnam?" asked another bar girl.

"How old you? You have wife America?"

A sign read, *Handling carefully, working exactly, most honestly clean. No. 1 Job Laundry.*

The bars had been named simply with an English noun, almost any noun. There was the Honey Bar, the Mexico Bar, the California Bar, Miami Bar, the Diamond Bar.

The bars were hurting from the off-limits restrictions, and I knew until a mutual agreement was reached, the price of venereal disease would be high in Pleiku.

There was talk at division headquarters of breaking down and moving 3 Tango. The monsoon season was coming, and our leadership knew enough about it by now to realize we would be stranded in such a remote camp near the border, but events began on the 12th that made everyone temporarily forget the relocation. Another enemy offensive was developing.

Both the 1st of the 22nd and the 1st of the 12th were in combat, the enemy attacking them and not withdrawing. That meant we had at least six infantry companies in action, and we were taking casualties again.

The Dustoff helicopters carrying wounded and dead clattered down out of the air again to 3 Tango, every hour their numbers increasing.

The 2nd of the 8th was brought in out of the field to begin their training on M-113 armored personnel carriers, and I met them at base camp, anxious to see my old squad again.

I found C Company as they were being issued clean uniforms. They had moved into tents, and their dirty weapons, web gear, and ammunition lay all over the tent floors.

Ski, Kircher, and Gemmel were all okay. They had not been wounded in the fight to save the 1st Platoon, but many of the 2nd Platoon had been.

They were hungry, and one "recon" team raided a closed kitchen supply tent. It was dark, and they could not read the labels on the cans. They stole 3 one-gallon cans of food. They had one can of powdered chicken soup, one can of raisins, and one of cake mix.

They ate all of it.

Needing a place to sleep for the night, I walked to 2nd Brigade headquarters, and searched until I found my friend Wally Wicks, the brigade mail clerk, the fattest of jobs.

He lived in a GP medium tent with plywood floors and electric lights, only sharing the big tent with a couple of other clerks. They had it partitioned off like an apartment.

Wicks was tall, bespectacled, and smiling. He had a soft job and a future. I had my tiger fatigues, web gear, NVA rucksack, and CAR-15. We had grown a world apart from each other.

We ate, then went to the brigade movie, and sometime after midnight, came back to his tent. He told me to use one of the empty cots there, since one of the clerks was out at The Oasis, and as I lay down on the cot and pulled my poncho liner over me, Wicks turned out the light. I went to sleep thinking that he deserved his job. Wicks would have died in the infantry. He was too nice a guy.

I hadn't been asleep long, or at least it didn't seem long, when a siren began to wail. I sat straight up on the cot.

"Go back to sleep," Wicks said. "That's the alert siren. It's just a drill. We have to go out to our bunkers and get counted."

I lay back down, covering my face with the poncho liner, and dozed off. Then, the light came on again and someone kicked me hard, with malice, on my foot. I threw the poncho liner back.

It was a short, fat black first sergeant, and he was furious. "Get up! Get up!" he was yelling at me. The kick enraged me. I wasn't even really awake. I grabbed my CAR-15 off the floor, tossed the poncho liner aside, and jumped up, pointing the weapon in his face.

"Go play your war games with somebody else!" I snarled, and I think I was about to shoot him.

When he saw I wasn't one of his clerks, he turned and ran out of the tent as fast as he could. I sat on the cot, now more awake and feeling guilty. I had just threatened the life of the first sergeant of brigade headquarters.

Thankfully, he was a new man, and didn't know me, but he would probably be back with help soon.

Disgusted, I picked up my equipment, walked out

into the night and found an empty bunker, rolled up in my liner, and went to sleep.

Well after sunrise, I slipped back to Wick's tent. He was sitting at his field desk. "God," he said, "I thought you were gone! The first sergeant has everybody looking for you."

"Did you tell him who I was?" I asked.

"No," Wicks said, "I told him you were from Special Forces."

"Thanks," I said. "I'm going back to the field now anyway."

"Be careful," said Wicks. I shook his hand and walked out of the brigade area as quickly as possible, back to the 2nd of the 8th street a few units away.

My old squad was still there, resting, and I told them what had happened with the first sergeant to give them a laugh.

I had to get back to 3 Tango, glad to have met my squad. I said good-bye to them, unsure of when we would meet again. It was a sad parting, because I knew they had to go back into combat, as I did. They were my friends and I didn't want anything bad to happen to them.

"If you ever hear of anyone getting killed hiding behind a tree, that'll be me," Kravitski had said as I shook his hand and walked to the helicopter pads. I would rather have embraced him.

At 3 Tango, the war was getting hotter. The LRRP platoon was notified to be on general alert. I went to my cot and tried to get some sleep, feeling I'd need it.

I could hear helicopters still coming in up at the aid tents, just like in February, bringing in their bloody cargoes.

"Getcha gear," a voice shouted, "we have to guard the water point!" I sat up on my cot and heard the message repeated at the next tent.

"Guard the goddamned water point?" one of my teammates griped, "we're not supposed to pull shit details for brigade!" I silently agreed as I gathered what I thought would be sufficient for a long night watching over washing machines.

"Let's go!" someone called, hurrying us along. "Meet at the operations tent!" I threw my ammo belt over my shoulder and picked up my bedroll and CAR-15. We filed out the door and headed for the brigade tactical operations center.

The sun was low in the sky as we gathered, a tinge of red just visible in the clouds. There were only a dozen of us. Everyone else was out on patrol.

A captain from S3 stepped out of the tent. "We think we're going to get hit tonight," he said, "and we need everybody on the line. The water point is weak, so we want you people down there to hold it."

The announcement didn't impress us. It seemed like another one of brigade's endless alerts. "Take your Star-lights with you," the captain warned. "You'll have help from Headquarters Company and the regular crew that lives at the water point."

I considered briefly loading up on more ammo, but I had ten magazines. Most importantly, I had my poncho for sleeping off brigade scares. Our group turned and walked back to the LRRP area to pick up the last two Starlight scopes left in supply.

At the bottom of the hill, a good five hundred meters from 3 Tango, was the water point. Its isolation was broken only by a dirt road back to the main camp and a single communications wire.

There were many huge laundry machines there, a wa-ter-purification unit, and a couple of shower tents beside the stream. The only fortifications were bunkers that surrounded the place.

It was just getting dark as we settled into the bunkers. I picked the outpost bunker at the apex of the horseshoe-shaped stream. All the other dugouts were behind us. As I laid my equipment down, I met the other three men who had chosen the outpost. Brown was an infantryman, obviously a veteran; and Hall was a Brigade Headquarters Company clerk; and our own LRRP supply sergeant, Snake.

Since we had all eaten, and darkness came so rapidly, there was nothing to do but to sit and talk, and let the night pass. Brown was quiet and withdrawn and talked in monosyllables and grunts. The clerk was talkative and a bit excited about being sent to the water point. He was new in Vietnam. Snake seemed nervous.

Our subjects of conversation were those common to soldiers. Hometowns, backgrounds, and our jobs in the army. The energy ran out of the talk early. We arranged guard shifts and found places to sleep. Everyone else decided to stay in the bunker, while I elected to sleep outside.

Brown took first guard. I lay on my poncho, looking at the stars and listening to the stream swirl past. I went to sleep with no apprehension.

I was touched gently, and came awake from my light sleep. The night was still clear and starry. I realized it was my time for guard. I checked my watch as Brown crept inside the bunker. It was well after midnight. I took my weapon and climbed atop the bunker, looking over my surroundings in the dark. The jungle around me was invisible in the night. I sat still, listening and looking. Time passed slowly.

Then I heard the sound. It came from somewhere out there, but was first indistinct and directionless. It was the rapid reports of a mortar being fired as fast as the crew could serve it.

My heart almost stopped. I was hearing the rounds being fired before they hit the ground. *"Incoming!"* I shouted to wake everyone, *"Incoming!"* I jumped off the roof and dived in the bunker's back door, tumbling over Brown and Hall.

Mortar rounds hit the ground almost in one group, patterned from us all the way up to 3 Tango. Ear-numbing blasts filled the air with dust and the shock of concussion.

3 Tango was the principal target. It was as if a crowded neighborhood had come under fire. Tents, temporary buildings, the old church, bunkers, trucks and jeeps, supply dumps, and field kitchens. All too close together. They couldn't miss.

Then the inevitable happened. The night was gone! Ten thousand gallons of JP-4 jet fuel took a hit and the explosion was brighter than daylight. We were awed by that hellish sight. Flames shot up as high as we could see. It couldn't have been worse if a volcano had erupted inside the camp.

Still mortar bombs fell out of the air. The pounding continued. The ground shook with each impact. A dense cloud of smoke obscured the sky, reflecting the inferno's blaze down on us all.

"My God!" Hall exclaimed, "what'll we do now?" Brown strained his eyes, peering out the front slit, a desperate look on his face. "Shut up, goddammit!" he hissed, "they might be out there!"

My eyes recovered from the glare, and Snake and I joined Brown. Hall was clearly scared to death. "What's gonna happen now?" he blurted. "Where are our planes? Why isn't our artillery firing back?"

"The artillery people are in their holes just like us," I said, surprised at the calmness of my own voice. "We'll get air support soon. Take it easy!" Hall stayed down and breathed in sobs. It was his first combat.

The NVA mortars lifted their fire off the hill and brought it to bear directly on the water point, never missing a stroke. This time it was all on us.

Mortar shells struck like lightning. We lay in the center of the bull's-eye. Pieces of the water point's equipment flew through the air. Sheet metal from the washing machines, canvas from the tents, wood from the pallets. The smoke was blinding.

The detonations kicked us in the stomach and struck our heads like blows from clubs. "Where's our artillery?" Hall cried, beating the sandbags from terror.

"Take it easy!" I repeated. "We'll get help soon!" I didn't believe we would, but I wanted to calm him down.

A bloodchilling, methodical series of explosions began off to our left. They were walking rounds down on us in even steps! Random death was bad enough. Planned death was unbearable.

I cringed. The bunker jolted violently from near misses. Dirt filled the air. I choked, trying to crawl under the spare sandbags. Then it passed.

My elation at being alive was indescribable. A group of shells had bracketed us and blown the burlap off our sandbags.

I paid little attention to the remaining attack. My ears rang. I struggled to look out. The fuel fire at 3 Tango was still going strong. The water point was covered with a blanket of dust that made seeing the next bunker impossible.

Brown was up and looking to the front. "I think something's moving out there!" he said. I poked frantically around in the dark. "Who's got any grenades?" I asked.

Hall rolled over. "I got some!" he said.

"Give 'em here," I demanded. He passed me his four grenades. "Do you see them?" I asked Brown. He looked out over the slit.

"Yeah! I see the son of a bitches! They're coming in right over there!" he said.

I ducked out the back, carrying the grenades. The bunker was a trap in a firefight. I wanted to be outside, where I could move. "Right front, ten meters!" Brown yelled. I used the bunker for cover and threw a grenade in that direction.

It exploded with a solid crash. "Direct front!" Brown shouted urgently. I pumped the next grenade out. The bunker trembled with the blast.

Brown didn't hesitate. "They're getting away!" he bellowed, firing his M-16 full-automatic. "Left! Left!" I had the third frag ready and arced it over the stream. There was no bang. It was a dud. I pulled the pin on the last grenade and heaved it. It went off, but Brown said, "Too late, they're past us!" I looked over the bunker to see which way the NVA had gone but it was too dark.

I realized now the perimeter was enveloped with small-arms fire. I dove back into the bunker for cover.

"Look out!" Snake yelped, and fired his CAR-15 inside the confines of the bunker, luckily getting his burst out the slit, but the blast deafened us in the closeness, and it raised a solid cloud of dust inside.

"Hold your goddamn fire," Brown said, "there's nobody out there right now! And put that thing on safe!"

Suddenly bullets flailed our bunker, kicking dirt through the viewslit as the fire tore into the sandbags and logs. We hugged the floor while a determined gunner raked us across.

I realized the source of the fire before it ceased. It was an M-60 machine gun from inside the water point! Another bunker was shooting at Snake's muzzle flashes, having forgotten we were beyond the bunker line on outpost!

"No more rifle fire!" I gasped. "Those idiots will kill us!" Brown agreed with a nod. Snake learned his lesson and laid his CAR-15 aside.

I heard a motor racing madly, and the clatter of a truck going at full power. I risked a look out the back of the bunker. The truck locked up all tires and slid into the water point. The burning fuel dump gave everything an unearthly orange glow.

The driver kept the engine running while the guard riding with him stood and shouted over the windshield, "Do you have any casualties?" His voice was barely audible over the engine and the roar of the fuel-dump fire up the hill.

Men came out from the bunkers and ran to the truck to pick up ammo and help a small group of wounded aboard. I heard someone say that the telephone landline was out. We had no communications with 3 Tango.

Their business finished, the driver jammed the truck into gear and spun the rear tires as he whipped the vehicle around and sped back up the road.

On our right flank, where the two Starlight scopes were, LRRP M-16s fired steadily. I hoped they were doing somebody great harm out there.

"The phone's out!" I told Brown. He grimly accepted the information as he watched the night. Hall was still on the floor. That suited me. He was out of the way.

Then it started again, the concussion of mortar bombs falling on 3 Tango making themselves felt all the way down to us like an earthquake. It was obvious the enemy had plenty of ammunition. All we could do was sit and wait, try not to flinch with each smashing round, and watch our front.

Finally our artillery went into action as the rounds from the hidden mortars ended. The 105mm howitzers made up for lost time with sheer volume. They were firing by guesswork, hoping for a lucky hit. Our tricky new counterbattery radar had never worked right after suffering a slightly rough unslinging from the helicopter that had delivered it.

The 105s continued for an hour. Then our air support came. It was Skyraiders from New Pleiku Air Force Base. They dropped napalm cannisters and strafed around, but it was clear they were hunting. After that it was quiet except for the drone of a lone spotter plane overhead.

We eyed the tree line suspiciously as the hours dragged by, wishing for the sun. I nodded off to sleep with Hall standing guard.

A tremendous explosion pitched me forward. I thought we had been hit by an artillery shell! Something big had gone off right outside our bunker.

"What was that?" Hall stammered, holding his ears. Brown looked out the back door. "That son of a bitch was close!" he said, amazed that our sandbags were still standing. The stinging of high-explosive smoke in our eyes and the pain in our eardrums testified to the nearness of the blast. We did not know what caused it.

Dawn did finally come. The sky turned lighter by degrees. First there was the outlines of the treetops. Then a few clouds became distinct.

I felt as if I had not closed my eyes for years. Brown gazed out the slit at the jungle. "Goddamn, I'm hungry," he stated to no one in particular. "All I want," I told Brown, "is a hot cup of coffee, and I'm going to sleep."

The sun was not yet visible over the mountains, but the world began to take on color again.

I stooped as I crawled out of the bunker. It felt great to get out of that rathole.

The hard clay was marked everywhere mortar rounds had struck. There were sharp, twisted fragments lying about to be picked up for examination. I pulled some out of the sandbags in our bunker.

A couple of the big laundry machines had been hit directly, and their doors and outer panels were gone. Clothes from the machines were scattered over the ground.

We found the telephone landline, cut by a mortar round that had hit it so perfectly it couldn't have been aimed any better.

Shower tents hung crazily on their poles. I was too tired to even be disgusted. No one spoke very much. We were all in a sort of subdued daze.

Then the bodies of two dead NVA were discovered. They lay only five meters to the exact left of my bunker. We grouped around them, staring, curious.

"We must have got them with the Claymore!" a man declared who had been in the next bunker to our left rear. "They came crawling through about four in the morning! I popped a Claymore on the noise! Shit, I didn't know I actually got anybody!"

I understood then what the big blast so early in the morning had been. The mine had exploded almost even with our bunker wall.

Actually, the two NVA had crawled past the mine. The backblast had killed them. Their skin was dark red and bruised. They only had a few fragment holes in them. They wore shorts and T-shirts. One had died in the act of crawling, and still held the pose. The other man was balled up in a fetal position, his face a grimace of pain.

Two folding-stock AK-47s were found in the grass near them. A big ball of plastic explosive was discovered also, wrapped in a cloth. The dead men were the people I had driven off with grenades. They must have laid low and waited for a better time and a less aggressive defense before trying to move in again.

A soldier produced a camera and the scene was recorded for the future, like a trophy.

It was almost 0700 in the morning and there still was no word for us to pull back from the water point. Fatigue and hunger made us impatient. "I'm going back up the hill. They don't need us anymore," I told Brown. He thought about it.

"I better stay until they come and get me. You go ahead," he said.

I went to the next bunker and asked the LRRPs in it if they wanted to go. In a few moments, all twelve of us were ready to leave. We trudged up the road into 3 Tango.

"You get any with the Starlight?" I asked.

"Yeah," said one of the riflemen. "I could see them standing out there in the trees at about a hundred meters. Hell, they didn't know what was happening. They didn't even try to take cover. I guess they thought it was stray rounds."

We passed through a wary group of infantry on the bunker line as we entered 3 Tango. They too had that all-night look in their eyes.

A double-door refrigerator had taken a hit on its side. Insulation and twisted metal protruded through the gap. Some outfit wouldn't have any more ice.

Tents had been blown down. Canvas hung in the trees. Torn sandbags were everywhere. Commo trucks parked in a glade between the motor pool and our LRRP tents had hundreds of mortar fragment gouges.

The old church itself had taken hits, but the headquarters troops inside were protected, because they had built sandbag walls and overhead cover in the building.

Even with this precaution, the brigade sergeant major, a man I knew well and respected, had been wounded when a roofing tile hit him in the forehead from a mortar explosion in the rafters of the church.

The medics carried him away and I never saw him again. He had been a decent and reasonable man, and a great help to me when I had been part of Headquarters Company.

I was relieved to find our own tent still upright. I pushed through the flap and went inside. I wanted to just drop on my cot and sleep.

Instead I laid my gear on the cot and walked to the back door of the tent, and held the flap open, pausing to yawn. On the other side of a barbed-wire fence was the brigade mess, KPs righting the overturned mess tables.

A mortar shell exploded right in the middle of the KPs as they worked. Then a second round fell, and then another. *It was starting again in daylight.*

I jumped out of my tent and into the covered trench just outside. I found it already full. It was a small hole in the ground in which we had to hide. The roof was a flimsy affair of plywood and a single layer of sandbags.

The inmates were all LRRPs. They huddled, jaws tight, not looking at each other. Then I saw the source of the embarrassment. Our platoon sergeant was whimpering in the far end of the ditch. He had obviously stayed the entire night in the trench.

He was digging a hole in the earthen wall with his fingers as the new attack immersed us in an avalanche of mortar shells.

His function with the platoon was only administrative; he went on no patrols. He had come from an infantry company, obviously to avoid field duty, but he did wear tiger fatigues and a bush hat, and carried one of the hard-to-get CAR-15s.

Now he was exposed for his gutlessness. I was angry.

Not so much that he was worthless, but that his breakdown could affect someone else.

A shell hit just outside and rocked us all. It was followed by a scream and a man falling through the trench doorway on me, shouting, "I'm hit! I'm hit!"

It was Tan, one of our Vietnamese interpreters. He had been dashing for safety when a mortar round struck right beside him. He was bleeding badly and was in extreme pain, his back full of pieces of metal.

I tried to get a bandage on him, but I would have needed a half dozen. He arched his back, eyes clenched shut, mouthing incomprehensible words. His CAR-15 was scarred with fragments.

With a wounded man, a near-crazy sergeant, and a mortar attack in progress, I did not understand how it could get much worse in our hole. I learned. They hit the ammo dump.

It was all blowing up. Entire stacks of shells exploded and threw more hot ammo around the camp, to burst on impact. I managed one look out a crack in the roof. The sky was covered with smoke and flame. It was a living nightmare. Debris flew overhead in all directions.

Tan wouldn't hold still. I was afraid he was losing too much blood. The sergeant was dug further into the wall. I had had enough. "Help me get Tan up," I asked the man nearest me, "I want to get him to the aid station."

I listened carefully, trying to pick a lull in the explosions. It sounded as if the mortar attack had stopped, but the ammo dump was still raising hell. I got a good grip on Tan and decided it was now or never.

I leaped out of the trench, running as fast as I could. I had over a hundred meters to go, uphill, before I would make the aid station.

Things were still detonating. A shell hit nearby and I stumbled, Tan rolling away from me in agony. I scooped him up and took off again.

Goddamn, if they're going to kill me, I'll be doing something, not cowering in the hole, I thought. Anger overcame fear as I thought about the medics. If they were in their bunkers, I swore to pull them out.

I fell to one knee and Tan screamed again. He fought me, delirious with pain. I saw the tents with the red crosses just ahead.

I jumped a sandbag wall and ducked inside the first tent. Its floor was covered with injured men. Medics worked feverishly. They showed no concern for their own safety. I was almost moved to tears at the sight.

A medic motioned for me to lay Tan down. I knelt and gently put him on the ground. I was out of breath. I saw a man dressed in tiger fatigues mixed with the infantry casualties. I tiptoed through the wounded to him. It was Harmon. Undressed mortar wounds bled on his stomach.

Harmon looked up at me and smiled. "It don't look bad," I said to him, "take it easy." He closed his eyes. I made my way out of the congestion of the aid station.

As I walked back to the LRRP tents, I realized it was over. It was actually quiet. Everybody was still in their holes; it was as if I had the camp to myself.

Then I saw my tent. It had stopped a mortar round. I walked in. The air mattress on my cot was flat, deflated by fragments.

Cans of shaving cream in our personal gear had exploded, dripping white soap suds off the ripped canvas tent sides like melting snow. Flashbulbs were shattered in their packages, uniforms were perforated and scattered. There seemed to be nothing in the tent that wasn't hit.

An M-16 buttstock was smashed, the recoil buffer spring sticking out. A helmet was hammered almost dead center with a chunk of Chinese mortar fragment, as if it were driven in with a sledge hammer.

On my cot, my own .45 pistol was ruined. A fragment had struck it beside the magazine release on the frame and actually bent the pistol in a slight U shape.

I lay down, and with the morning sun streaming in through the tattered hole where the tent roof used to be, went to sleep.

* * *

Someone shook me awake. I looked at my watch. I had been asleep for almost two hours. "Let's go," said the LRRP, "we got a briefing."

I sat up, rubbed my eyes, and with my CAR-15 in my hands, I detoured over to the mess tent and got a canteen cup of coffee. The briefing was held near the church building, by an S5 captain. S5 was supposed to be public relations, but in our case, it was really an intelligence function.

All the LRRPs were there, and a few troops from brigade headquarters.

The captain said we were all going on a raid. Two "Deuce-and-a-halfs," our standard two-and-a-half-ton heavy trucks, were ready to take us. The target was a nearby Montagnard village; he suspected it hid an enemy mortar position, and that there might still be NVA there.

There was one road into the village. It was surrounded by jungle. The first truck in would drive through the village to the far side before stopping, and those on it would jump out and spread right and left to cover the flanks.

The second truck would brake at the front of the village and its men deploy left and right. With this technique, we would all be inside fast, and cover four directions with our raiders.

Following the entry of the second truck, the captain and his driver and interpreter would arrive. We were to round up all the people in the village and herd them to the center. That was the extent of the plan.

"Sir," asked one of the LRRPs, "what if somebody runs?"

"Shoot 'em," said the S5 officer, and we boarded the trucks, checking our weapons and grenades. I was tired and hostile, a bad way to feel before battle.

Like racers, the truck drivers plunged us along the dirt road into the jungle, limbs and branches smashing at us. One took my flop hat right off my head, and I reached for it, but it hung in the tree. The men on the second truck grabbed for it, but missed.

We could hear the beat of rotor blades as Hueys whipped overhead, looking for signs of retreating North Vietnamese. It was full day now, and 3 Tango was making an effort at revenge, like an angry giant looking for the snake that had bitten him in the night.

The village lay ahead, a quick impression of huts through the trees. Rifle bolts slammed closed as we chambered ammunition.

Bouncing and tilting, our truck sped into the village. I saw log bunkers buried in the ground and my heart almost stopped, but the bunkers were empty. They were for the villagers who lived there. I had never considered they would dig bunkers for their own protection, like we did, but it made sense.

Our driver jerked the truck around the bunkers, and I saw glimpses of dark-skinned Montagnards, naked children, and fleeing chickens.

Hard on the brakes, our truck slid and stopped, and I jumped over the side, not feeling my feet hit the ground. We were the point truck, and my section of the village to cover was the left rear quarter, from six to nine on the clock, with the entry road at twelve.

I could instantly see the village was roughly circular, with the huts facing inward, toward the bunkers. The men on my section spread out. I wondered if we should be looking outward, as well as inward, when someone dashed in between the huts and into the jungle.

He was moving so fast, just a blur, that all I could tell was he wore a loincloth, had on U.S. jungle boots, and carried a long, tubular object, maybe a B-40 rocket-launcher tube.

I snapped up my CAR-15 to fire, but instead yelled, *"Halt! Halt!"* My trigger finger tightened. He ran on, zig-zagging downhill into the jungle, jumping like a deer.

I don't know why I didn't fire. I ran after him, crashing through the foliage, shouting for him to stop. Suddenly I realized I was doing just what I needed to be doing to run into sudden death. I stopped, and *he* stopped, looking back at me.

It was a Montagnard boy, just a boy. He was holding a staff of bamboo, the kind his people used to carry water. I was flushed and breathless. I motioned for him to come back, and he smiled at me and walked up the hill. Jesus Christ. I was just twenty, and I had almost shot a boy younger than me. I delivered him to the group of natives who had all been ordered to the center of the village.

As yet, there had been no shots, no gunfire.

The S5 captain stood beside his jeep, his interpreter talking to the people. They were mostly old men and women, and some children. They wore drab blankets and loincloths. It was like looking at prehistoric mankind. They were impassive as they listened to the interpreter.

Their huts—their *homes*—were being searched. I took my place back in the cordon of LRRPs watching the village perimeter. The searchers were finding no evidence of the enemy.

An old man was helped out of his hut by his family. His hair was white and he had a thin, tattered blanket over his shoulders. On one of his feet was a dirty bandage, the result, the interpreter told the captain, of an American shell splinter from the night's bombardment.

The captain ordered the old man placed on the back seat of his jeep, to be taken in for treatment.

The old man's family brought him a jug of water and a few sweet potatoes wrapped in a rag, because they didn't know if we would feed him or not.

As we prepared to leave, and the S5 officer sat in his jeep, a young Montagnard girl, perhaps ten years old, came running out of her hut, shouting loudly at the interpreter.

Our convoy waited as the highly excited girl gestured and pointed to the truck beside mine. The captain walked from his jeep to the truck.

"She says one of you guys took a couple of machetes from her hooch," said the captain. "Who's got 'em?"

An NCO from brigade headquarters sheepishly handed the machetes down to the officer. I remembered the incident in the infantry when one of my company had stolen bracelets from a Montagnard girl. The wooden-handled, hook-bladed machetes were only curios to us, but to the poverty-stricken Montagnards, they were as precious as a car would be to a family in the States.

The theft of the machetes humiliated me. I wanted to apologize or explain to the people somehow, but we were already rolling. We drove out of the village with the old man behind the captain, holding himself with dignity.

On the road out, our driver slowed enough for me to pick my hat out of the tree.

A helicopter flew in one of our LRRP teams that had been out during the mortar attack on 3 Tango, but we learned from them they had not missed any action.

They said they were at one of our firebases that had been heavily mortared on the same night.

"They hit the ammo," one of the team said, "and the trucks the ammo was on were blown all over the place. You ever seen a deuce-and-a-half turn a flip in the air? Goddamn!"

The four of them sat together on a low sandbag wall, and were as glad to be back at 3 Tango as if it had been Fort Benning. Their jokes were too nervous, their laughs too quick. They were alive, and they were giddy with the enjoyment of it.

---

17 March 1967: Situations

The 2nd Brigade was involved in heavy combat along the Cambodian border.

The 1st of the 22nd, my original battalion at Fort Lewis, had suffered terrible casualties. Almost everyone in A Company, to which I had been assigned, was killed or wounded. By the 18th of March virtually every man in it was a replacement.

The 1st of the 22nd, and the 1st of the 12th, were locked in fierce fighting with the North Vietnamese. A battalion from the 25th Infantry Division, their 1st of the 35th, stood in for the 2nd of the 8th, which was no longer in the field.

I flew back to base camp the next day to take care of some errands for the platoon at brigade headquarters personnel, and decided to visit a friend who was still with A Company, 1st of the 22nd. His name was O'Shea, and he had survived because he was a supply clerk in base camp, not an infantryman.

He had never fired a shot in anger or seen an enemy soldier in all his time in-country, and he had arrived on the *Walker* with me.

When I told him I could use some equipment for the LRRP platoon, he told me he had heard there was a load of it at the battalion headquarters supply tent. I thanked him and left, walking through the company streets until I saw the 1st of the 22nd's sign, and knew where to come back to tomorrow.

As the members of our LRRP platoon lost equipment, wore it out, or had it damaged in battle, getting replacements was difficult. Our parent units had issued us complete sets of clothing and equipment, and once we were away would not issue more.

We often sent out individuals from the platoon on "midnight requisitions." All of us stayed alert for usable equipment, even if it was just an extra shirt or canteen cup.

Having to be our own source of supply was one of the results of being a provisional unit. It made us feel that much more independent.

---

18 March 1967: Remains

With all the 12th infantry battalions in the field, their section of base camp was as still as death. Not even a breeze moved the hot, stale air between the tents. The place smelled like baking canvas.

I found the supply building. It was actually a wooden frame roofed with a GP medium tent. A clerk worked quietly inside. It seemed very dark in there after the brilliance outside.

I walked in amid stacks of crates and boxes. "I'm from the LRRPs. I was told I could get some equipment from you." I said, breaking the silence of the afternoon.

The clerk looked at me with resentment. "It's out back. Take whatever you want," he said, pointing at the door.

I walked between piles of laundered uniforms and stepped down out of the building. On the bare earth lay several ponchos covered with web gear and helmets.

All of it was dirty and shot full of holes and starched with dried blood. I knelt beside a pile of the morbid gear and picked up a canteen and cup, pressed together forever by a bullet. No good at all.

There was a helmet, the suspension inside still holding several envelopes and personal letters, but it was all glued together with an amazing amount of black, sticky blood.

I saw another helmet with a hole punched through it, making two exit holes where the bullet must have fragmented as it passed through the skull of the wearer, but the detail that chilled my heart was the name on the sweatband. I had known the man.

Smashed rifle magazines lay around, all useless. A paperback novel was mixed with the equipment, torn apart by a direct hit. I found the steel core of a Tokarev pistol bullet still in it.

I lifted a pistol belt, made inflexible with dried blood, and tossed it back into the pile. Ants swarmed into the packs, going for C rations punctured by bullets.

Each grisly item told a unique and ghastly story. The grotesque appearance of a set of web-gear suspenders so stiff with crusty blood they still held the shape of a human torso was sickening.

This was not equipment, it was remains. It should

have been buried. I left the supply tent and walked back down the company road to the airstrip.

I'd have to get my extra equipment somewhere else.

21 March 1967: Situations, Part II

The infantry units were still in contact on and off with the North Vietnamese. Our LRRP teams were spotting the enemy daily, and everybody's casualties—except the LRRPs'—were mounting.

As if charmed, our teams kept going out, bringing back intelligence, and killing enemy soldiers as a side effect.

The monsoon was coming, and the smell of rain was often on the breeze. 3 Tango was being dismantled, truckloads of equipment leaving every day.

When the rains came back, the dust that plagued us would become mud, but in March the dust was still supreme. It was ankle-deep on the roadsides, the winds stirring huge clouds of it like desert sandstorms.

Moving vehicles had dust plumes behind them ten meters high. Everything was the color of reddish dust. It ruined weapons, food, and crept into the tightest corners of equipment.

Whenever a helicopter landed, the dust was unbelievable. The aircraft would vanish in a violent opaque mass of red-brown atmosphere, the dust rising above the trees, moving outward, impossible to breathe in, slowly settling, coating everything.

Vehicle drivers' faces on the daily convoys were cracked masks of dust, only their eyes displaying humanity.

The Military Intelligence tent, the LRRP platoon area, and the mysterious RRU tents were all grouped together, like a compound within a compound at 3 Tango,

but the RRU was separated from us by another barbed
wire barrier.

RRU meant Radio Reconnaissance Unit, which was
actually a cover for the ASA, or Army Security Agency.
What they were doing was monitoring everybody's radio
frequencies.

They were nervous types, scared of their own security
clearances, but they had to come out and eat sometimes,
and when they sat at the mess tables with us, they were
very careful never to talk about their work.

We had a small battery-powered record player set
atop a narrow crate in my tent. It was fed by stolen BA-30
batteries (the army version of the D cell), and on it we
played a few 45's and a couple of albums bought by our
guys while on R & R.

Having the record player was a godsend, and we
played scratched recordings of "Devil with a Blue Dress
On," Simon and Garfunkel's "Parsley, Sage, Rosemary
and Thyme," or Beatles music.

One day, the record player began to do odd things,
somehow picking up English-language radio traffic that
was so powerful it would blare out and override the record
we were playing. We recognized none of the call signs, but
we realized we were getting only half of the conversations.
It was disturbing what pleasure we got from our records.

At chow one day, we told one of the RRU/ASA men
about the strange conversations we were overhearing on
our record player. The man almost choked on his food,
and left the table in a hurry.

We lost the interference that afternoon. There was an
explanation.

An RRU linear antenna had been strung just over our
tents. The powerful electromagnetic transmission waves off
the antenna were activating the simple crystal pickup in
the tone arm of the record player, and causing the captured but unwanted signal to be sent on to the amplifier
and speaker.

The RRU had been bugged by a child's-quality record player. The antenna was relocated. We got a good laugh at RRU's expense, but they never saw the humor in it.

22 March 1967: Missing Team

Sergeant Britt, Keough, Davis, and Hatchett from our platoon went out on patrol and disappeared.

They had taken not one, but two radios. An infantry unit from the 1st of the 8th, part of the 1st Brigade of the 4th Division, moved into their last known area to try to find them, their bodies, or some signs of them.

The infantrymen ran into enemy, and soon a few firefights became a battle; the 1st of the 8th was in full contact.

A helicopter flying over the fight saw a smoke grenade burning, and dropped low enough to recognize Britt's team signaling them. Both radio sets had failed, and the LRRP team was trapped in all the combat.

When they were flown back to our platoon area, they told how they had observed about forty North Vietnamese soldiers while they were on patrol, including some armed women.

Without radio contact, Britt couldn't report them, but had his team follow their movements as long as he could. After thirty-six hours without radio contact, Britt heard gunfire and realized his small team was on the outskirts of a developing infantry battle. His men were trapped between the North Vietnamese and the American unit, and either side would shoot the LRRPs, since the NVA would know they were American, but the Americans would think the LRRPs were the enemy, because of the different way they dressed.

23 March 1967: Back to The Oasis

We were told to prepare to pack and leave 3 Tango. We had to destroy our bunkers, drop the tents, and burn all of our wood frames, props, and structures.

28 March 1967: Road Mines

3 Tango was gone. The airstrip, the asphalted helicopter pad, all the graded company streets, the places where I had seen and handled our casualties from February . . . all plowed down and destroyed.

Over the period of a few days, we had worked ourselves to exhaustion, slashing sandbags to keep the enemy from trying to reuse them, and fueling huge fires with the carpenters' labors of tent frames, wooden latrines, signs, and bunker supports.

The church was empty again, as hollow as the day we had discovered it. All the work invested in it, the plywood paneling, the rows of offices inside, the reglassed windows, all were ashes or shards.

The grass would grow back soon, bushes would cover the holes where the bunkers, trenches, and roads had been, and the landing zone and airstrip would sprout vegetation. The North Vietnamese would also come back, free to roam there again.

We were gone.

The convoy back to The Oasis was an all-day ordeal. I rode as guard on a truck, rolling along behind another truck, looking at the jungle and mountains. The countryside was wild and remote.

The dirt road was narrow and badly rutted. The choking dust made the drivers try to keep their distance from each other, but fear made them want to stay close together.

It seemed that every twenty meters there was a deep mine crater. Along the roadside was the sort of wreckage our army should have removed, but had left instead. The ditches were literally filled in places with pieces of vehicles that had hit mines.

There were hoods, fenders, bumpers, wheels and tires, track links from tanks, even twisted frames.

I heard a muffled explosion behind us, and looked over my shoulder and saw a tall column of dust go up. A 2½-ton truck had just been disabled by a mine.

Almost at the same moment, six vehicles ahead of me, another truck hit a mine. My driver tried to dart our truck out of line, thinking he had to get us quickly around the traffic jam ahead, and just as suddenly stomped on his brakes. A tank, coming up from behind us, raced by, nearly smashing our truck.

There were some gunshots, and smaller explosions that I took to be mortar rounds landing near the road, but we were moving ahead fast, and as we drove around the truck, I saw an injured man lying off to the side, clutching his legs.

We kept driving. I counted the major parts of vehicles I saw beside the road, and estimated by the time the day was over that the United States Army had lost a minimum of fifty trucks, tanks, and other vehicles just along that single stretch of "highway," over the last few months.

There was an M-60 tank with its engine and transmission blown completely out of it, parts lying beside the hull, all of the access hatches missing over the engine deck.

A steel frame bridge lay crumpled in a deep gully, a new bridge thrown up so we could cross. I wondered how many bridges had been built there.

We passed one town. It was not inhabited. Much of the town had been built of brick, with plastered walls and tile roofing. Now it was all shattered, pockmarked with bullets and shrapnel, heaped in worthless piles.

The sights were eerie, puzzling, mute evidence of battles fought and forgotten.

It took us two days to dig the new radio bunker and get our tents erected. The new LRRP platoon area at The

Oasis was better organized, and larger. We even made a duplicate of the radio bunker and designated it the "television bunker," because there was a low-powered television broadcasting station now at Dragon Mountain Base Camp. It was on the air several hours a day, and we all donated money for a black-and-white television set.

We did not take our small unit of Montagnard mercs with us from 3 Tango. They went on to another SOG outfit. We did keep a few of the Vietnamese and Americans who had been attached to us as part of our SOG duties.

Now we were thirty miles from the border instead of a few kilometers, and our new area of operations would be mostly in Pleiku and Kontum provinces.

Tan, the Vietnamese interpreter I had carried to the aid station at 3 Tango during the mortar attack, came back from the hospital, his shrapnel wounds healed.

We also got Sergeant Littlejohn back, and I gave him his carbine. He had been hit in the side with an AK-47, the bullet itself not making half the scar the surgeons did getting it out of him.

Another change for us was the introduction of Captain Clarke, who came to take over command of the platoon, making Lieutenant Lapollo the executive officer.

I went down to the creek at the bottom of the hill and washed with the rest of our work party after we finished the sandbagging, knowing that a few minutes after we started the long, hot walk back up the hill, we would be coated with dust again from the passing trucks, but the bath was worth it.

Tom Harris, my friend from C Company, finally joined the LRRPs. We had gone to LRRP school together.

One of the basic principles we maintained in the platoon was the option to quit. We had come to the platoon as volunteers; we could just as quickly leave.

While not many did, one of my friends, Brown, who had originally been with the Aviation, doorgunner on a Chinook, lost his resolve one day. This is how it happened.

THE CHOICE

Four men dressed in tiger fatigues and soft hats walked out of the firebase perimeter, cradling M-16s in their arms and wearing heavy rucksacks. The tension began.

The morning was hot and the sky almost cloudless. Their footsteps crunched loudly in the defoliated kill zone around the encampment.

The rain forest lay ahead, still dark and forbidding even with the peak of day approaching.

Soon they were in knee-high yellow grass, the buffer between the jungle and the firebase. Their eyes searched the tree line.

One stomach couldn't take it. Brown stopped. The other team members hesitated and looked at him.

"What's wrong?" a man asked, his eyes in shadow under the hat brim. Brown agonized for a moment, swinging his rifle limply by one hand.

"I can't do it anymore," he said. Glances were exchanged. They stood in the open, the forest waiting.

Brown looked into the faces. He saw sympathy. He saw coldness. "I can't do it. I'm through. Let's go back in," he said.

As slowly and deliberately as they had come, they trudged back into the firebase. The infantry on the line watched them return without comment.

"What are you going to do?" a team member asked him. Brown sat down on some sandbags. "Go back to the Chinooks, I guess. Get my job as a doorgunner again."

The team leader turned to the radio man. "Call brigade and tell them we need a man. Brown'll go back on the chopper."

Brown was beyond conversation. He sat and stared, his decision made. The other men on the patrol gave him the grace of silence.

We organized as a five-man team for this mission, the objective not reconnaissance, but ambush. We were going out as a hunter-killer team.

There was a dirt road that led away into the jungle from the Special Forces camp being built near The Oasis. Enemy mining parties were active on it, coming in at night to bury some of those powerful road mines that could blow the wheels off our trucks.

We were to walk the road at night, for a length of six kilometers if we could, try to intercept a mining party in action—and kill them.

The road was rocky, and it was difficult to walk it quietly in the dark. I was point again, the rocks almost tripping me and generally impeding silent movement.

I had already realized how crazy the idea of walking the road at night was. A mining party would have security out on both ends of their dig, and the first I'd know about it would be muzzle flashes from their AK-47s.

Even though the night was cool, I was sweaty from nervousness. We took rest breaks every thousand meters.

At one of our breaks, we heard the distinct sound of incoming mortars, and suddenly the road was bracketed with explosions.

Sergeant Mott, who had recently been promoted to staff sergeant (E5 to E6), stammered that someone at The Oasis had made a mistake, and had failed to tell the mortar crews not to plot fire on the road.

It was standard practice for both the mortars and artillery to drop harassment-and-interdiction (H&I) fire on mapped targets either day or night.

The mortar rounds walked away from us, in twenty-five-meter steps, but we didn't know if they would come back, so knowing we were at maximum range, we ran down the road in the dark, trying to make sure we outdistanced the mortars.

We walked with me still on point until midnight, decided then we had gone far enough, and crept off the road into the forest, arranged guard, and went to sleep.

I was picked up off the ground by an explosion so close it cut down the small trees near us with fragments. I bounced once, grabbed for my weapon, and in that instant we were surrounded by more explosions. This time it wasn't mortar. It was 105mm artillery.

Sergeant Mott frantically grabbed the radio handset, calling brigade, managing to blurt out for them to cease fire, that the rounds were hitting us.

The shells still came smashing into the night around us, as if we were the specific target. Mott started to whimper, and sensing he was going to try and run, two of us held him down, trying to tell him what we didn't believe ourselves—that everything was going to be all right—and Mott was swearing he was going to quit the LRRPs if he got back.

We stayed there the rest of the night.

We moved out at 0800, avoiding some Montagnards who were walking through the woods toward the road, and continued on parallel to the road.

The foliage became thick, and it took hard pushing to keep moving. We made only a thousand meters all morning. We found nothing but ancient Montagnard trails. Finally, aggravated, exhausted, and dripping with sweat, we stopped in the late afternoon, found some good ground, and set up another overnight defense perimeter.

Before dark, listening to the radio traffic, we learned two things. One of the new division LRRP teams had to be extracted because they had lost their map. I laughed about that. Some LRRPs.

Second, we got news that Sergeant Sanderson's team had made contact with ten enemy, killed six of them, and had captured a light machine gun.

That raised the platoon toll of enemy killed to seventeen. We still had no dead of our own. Littlejohn had been hit in the side, and Bonnert had been shot in the thigh, plus another man had a slight graze on his arm, but that was our total casualty list.

Bonnert had come back about the same time Little-john had returned. He had been point man on his team, and taken a bullet through his thigh in an ambush, but that had happened before I joined the platoon.

Bonnert had told me the story of his ambush, and it was a disturbing one.

He had sensed the ambush a moment before it happened. "It was too quiet, too still," he said. "I knew we were fucked, but before I could say anything . . ."

Bonnert was point, and was hit in the thigh, his leg collapsing under him. "I tried to run, but I couldn't," he said, "but I realize now, if I had gotten back to my feet quickly, I would have been killed."

The NVA broke contact, but Bonnert said he was left for dead by his team. "I managed to get out of my ruck-sack," he said, "and with the weight off me, I could crawl."

He did crawl, and happened to find his team at the assembly point they had prearranged not long before the ambush.

"My team just ran out on me," he said, and told me who they were, and to watch out for them.

"Those bastards," he said. "They never even checked. You don't ever leave a man behind like that. *Never.*"

---

1 April 1967: Recall

During the night I was attacked by ants who crawled over me constantly.

We shouldered our equipment and left our night posi-tion at 0830, and struggled through dense foliage until 1300, having advanced only about a thousand meters.

We were low on water, and trying to find a river indi-cated on our map. When we called in our afternoon situa-tion report, the order was given to us to return, that our mission was canceled.

I couldn't believe it. There we were, far out in the

middle of some of the thickest jungle I'd seen since a brick wall, and the word was come home.

A spotter aircraft flew over us, and when we asked him by radio for verification of the nearest clear landing zone, he gave us one only three hundred meters away.

Brigade headquarters said they could not spare a helicopter, and they wanted us to walk out. It had taken us a day and a half to get where we were, and headquarters had the nerve to ask us if we could get back by late afternoon.

I held my CAR-15 ahead of myself and pushed down the vines and saplings, moving ahead like a human bulldozer. With no noise discipline at all, I made three thousand meters in four hours.

Thorns ripped me, vines brought me down, branches blocked me and stabbed me, but I made the distance.

When we finally found the road again, I was a bloody, shredded mess. I collapsed in the high grass and worked my way out of my pack, and lay there panting. I pulled the thorns out of my hands with my teeth. My neck was burned where vines had lashed me like ropes.

Mott radioed back at 1600 hours. We were still several kilometers from The Oasis, a long, hot, dusty walk up an unsecured road. We didn't have any water, and the heat and thirst were excruciating.

Brigade promised a vehicle would come for us. An hour later, nothing had showed. We called again, and were told again the truck was on the way.

We later learned the truck went on the wrong road.

We walked about 1500 meters toward The Oasis before hearing a convoy coming. We really wanted to ride, but there was the possibility that if the convoy saw us, they would mistake us for North Vietnamese and shoot us down.

I volunteered to be the one who stood in the road to stop the convoy.

I took off all my equipment, held no weapon, and opened my shirt so the men on the vehicles could see I was light-skinned, not a brown Vietnamese. My face and arms were tanned so darkly I knew I had to show some light skin somehow.

The team hid behind a low hill beside the dirt road. I was prepared to run if I was fired on.

The first vehicle I saw was a huge tank retriever, a large track vehicle fitted with a short crane and heavy-duty winches. The VTR (vehicle, tank retriever) was armed with a .50 caliber heavy machine gun manned by the helmeted figure standing in the deck hatch.

A Fifty is pure light artillery, and does not deserve to be classed as a machine gun. The destruction a Fifty can cause is impressive. It can shoot through hills, bunkers, all with no problems.

The VTR commander rode casually holding his Fifty, but then the vehicle stopped abruptly as he saw me, snatched his gun around, and pointed it straight at me.

He was still a hundred meters out, and I thought I could see down the bore of that big machine gun. I didn't move. If I had wavered, he would have pulled the trigger, and I would have been racing through the trees, .50 caliber slugs uprooting everything around me.

I saw the man speak into his helmet mike, and the VTR started crawling forward, uncertain of me. Finally, the VTR resumed speed, the gunner raised the barrel of the Fifty, and my heart started to beat again.

The convoy gave us a ride back to The Oasis, and we were covered with road dust so perfectly, we looked as if we had been spray-painted, but it was better than walking.

The first thing I saw as we walked into the platoon area was a group of our men and a few officers from brigade examining a bipod-mounted, top-magazine-loaded, heavy-barreled automatic rifle. The weapon was set atop a low bunker, and it had attracted a crowd. It was the "light machine gun" Sergeant Sanderson's team had captured.

I paused and took a look at the weapon. It was actually an antique French automatic rifle of World War I vintage, but it was in good shape, and I heard one of the brigade officers say they were going to send it to the West Point museum.

After getting a drink of water and dropping my weapon and equipment beside my bunk, I felt better, and indeed was proud of Sanderson's team. I decided to find one of them and ask about the details of the fight.

I looked into the next tent, and saw one of the men I knew who had been on Sanderson's team, actually one of our few prior wounded. He was the man who had been grazed on the arm the day Littlejohn was hit.

I have not used his name because of this incident.

"Hey, killer!" I said, "looks like you guys really put the hurt on Charlie!"

He was sitting on the end of his cot, looking at the ground. He turned his head and stared at me, eyes wide open in fury.

"Get out of here! Get out before I kill you! You don't know! Get away from me!" he shouted.

Shaken, I backed out of the tent, and one of the men took me by the arm and pulled me away.

"That gun was being carried by a Montagnard who was the point," said my friend. "There were only three cartridges in the magazine of the weapon, and they were corroded together. That was his personal weapon. He wasn't with the VC."

"What happened?" I asked.

"Sandy and his boys had an ambush set up, and heard the people walking into it before they saw them. The point man was carrying that weapon. They opened up and killed the point and everybody in the bushes behind him. Turns out it was a Montagnard family. All the rest of them were women and kids."

Sickened, I understood. I didn't even know how to apologize to the man I had just called "killer."

But they sent the damn automatic rifle to West Point anyway.

Again we were designated as a hunter-killer team. Captain Clarke decided to come out with us, so our organization was Sergeant Mott as team leader, me as point man, Streeter, one of our black LRRPs, as radioman, and the captain as a participant/observer.

Captain Clarke had been a bow hunter in the States, and a transportation officer in Vietnam. He had been lightly wounded in the leg while on a convoy, and while healing in the hospital had volunteered for long-range patrol.

Since brigade thought we needed an officer who had more rank than a first lieutenant, we received Clarke. He was tall, brave, and ready for the assignment.

Captain Clarke wanted to actually go on patrol himself, something Lapollo did not do often, except to familiarize himself with what kind of conditions we worked under in the field.

Clarke had gone on an earlier patrol with Speck, whose sprained ankle had healed while he worked in the radio bunker. Keough, recently back from the Nha Trang Recondo School, was point for Clarke's team.

They had only just come off the helicopter, and were moving through a wooded area, when they walked face-first into a North Vietnamese patrol.

Keough blasted the enemy point man with his CAR-15. Machine gunners were taught to fire a "burst of six." Keough had the technique on such surprise encounters of emptying his entire magazine, or as he called it, a "burst of twenty."

The enemy point man went down very dead, and for a moment, both patrols were scurrying for cover, still facing each other.

Speck knew the thing to do was escape at the first opportunity. LRRP teams were not supposed to stand and fight.

Captain Clarke had other ideas. He suddenly grabbed

Speck by the arm, and shouted for the team to *attack* the enemy.

Speck was more experienced. He did not move from his fairly safe place nose-down in the dirt, but Clarke jumped up and charged the North Vietnamese, throwing hand grenades.

"I knew he was crazy then," Speck told me, "but I couldn't let him go all by himself. I jumped up too, and went in behind him."

Speck and Clarke killed five enemy soldiers with grenades, saturating the bushes with a barrage of them, until, as Speck put it, "Arms and legs flew out."

Then they retreated to a pickup point and called back the helicopters.

Now, it was my turn to go out with Captain Clarke.

I thought bravery was all well and good, but it had to be tempered with wisdom and a good survival instinct. I didn't want to be killed because Captain Clarke saw a chance to assault an enemy position.

I knew Sergeant Mott was scared of going out with Clarke, but Mott wanted too much to impress him, so I knew we might be in for a general hard time on this patrol.

Two Hueys landed on our insertion, my team on one, another team on the other. The terrain where we landed was flat and burnt-over, with many good places to set a helicopter down. The forest was close.

The other team went east. We went west, and as point I led my team about a thousand meters through the jungle to a good, well-used trail.

It was almost dark, and we split up to cover a fork we found in the trail. Sergeant Mott and Captain Clarke stayed at the intersection, while Streeter took one branch and I took the other. We were covered front and back, and settled into a quiet walk.

I boiled water for a dehydrated ration, and was waiting for it to reconstitute when there was a single, loud gunshot from Streeter's position. I didn't have a direct line of sight to him, our positions separated by brush, and as I went down, flipping the safety off my CAR-15, I didn't know what had happened.

"Are you all right?" Mott called to Streeter, who came running back to him, out of breath.

"There was three of them!" Streeter said. "First couple of guys were 'Yards, carrying baskets on their backs, the last guy was a VC, he had a carbine! They walked right up on me!"

I crawled to his position. There were two baskets abandoned by the escaped Montagnards. One had a few edible roots in it. The other had once contained fresh meat, but now there was only congealed blood and fat.

"Maybe they'll come back," Captain Clarke said.

And probably bring all their friends in the North Vietnamese Army, I was thinking.

Clarke believed the VC would think we had run. He decided to set up an ambush and wait for them. We planned the ambush carefully, moving away from the trail fork a distance, and arranged all of our Claymore mines to crisscross their sweeping blasts of steel shot there.

We stayed in ambush, and very late that night, we heard movement.

I laid my hand on my CAR-15, waiting. It sounded like a point man creeping off the trail, coming directly our way.

All of us tensed, weapons ready. The rustling of the grass and bushes was slow, careful, and steady, except for the times it would go silent for a few moments. I could imagine the point man walking like I did, pausing to listen every few steps.

Since we were lying down in the dark, the enemy would not see us until we fired.

Soon, the noise was only a few meters away. I prepared to fire.

A wild pig snorted, sensing us, and walked away, sounding exactly on his travels like a deliberate, slow-moving point man in the night.

3 April 1967

We disarmed our mines and moved on into the Ia Drang Valley, walking much farther than we would have normally gone. The distances were Clarke's idea. By late afternoon we were exhausted, and found a spot to rest, and set up another ambush.

4 April 1967

The foliage became so dense it was virtually impenetrable as we began the third day of the mission. At times, as point, I moved forward on my hands and knees, or actually on my stomach.

The briars, vines, grass, and saplings made a carpet two meters high.

I lost an ink pen, broke the glass on the face of my compass, and lost my stainless-steel folding-blade pocketknife.

Mott lost his compass.

A helicopter flying overhead trying to contact another one of our teams gave us a visual sighting on an abandoned Montagnard village, and we changed directions toward it, but when we came out the rough foliage, we found nothing but burnt-out clearings and many well-traveled foot trails.

We moved into the brush to observe any trail activity, when we heard voices coming from out of the forest behind us.

Clarke, Mott, Streeter, and I all raised our CAR-15s, no word among us necessary. There were two men walking on the very trail we had chosen to watch.

I could see their shapes through the jungle. Neither man was armed. The voices were Montagnard. The lead man wore an oversize U.S. olive-drab T-shirt, and was carrying a native machete.

The man following him was bare-chested, dressed

only in his loincloth, and walked carrying a tall stick. Both were talking fast and loudly. The lead man looked into the bushes, and saw the four of us, our weapons all pointed directly at him and his friend.

The first man halted as if he had been paralyzed. The man behind him bumped into his back, stepped away with a puzzled expression, then he saw us and froze.

The first man tried to smile and speak, but we did not respond. I was aiming center mass on him. The smile vanished and he raised his hands.

For a moment, their lives were in Captain Clarke's hands. If the captain had fired, I would have fired. The Montagnards were not armed, but that didn't automatically make them friendly.

Clarke took his left hand off the foregrip of his CAR-15, and waved the men away with a short flick of his wrist, never taking his weapon off them.

They sprinted away.

We had no way of knowing if they were sympathetic to Americans, or if they would go straight to the North Vietnamese Army. We had let them live because they seemed to be innocent.

To survive, we had to leave the area. I took point, and we began putting distance behind us, moving on the banks of the Ia Drang River.

I was fed up with Clarke. He was making us take chances I felt were unnecessary, and like a yes-man, Mott was agreeing with him.

At one spot, when we paused to refill our canteens, Clarke didn't like the looks of the water at the edge of the river, so while we filled our canteens from the concealment of the banks, he walked out onto a log to the clearer, swifter water. He was in plain sight as he knelt to fill his canteens.

The Ia Drang Valley was a dangerous place. The 1st CAV had been mauled in it, and our own units didn't penetrate it very far. It was established enemy terrority, and Captain Clarke was revealing the presence of our patrol.

"If he gets shot," I told Streeter, "I'm not doing anything about it. I'm just walking away." He grunted in agreement.

We covered eleven kilometers that day before we halted, all of it following enemy trails beside the river.

We had to move steadily until sunset to get that sort of range, and by the time we stopped, we were so tired none of us could stand.

At dark, we crawled off into heavy foliage, and wired out our Claymores to cover the approaches. Away from the better water of the river, we had to get our water for cooking from a swampy spot nearby. It required pushing back the green slime on the surface, removing the sticks and moss, dipping in a canteen cup, and filtering the water into the canteen through a cloth. After that, to kill the bacteria in the rich swamp water, we would drop in one or two iodine tablets. The taste of iodined-laced swamp water was nasty. I had to make coffee or cocoa with it before I could comfortably drink it.

During the night we heard—very distinctly and quite near—an enemy mortar firing. It sounded about five hundred meters away. Some American artillery came in too, and it was long-range heavy guns, like 8-inch or 175mm pieces.

It hit in the valley, and the concussion shook the leaves where I sat.

The termites appeared before dawn. When I woke up for guard at 0230, they had come out of the ground and were everywhere. They were all clicking their jaw pincers and it made a sound like a constant buzz. They could eat into packs, going right through nylon or canvas, even plastic bags.

If I lay still, they would crawl all over me, but not bite. I touched my finger to the ground once, and one of the soldier termites snapped its pincers into my fingertip with incredible strength. It was not unusual for the Montagnards to use them to close wounds, the way we would use stitches. Once the termite had bitten into both sides of a cut and pulled it together with its wide, curved pincers, the Montagnards would break the body of the in-

sect away from the head, leaving the pincers there to hold
the wound clamped shut.

I woke the next morning, had my first case of bleeding
bowels, and knew I had to get to the 4th Medical when we
returned.

Brigade radioed and told us we would be extracted at
1400 hours, so we held our position, listening to radio traffic, and wondering if the enemy would come along and
make us have to blow our Claymores.

We learned that Viking 3, our sister team on this mission, had been extracted the day before, the team having
made enemy contact, killed one North Vietnamese, and
captured a weapon. The team got away from the enemy,
called in air strikes and artillery, and came back without
losing a man.

The extraction ship found us with no problem after
we moved to one of the burned-over clearings, and soon we
were back at The Oasis, washing, eating, and relaxing.

Sergeant Sanderson's team that had killed the
Montagnards by mistake was issued medals while we were
gone. The brigade commander insisted on giving them all
Bronze Stars.

Whitlock, a clowning LRRP who had gone on
Sanderson's team as the radioman, and who did no actual
firing because he was with the radio, cried when they gave
him the medal, because he knew the awards were really to
cover the accident.

7 April 1967: Warning Order

Mott told me to get ready for another patrol, and to
pack to be gone five days. Our target area was to be south
of The Oasis where our LRRP teams were having so much
contact.

Almost all of the platoon was assigned for this mission, which meant we would be deploying three or more teams.

I accepted the news, and tried to enjoy what relaxation I could around the platoon area. Usually, I found a friend to talk to. It was good therapy.

One of the men who joined us after we began working with the Special Operations Group was a fellow named Ghoul. That was his real name.

It's not that Ghoul was hard to speak to, it's just that I couldn't think of anything to strike up a conversation with him about.

Ghoul was tall. His eyes were dark and sunk far back under his eyebrows. I had never seen their real color. His hair was black and cut military-short. No tiger fatigues would fit him. He usually wore plain jungle fatigues.

Ghoul was a professional sniper. He would leave our area and be gone for several days. When he returned, somebody out there would be dead. Four Vietnamese security men went with him everywhere, even in 3 Tango.

I had watched all five of them sit and play a spirited game of cards, Ghoul cursing in English and the others ranting in their language, shouting at the top of their voices, playing cards flying everywhere.

Ghoul never carried his rifle with him. It stayed wrapped up in his tent beside his cot, but his Viets seemed to always drag their carbines around in the mess tent, in the TV bunker, at the card games.

His men dressed in anything. They wore black pajamas, khaki NVA uniforms, tigers, whatever. I had never seen any of them saddled with a rucksack. I believed they carried whatever they ate in their pockets.

Ghoul's missions were not like those of a combat sniper. Harris had told me that. Ghoul went after certain individuals. His usual method was to stake out a village or a trail that he knew his victim used and simply wait. Harris said he preyed on Communist tax collectors, VC cadre, and corrupt or suspect officials of the South Viet government.

His security men could mix with the local people to

clearly point out the target. I understood they let Ghoul do the actual killing even though they had the opportunity sometimes themselves.

We kept score of the platoon's kills. A patrol returning with a bodycount was welcomed, and the tally raised. But Ghoul's kills were never added or discussed.

---

8 April 1967: Mission

Five of us went out, Sergeant Mott as team leader, myself, Supply Sergeant Snake (who wanted the experience of going out once), and two new men, Sergeant Rilley and Specialist Ramey.

The platoon had started to get some new blood. We were thankful for them, and were mixing new men with veterans to get them trained.

In my search and experimentation for a reliable and better weapon, for this patrol I took out an M-3 .45 caliber "grease gun" I had borrowed from one of our Vietnamese.

The grease gun was World War II vintage, and no longer issued in the United States Army, except to tankers. It seemed lighter and handier than a stockless M-1A Thompson offered to me by a brigade weapons trader. The Thompson had felt like an anvil.

I also borrowed an ammo pouch for the grease gun; it held three 30-round magazines. I would discover the weight of the ammunition alone was enough reason not to carry a .45 caliber anything. I had saddled myself with less total rounds of ammunition than if I had carried a carbine, and three times the weight.

We were issued a new type of mine for this mission, the M-14 "shoe" mine. It was a small, lightweight, plastic mine that was intended to blow off part of someone's foot. We were going to set them out at night on approaches to our positions, to use as warning devices.

The helicopter that brought us in also picked up Sergeant Britt's team at the same place. Britt was carrying a captured M-1 Garand his men had taken after killing a Vietcong. That made over twenty kills for us so far.

The trick of direct exchange (DX) was a good one, because it replaced one team with another, and made the enemy think the first team was gone.

I took point again. It was my favorite position. Many men were afraid of point because it was where most of the shooting started, and the responsibility of the point man was heavy; if he made an error, the whole team would suffer for it.

I didn't realize at first that Mott gladly let me take point. It began to be clear to me later that Mott wanted me on point for two reasons.

First, he knew I would fight if I encountered the enemy.

Second, he wanted me killed if possible, because he was still afraid I might expose him.

Just before our surprise contact with all those North Vietnamese on my first mission with Mott, he had been waiting for his promotion, and had probably been worried that if I revealed how he had reacted under fire, he would not be promoted.

And he was worried enough about it to threaten my life. I didn't believe he would kill me himself. He would try and create the situation where the enemy would kill me, and that meant giving me every dangerous assignment that came along.

Though I would be his point man, scout and risk-taker, I didn't confront him with a reply to his threat. I didn't care. I would do my job, and that involved risks.

I led the team to high ground, found a trail, and we followed it down to the water. This was a prime place to catch somebody. We found old enemy fighting positions near the stream crossing, and decided to lay in an ambush there.

It rained heavily after dark, soaking us where we sat, but we had a good position, and we didn't move.

Late that night, we heard a mortar firing steadily, but

could not hear where its shells were landing. It sounded as if it were at least two thousand meters from where we waited in ambush.

After I had gone to sleep, and one of our men was on guard, a supersonic 8-inch howitzer shell hit a hill nearby, waking us all, and as I lay there, surprised, a few more fell.

The valley echoed with the tremendous blasts. It was H&I fire, and again, we were on the receiving end.

After daybreak, we slowly moved uphill, back to higher ground, and reset our ambush, sprinkling out our M-14 mines and backing them up with Claymores aimed to massacre anything lying or standing in the kill zone.

We stayed the day there, waiting, watching, thinking. We sincerely wanted a kill. A Vietcong or North Vietnamese taking our trail would be as good as dead.

Because I was separated from the team farther than usual due to the hillside and ambush arrangement, Mott told me to stick a blasting cap into the two-pound block of C4 plastic explosive I carried in my rucksack and give him the wire to attach to his Claymore clacker.

The reason he gave me was that if I were killed, he could destroy my equipment. I didn't like it, but I did it. We had done things like this before, but rarely, and usually it was only on rucksacks that held Starlight scopes or code-books.

With the wire fixed, I crawled downhill to my position. I was worried about Mott, who literally held my life in his hands, because if any shooting started, I knew he would squeeze the clacker and claim I had been hit.

As soon as I was in place, I disarmed the cap. I could not trust him. Not at all.

We held that ambush through the night, and, having turned up nothing, took in our mines the next morning, radioed our situation report, and were given the message to cancel the rest of the mission and find a landing zone for extraction.

Soon a small, single-engined spotter plane was over us, and we used it to get a radio-direction-finding fix, and have the pilot locate a nearby LZ.

He gave us a compass azimuth to an old American position, and we started toward it, but the brush and grass were so thick we made no real distance, and decided to cut a landing zone out of the growth ourselves.

It was what we called a "pocketknife LZ," and we used our sheath knives to chop out a place, and stomped, snapped, and pushed down what we couldn't cut out. It took four hours to cut the clearing.

The Huey and gunship escort came at 1530. The air was hot and thin, which is bad for helicopters. They don't get much lift then, even at maximum power. The Huey slammed into the ground as it landed, but the pilot corrected, swung the ship around, and we scrambled out of the grass, trying to get to the doorways.

The pilot couldn't stabilize the ship, and it continued to swing, the tail rotor coming at us like a huge, lethal fan, and we ducked and weaved, dodging to go under his tail boom, escape the rotor, and jump in the doorways.

Once aboard, we relaxed on the cooling ride back to The Oasis.

Coming off the ship, we reported to the radio bunker, and discovered we had been recalled because we were needed for insertion in another area, and we were to prepare to go back out as soon as possible.

The new mission was to go into the Cateka Tea Plantation and try to find some of the Vietcong cadre that lived there.

The VC had used the tea plantation for years, and reportedly had sophisticated printing presses, electrical power generators, and machine tools in operation within the safe boundaries of the plantation, because it was "off limits" to U.S. military operations. The plantation was private property protected by an agreement with the South Vietnamese politicians that ran Pleiku Province, making it untouchable to the American Army.

U.S. forces could not shell or bomb the plantation, send infantry soldiers onto it to damage the tea bushes, or harm it in any other way, such as allowing tanks to drive across plantation property.

We had taken sniper fire out of Cateka before, and we were reasonably sure road-mining parties worked out of it.

Intelligence from friendly Vietnamese reinforced what we knew. The Vietcong had a first-class "safe house" on that plantation. The workers even attended Communist political meetings, often during the day when they should have been working. They had little choice. If they didn't assemble on cue, they would be killed.

We also knew the reason the plantation was allowed to operate while thousands of other Vietnamese places of business had been destroyed was that the Cateka Tea Plantation paid protection money and taxes to the Vietcong.

Finally, we were going to try to do something about it.

Cateka was about to be visited by a number of LRRP teams.

Our teams didn't go directly into the plantation at first, but scouted the trails and roads that led on and off the property.

There was no cover and little concealment in the tea bushes themselves, which were grown in well-tended lots, divided by dirt roads, and watched over constantly by workers.

As soon as our teams began to skirt the perimeter of the plantation, they made discoveries. The Vietcong indeed had what our sources claimed they did: an electrical generator, power printing presses, and machine tool equipment.

There was a VC cadre unit that lived on the plantation and collected taxes from many areas in the Pleiku Province. They were not a combat unit, but a political and organizational one. They carried pistols, but a few had U.S. carbines, and wore ARVN*-type uniforms—in case they were spotted, they could pass themselves off as local militia.

The Cateka recon missions were shorter than our

* Army of the Republic of Vietnam

usual patrols, because they were so much nearer The Oasis.

I went out with a sniper team to a village in the hills behind Cateka. Our orders were to lie in wait and protect our sniper, while he watched the village for his special target. He knew whom he was looking for. We didn't.

On a tree-covered hill overlooking the village, we dropped into the waist-deep greenery, and settled into comfortable positions. The sniper prepared himself a field of fire, camouflaged it, and relaxed. He had one of the accurate, specially-built M-14 rifles with a powerful telescopic sight on it.

Our sniper had permission to fire. The other teams playing duck-and-hide in the tea bushes of the plantation had been told not to fire unless fired on. I was reminded of one of the LRRPs coming off a Cateka recon, his face strained and his temper sharp, holding his hand at waist-level and saying, "You know how high a damn tea bush is? This high!"

I watched the village below us. It was large and well laid out. I could see gardens and fences. The people there went on with their business, unaware of the telescope that tracked them from their wells to their back doors, and up and down their streets and alleys.

Apparently our sniper's target never showed. After a day, we crept away, the planned execution never taking place.

After our patrols had been hiding along the plantation tree line and seen the Communist political officers openly talking to the workers, they wanted to go back to raid, but no permission from our command was given. To launch a hostile action inside the plantation required approvals that started at Saigon and came back to the Vietnamese Pleiku Province chiefs. We never received permission.

This situation angered Captain Clarke and all the rest of us, but it was only one more bitter disappointment in a war that was full of them.

The team that had just left the area of operations I was going into had enemy contact there twice, and had been extracted.

We were going west to the border, south of the old 3 Tango location.

Sergeant Willie was my team leader this trip, and was tremendously different from the paranoid and moody Mott. Willie wore a gold earring in one ear, and liked to fight.

Harris finally managed to get on a team with me, the first long-range patrol we had done together since December.

Tailgun for our team was Shin, one of the new men from the infantry, but a combat veteran.

While preparing my equipment for the mission, I studied the wrench flats on the 4-inch sound- and flash suppressor on the muzzle of my CAR-15. I went to the motor pool, borrowed a wrench, and unscrewed it; then I replaced it with a normal, one-inch rifle flash suppressor.

I figured that at the expense of some muzzle blast, I had saved length and weight on my weapon. There wasn't time to test it, but I managed one shot out of the perimeter.

The muzzle blast was terrific, but manageable. I decided to take my modified CAR-15 on patrol.

We were inserted by helicopter at 1030, and the two escort gunships with us cut speed at the same time we did to create the illusion the entire flight had simply slowed, covering the fact our ship had dipped close enough to the ground to let four men jump off.

I had stood out on the landing skid as our helicopter rushed over the treetops, and let go as I heard the door-gunner yell for me to move. I hit hard, literally sprawling, gathered myself, and ran for the woods.

Shin and Willie crashed up to where I was waiting, holding my CAR-15 ready to open fire if I saw anything coming our way. There was no sign of Harris, who had our radio.

The three of us made a quick defense perimeter, keeping low in the bushes, watching the helicopters fly away. A moment later, Harris came stumbling toward us, his face contorted in pain. "I think I broke my leg," he said.

Willie examined his leg. Harris was hurting, gritting his teeth. Shin and I kept security. Satisfied that the leg wasn't broken, Harris laced his boot tightly to give himself more ankle support, and we had to wait for him to rest.

The jump out of the helicopter had been too fast and too high. I had hurt one foot myself, and later, when I would take off my boot to inspect it, I would find the bottom of my foot bruised.

We were on operational control (opcon) to the 1st of the 22nd Battalion headquarters, following their orders and gathering intelligence for them.

We were cautious, but our "up the mountain, down the mountain" type of highlands patrol continued. We had some sweeping views across the valleys, our terrain rocky, high, and lightly wooded.

The first of the monsoon rains hit us, making rivers out of gulleys, and preventing us from seeing or hearing well.

After enduring the rain for the best part of a day and night, I was trying to sleep in a wet hammock I had strung on a steep hillside, and at about 0530 in the morning, it fell, rolling me to the wetter ground.

The four of us were shivering from the cold of the highlands night added to the natural chill of the rain.

As soon as there was enough light, we packed and walked down to the valley, and began to follow the river because it was easier to move through than the heavy foliage on the riverbanks.

We were in the water for hours, moving quietly, holding onto overhead branches and vines to keep our balance as we stayed close to the banks and the concealing vegetation there.

I was point man, and I constantly looked up the banks

as far as I could see into the jungle, but my attention was wavering because I was feeling sick. Finally, I turned to Willie and told him I was very ill.

He signaled for me to take the team up the embankment, toward a cavelike hollow in the rocks. We climbed up into it, stripped off our equipment, and collapsed for a break. The rains were coming down again, and we made a fire to warm us.

I noticed an itching on my knee, and reached down to scratch it, feeling the fat blob of a large leech under my trousers.

I rolled the leg of my trousers up over the leech. It was bloated with blood, locked firmly beside my kneecap. I pushed at it gingerly with my knife, but it would not release.

The leech had apparently changed places once, and left a small purple mark still oozing fresh blood near where it was presently. I squirted some insect repellent on the leech and it dropped off.

We soon had a smoky fire in our cave, which angered a nest of hornets that had residence there before we did. The hornets gave way completely only after they learned we were serious about staying.

Shin, Harris, Willie, and I had to spread out in the small cave, and slap and swat at the hornets, killing dozens of them as they attacked out of their nest. The cave was too good to give back to insects.

After the rains, and some hot coffee, I felt like moving again, so we slowly made our way down to a shady cove in the rocks and camouflaged a poncho shelter so we could dry our clothes and equipment.

On the fourth day of the patrol, we walked downriver 1500 meters, and found bundles of sharpened bamboo stakes.

Later, we almost lost Harris during a river crossing. I picked a spot to cross the river near the edge of a dramatic waterfall. There was a rocky ridge under the surface of the water that made our crossing possible, but to slip could mean being carried over the waterfall.

The rains had swelled the river, making the rapids and falls more fierce.

I made it across, scouted the opposite banks, and signaled for Harris to follow. He walked toward me carefully, balancing, and had come near enough to reach for my hand.

He fell into the water, and I saw him wash over the edge of the waterfall. I dropped my CAR-15 on the bank, and grabbed for him. I fell backward into the deep but less-turbulent water upstream of the underwater ledge on which I had been standing.

Shin had come far enough across by that time to reach for Harris, who was totally submerged, only his radio antenna sticking above the surface. He was holding on to a rock for all he was worth, his feet over the edge of the waterfall.

I jumped out of the water and helped Shin pull Harris up. Willie had watched the entire affair, covering us, from the opposite shore.

Harris was gasping and choking when we dragged him to the shore. He had not even lost his weapon. The sight of him clinging underwater to that rock, battered by the current, had been incredible.

"What were you thinking about down there?" I asked him.

"I wasn't worried," Harris said. "I knew you guys would get me out . . . I just had to hold on."

We set up another poncho shelter on a sandbar near the water, camouflaged it, and split into two teams to watch up and down river, and stayed the night there.

The leech spots on my knee had hardened in the center, and were very tender around the edges, resembling rotten spots on fruit. I'd had many leech bites before, but this one was the worst. It would be months before the marks would really heal.

On our way to the area we had planned to use as our pickup zone, we encountered a section of the river that had almost been diverted from its course by a B-52 strike. Instead of a river, it had become a wide, bomb-cratered swamp.

As we walked into the water, I saw a hazy, buzzing greenish cloud hovering ahead, spanning the river and the treetops. It was a mass of flying insects, still in turmoil, unwilling to land.

We had to go through them.

Squinting and closing our mouths as we splashed into the muck of fresh grass and liquid mud, the insects swarmed us. There seemed to be hundreds of different types of them, trying to crawl into our ears, eyes, nostrils, and corners of our mouths.

Swatting at them was no good. There were too many. We walked through the maddening, boiling mass of them, almost blinded, our skin crawling with thousands of pricking, probing legs and wings.

When we emerged from the other side, the insects left us to go back to the cloud, as if they were in agony over the despoiled river.

It was the first time in my life I have ever felt sorry for bugs.

We realized without surprise the next morning that we were probably being followed when we saw movement and heard noises behind us. It was possible. We had been on the river too long.

It was the end of the mission anyway.

Willie gave the order and Harris radioed our position and extraction request, which meant we were now committed to stay put. I hoped the helicopter would arrive before the enemy did.

Our pickup spot was a grown-over sandbar beside the river. An hour later, we heard the helicopter. The NVA could hear it too. I stood in the open and marked our position with a panel as the swaying, thundering-loud Huey settled onto the sandbar.

Shin was tailgun. The rest of us ran to the ship, then he followed. The rotors were spinning, the jet turbine screaming, and the Huey was bouncing, but we were not taking off.

Turning in his seat, the pilot gestured that two of us had to get off. I understood at once. The air was too hot and thin to allow the rotors enough bite. To fly at all, the ship had to be lightened.

I was point and Shin was tailgun, so we jumped.

The Huey trembled and started to rise. It was going to be a long walk home, if we made it at all.

Then Willie and Harris jumped too. They were not going to split up the team. Willie grabbed me.

"Get back on the ship!" he ordered.

"Why?" I shouted, my voice faint in the noise of the engine.

"Me and Harris have the radio! You don't! Tell the pilot to take you downriver and then come back for us! I'll change positions!"

That made sense. Willie was a good team leader. He made me realize how bad I'd had it with Mott. The Huey took Shin and me out, and went back for Willie and Harris.

I trusted Willie and I liked him.

UNAUTHORIZED MODIFICATION

Back from patrol, Harris, Shin, and I went to the garbage-dump firing range at the far side of The Oasis to do a little target practice.

As my friends began firing, I raised my CAR-15 and pulled the trigger. It fired once, with its new horrendous muzzle blast, but failed to recycle. I had to eject the spent brass manually.

It would fire, fail to recock, or fire and recock once. I could not get it to function normally on semi or full automatic. It took me a few moments to realize the problem.

The four-inch-long sound- and flash suppressor that I had removed before the mission compensated for the short barrel length by providing enough gas backpressure to allow the weapon's gas system to recycle.

I had almost killed myself for an unauthorized modification done on a whim. What if we had gotten into a firefight? I vowed to replace the proper suppressor that day, feeling like a fool.

Shin and Harris laughed at me, shooting up their old ammo. They saw a dud 40mm M-79 grenade projectile in the dump. It was lying out at about twenty-five yards, a small target.

"I wonder if it'll blow if I shot it?" Harris asked.

"Blow it? You can't even hit it from here," Shin said.

They began firing at the high-explosive shell, kicking up dirt with near misses, arguing with each other about the chance of the grenade exploding.

It did, making a ball of flame and gray smoke and flinging fragments at us. It happened too quickly to even duck.

At least I wasn't the only fool at the garbage dump.

26 to 30 April 1967: Radio Watch

It was raining more, and the dust was settling. The promise of June and my passage home was foremost on my mind. Radio-watch duty was both tiresome and exciting, taking the team situation reports, listening to coded signals, and sometimes trying to broadcast over frequencies being used by the North Vietnamese in order to jam them.

By slowly turning the dial on our powerful radio set, it was possible to tune in both propaganda and field combat communications of the enemy. I could even hear background voices as the radio operator spoke in the microphone.

Hearing their clinking of cookware, laughter, or commands being given near the radio operators was fascinating, as if I were there with them.

PANTHERS

One of our teams radioed us with a shocking but comical message. At least it was comical to us in the radio bunker.

"What do we do about *panthers?* Over."

"Say again? Over," said the LRRP on radio watch.

"A panther has us up a tree. Should we just shoot him, over?"

"All of you are up in a tree? The whole *team?* Over."

"Yeah. All of us. We want permission to shoot him, over."

"Don't do that, you'll give away your position. Wait, out."

The radioman ran for the captain, who came to the radio bunker, mystified as to how an entire team could be treed by one animal.

"Say again your situation, over," said the captain.

"We're okay now," replied the LRRP RTO. "We sprayed the panther in the face with bug repellent and he jumped down and ran away."

"Very good," said the captain. "Continue the mission."

"Roger," said the team, and they did.

THE FACE

The sight of wounded and disfigured Vietnamese in Pleiku was common enough, from hobbling veterans to pathetic women and children. I had finally become accustomed to them, the way I had become accustomed to the smell of the fish market, or the war itself, or so I thought.

As I walked down a Pleiku street one day on an errand, I realized someone was following me much too closely, which was a dangerous thing. I spun around and almost bumped into the man.

I was looking into a hole where his face should have been.

As if a crater had erupted from his nose outward,

there was one hole, and in it I saw nasal passages like open wounds, mixed with a few broken upper teeth and what was left of his tongue.

There was a sunken yellow eye peering out of the top of it all.

He felt his way around me and kept walking. To this day I have never seen a Halloween mask with the horror of that ruined face.

It was just another day in Vietnam.

2 May 1967: Silver Star

I learned Captain Clarke had recommended me for the Silver Star medal for the mission in February when we'd had enemy contact on Mott's team, and he'd also placed me on the promotion list to sergeant.

It was also on that date that I refused to go on any more missions with Mott. I was finished with him.

4 May 1967: Bronze Star

The awards board at Dragon Mountain Base Camp downgraded my award recommendation from the Silver Star to the Bronze Star with the "V" (for Valor) device, but the award still had to be approved.

Harris was out on a team that made enemy contact. The team point man met a North Vietnamese soldier in a heart-stopping face-to-face encounter. The NVA wore a tan uniform and a backpack. The LRRP point man killed the Viet with one burst, and the team took defensive positions near a stream to set up their radio and antenna and call in contact.

Harris was watching a trail across the stream when up stood another North Vietnamese in green fatigues, with a U.S. carbine. Harris fired his CAR-15 at the man, but it jammed after the first shot.

Harris quickly cleared the malfunction, and fired at the man again, but again the weapon only shot once and quit. The enemy soldier went to cover.

Sergeant Willie, who was Harris's team leader, lobbed a grenade at the opposite bank, and the enemy began to throw grenades back.

The two streambanks rocked with concussions as the grenade duel continued, Willie not giving ground, and the North Vietnamese refusing to retreat.

Finally, Willie landed a grenade that settled the fight, but not before he had been wounded many times by fragments.

When I saw Willie carried off the helicopter, both of his eyes were swollen shut, and his body and face were scarred with bloody punctures, his tiger fatigues tattered from the grenade fragments.

He was still trying to smile. "I got them bastards," he mumbled, "they ran out of grenades *first.*"

Harris was frustrated at his experience with the CAR-15, and angry his request to test-fire the weapon before going on the patrol had been denied.

Scabbed-over sores were appearing on Harris's legs. He went on sick call because of them, and got dosed with penicillin, but the sores did not go away. After a brief retreat, they came back stronger.

The medics didn't know what the sores were. We suspected they were some type of tropical disease. Finally, the sores developed on his arms, and he began getting feverish. The captain sent him to the 4th Medical, to a holding area they had at The Oasis for recovering patients or those too sick for the field but too well for the 75th Evac.

We told Harris we would visit him there, and a few days later, three of us walked to the other side of the big camp and found the "hospital." It was nothing but a group of GP medium tents in an isolated section of The Oasis. It was quiet, hot, and except for an orderly sitting at a field table in front of a small pyramid tent, it seemed to be deserted.

"We're from the LRRPs," I said. "One of our men by the name of Harris is here."

The orderly was reading a paperback novel. Beside his elbow was a large jar of Darvon pain capsules. He looked up at me, a little puzzled by our camouflaged fatigues and soft hats.

"Don't know," he said, "just look in the tents."

We left him and went to the first tent in the row. All of the tents had the sides rolled down, which seemed curious in the heat. What we found when we lifted the door flap and stepped into the darkness astonished then enraged me.

Along each side of the tent was a ragged cluster of cots. On those cots were soldiers, some asleep or unconscious, some in pain. The smell hit us like a slap. It was a combination of vomit, the rottenness of infected wounds, and bitter urine.

When the conscious men saw us, they began calling out, begging for water, reaching out with their hands.

I couldn't believe what I was seeing. We took out our canteens and started going from man to man, giving them water. I yanked up the tent side, rolling and tying it up, before I ran to the next tent.

Harris was there on a cot. He was in pain, but he recognized me. I gave him my canteen and his hand was hot with fever.

"What the hell is this?" I asked. "Where's the doctors? The medics?"

"Nobody's coming around," Harris said weakly. "Can you go and get us some water? Some Cokes? Cigarettes?" The other patients were trying to find money in their pockets, begging for the same thing.

"Yeah," I said, looking at men with bloodclotted bandages that were long overdue for changing.

"We been takin' care of each other," Harris said.

One of the other LRRPs found me, and started taking a list and money from the men. Just outside, a street or two away, were water trailers, mess tents, even PX tents with cold soft drinks.

"I'm going to get the orderly," I told Harris, and ran, livid with anger, to the pyramid tent and its shaded occupant. I grabbed him out of the chair, my CAR-15 held at the ready.

"Why isn't there anybody taking care of those men?" I demanded.

The clerk was terrified. He dropped his book. "I'm the only one h-here!" he stammered.

"Then, how come you're not doing your damn *job?"* I shouted, and pushed him against the tent. "Go get your CO now!"

He ran off into the tents.

A few days later, Harris was evacuated. His sores and fever were worse. I never found out what happened to him. I wish I knew.

---

6 May 1967: Carbines

Staff Sergeant Tilley and his LRRP team were operating twelve kilometers southwest of The Oasis. They had been in ambush, but when it was time for them to move on, and they had begun taking in their shoe mines and Claymores, the enemy walked up on them.

Tilley saw the first one. The man was wearing black farmer's clothing, a straw hat, and had a U.S. carbine slung over his shoulder, and American grenades on his belt.

Crouched in the bushes, Tilley fired a close-range burst of automatic fire at the man with his CAR-15 and somehow missed him. The Vietcong jumped back, and tried to unsling his carbine.

Tilley rapidly corrected his aim, and killed the man with a burst of six.

The dead man's partner turned and ran, the other LRRPs shooting at him, but Norton, who already had two NVA to his credit, aimed and brought the escaping man down with one shot.

Tilley stripped his kill, finding money, a good knife, a North Vietnamese Army belt, and an empty canteen which still had the smell of whiskey in it.

The carbine was a brand-new M-2 selective-fire, unscratched, tight, and obviously not long out of the packing crate.

As Tilley bagged the man's valuables, the enemy began to counterattack, and it sounded like a lot of them. The team left their mines in place, and retreated back into the jungle, making the current score twenty-six to nothing in favor of the LRRP platoon.

We were very careful of claiming "kills," the direct opposite of the infantry, which counted anything they thought they might have hit. It was a point of honor with us to only claim the kill you were certain of having made.

I examined Tilley's trophy carbine, and knew I wanted another one of my own. I had carried Littlejohn's carbine on short security missions and truck rides, but never in combat.

My CAR-15 had not jammed on me yet, but Harris's had, and I wanted more than ever now to get a dependable weapon, so I took an offer from one of our platoon members who had an M-2 carbine, and bought it from him for $20. It was hard finding enough magazines for it.

Carbine ammunition was no longer general issue in the United States Army, so I had to go to the Special Forces and the Vietnamese to get my ammunition. After some searching, I had a good, workable carbine that I took to the garbage dump and test-fired frequently; it always worked perfectly.

11 May 1967: Mission

I packed for another mission, going out with Sergeant Rilley as the team leader, Sergeant Padilla as the assistant team leader, and Huxtable.

I asked for and was given the point, hoping there was nothing hostile out there. I was told in the mission briefing not to bring my carbine, because Sergeant Rilley didn't want all of us not having the same type of ammunition.

Our mission went like one from the textbook, riding the Huey in, jumping off into unknown jungle, creeping under the darkness of heavily canopied trees, listening to each sound—or lack of sound—from the insects and animals, sleeping lightly on guard at night, eating soupy LRRP rations, and worrying about what size enemy unit we might encounter.

The mission produced no sign of enemy contact. I was thankful, marking days off on my calendar.

15 May 1967: Warning Order

I had not finished cleaning and sorting my equipment from the last patrol when I was given another. This was a special mission, five days on top of a high peak near the Chu Pong Mountains, acting as a radio relay station for our teams operating in the valley along the Cambodian border.

There would be no walking, only guarding the hilltop, drinking water from five-gallon cans that we took with us, and braving the weather.

16 May 1967: Hill 339

The hill was a stark, rocky jut out of the jungle, covered with sparse foliage and ancient trees. Three sides of the hill towered so wickedly they were almost unscalable. The one side that wasn't a sheer fall was the north ridgeline, a jumble of ups and downs like an obstacle course.

The pinnacle of 339 was a tiny, cleared flat area, just wide enough to allow a helicopter to set its skids down.

All around the small landing zone the broken rock fell

away so sharply a stone rolled off the top would not stop
until it had hit the treetops far, far below.

Three-thirty-nine overlooked everything, the view
from the top commanding the rolling, emerald-green valleys and hills of Vietnam.

Clouds cast shadows on the carpet of jungle below,
and in the far distance to the east, mountains were dim on
the horizon. The rugged Chu Pong mountain range, and
Cambodia, were west. There was no civilization as far as
we could see from the top of 339, only serene, patient nature.

Our three helicopters came in fast, just over the treetops, flying with the contour of the land. There were four
of us riding in the middle Huey. The two outside ships
were armed.

I was with Sergeant Conrad, Sergeant Padilla, Hart,
and Diamond, our radio man. We each had a five-gallon
water can. Everybody but me carried a CAR-15. I had
been assigned to bring my M-16 rifle for any necessary
long-range shots.

As we approached 339, the helicopters started to
climb, rotors beating the air furiously. I could see yellow
smoke at the top of the hill.

Huddled around the small landing zone, holding their
hats, waited the previous team, packed and ready to go
back to The Oasis.

Gently, our Huey touched down, dust and leaves flying, and inside half a minute we were off and the sunburned and bearded old team on.

In a din of jet noise and slashing rotor blades, the
Huey was gone as swiftly as it had come.

After the sound of the helicopters had diminished, it
was silent on the naked, sunbaked crest. We all stood quietly, amazed at the grandeur as we looked off the little LZ
to the mighty Chu Pongs and the jungle below.

The heat made us strip off our shirts as we went to
work. Diamond set up the radio, erecting the long-range

antenna. Padilla went looking for a good site for our command post. Hart and I scouted the area to plan a defense.

My rucksack still on, I sat down in a rocky depression to cover the north approach while Hart checked out some of the features of the hill. I had just relaxed, when something under me in the dead leaves *moved*, exerting enough strength to slightly shift me sideways.

I leaped up with my heart pounding, spinning to see what I had sat on. At first it looked like a massive roach, wiggling its legs wildly, but then I recognized it. It was a giant *scorpion*, its lethal tail just uncurling from being mashed into the leaves by my rucksack. The insect seemed to be five inches long, and built broad and powerfully.

Then I saw more of them as they retreated into the crevices of the rocks. They were the largest scorpions I had ever seen in my life. I seriously considered killing them all with a grenade.

I changed positions in the rocks, inspecting my new spot with more care.

Three-thirty-nine had a long razorback of pure rock going down the north approach. At one time, a platoon of infantry had been encamped on the ridge, and there was ample evidence of their presence in the scattering of rusty ration cans and rotting cardboard boxes. The hill had been too rocky for them to dig into, but in places they had tried, and even left the tree-branch frames they had built to cover their positions with poncho sunshades. Large, heavy rocks had been piled defensively around the shallow holes.

It was silent and magnificent on that great hill. We were respectful of this majesty, speaking quietly as we worked.

Our positions formed a rough triangle. Conrad and Diamond with the radio in a niche in the rock, Hart and Padilla together under a logged roof, and me by myself, protected by a low log barricade facing the approach, sheltered by a lean-to poncho keeping off the direct sun.

We had brought no Claymore mines, but I rigged grenade traps in zigzag patterns on the north approach.

Thus settled, our wait began.

17 May 1967: Distant War

A war started below us in the jungle in the late morning. First came heavily armed Huey gunships, equipped with automatic 40mm cannon, forward-firing quad machine guns, and multiple rocket pods.

They began to shoot into a section of jungle with white-phosphorus rockets, chattering machine-gun fire, and pounding 40mm nose cannons.

Artillery spotter planes buzzed in, Puff the Magic Dragon came with its terrible miniguns, and finally, F-4 Phantom jets arrived, circling warily above.

We found their radio frequency and listened. All of this firepower was being directed against an enemy ammunition storage dump, not an infantry unit or a base camp.

Before it was all over, a single spotter plane flew over our hill looking for enemy activity near us, but saw none.

By noon, we were alone again.

Later in the afternoon, opposite the morning's demolition display, we saw heavy smoke rising out of the jungle, and the distant, faraway rumble of a B-52 strike or a barrage of 175mm artillery reached us. From 339, we could see the war.

18 May 1967: Fire Mission, 105mm

Before dawn, far down on the valley floor, there were lights in the blackness of the jungle. The man on guard woke us, pointing to the lights. We realized we were seeing North Vietnamese troops down there using flashlights for night movements or labor.

We radioed in a report about the lights, and The Oasis told us no friendly troops were in the area and for us to call the artillery.

Padilla looked up the frequency for the 4th of the

42nd Artillery in our radio book, and I radioed them myself and requested a fire mission.

I was given one battery of five guns firing volleys. The
first round, a smoke marker, came in right on target, so I
gave "fire for effect."

The volleys came in groups of five, three times. I corrected fire, giving a five-hundred-meter drop on their gun-
to-target line for two more volleys. The lights went out.

18 May 1967: Fire Mission, 175mm

The rain swept in, forceful and blinding on our isolated little peak. The wind howled across the hillside as the
trees bowed to the downpour.

The sun was lost somewhere in the murky sky, and we
all sat, drenched and miserable at our positions.

Suddenly, something caught our eye. There was a dif-
fusion of campfire smoke rising out of the foggy jungle in
the valley below. The fog and rain almost concealed it.

It had to be the enemy, taking advantage of the low
visibility and lack of aircraft to cook some hot food. I ran
over to Padilla's tent and took the radio and binoculars. I
had called in one good fire mission and I wanted to do it
again.

I radioed The Oasis, described our sighting, and received permission again for artillery. This time, the target
was out of range for the 105mm howitzers, so they gave me
a battery of 175mm long-range guns.

The spotting round was a high explosive that fell a
kilometer short. I had plotted the location of the fires on
our map, which revealed there was a stream where we
could see the smoke. That made sense. The enemy would
be camping beside the stream, using it for water as they
cooked.

I corrected the fire, and asked for a ten-round mission,
a lot of fire from big 175mm cannons.

The guns were so far away I could not hear them

shoot. I could see and hear the impact of the shells, but only afterward would I hear the sound of the shell flying in. The 175mm shells were supersonic, and reached the targets before their sound did.

All ten shells exploded along the stream, three thousand meters from me. I hoped I had ruined their breakfast.

That afternoon, a Huey flew out to us from The Oasis. Captain Clarke was on it, and brought us two more water cans, his ship taking the empties and delivering the full cans without ever landing.

Each night, we packed all our equipment except for our ponchos and lightweight tropical blankets, so in case we had to leave the hill in a fight after dark, we could take everything important with us.

19 May 1967: Extraction

We were extracted off the hill at 1600 hours, our extra water ration having proved unnecessary.

The sun had been intense during the day, and with our shelters packed, the heat was brutal.

As the helicopter eased in to pick us up, its rotor blast felt like it was going to blow us off the hill. Two new men in the LRRP platoon were on my side of the helicopter, poised in the doorway, but seemed afraid to get out of the helicopter.

I shouted at them, motioning with my rifle, and they jumped. I climbed aboard, handed them their own full water cans, and in a moment, all of my team was on.

The helicopter pilot lifted us off into space, and dived for the jungle to gain airspeed. For a moment it felt like the ship was falling, then I could feel the rotors getting a bite, and we leveled out.

We were sunburned, bearded, and dirty, but happy.

The doorgunner looked at me and smiled, as if wondering what made us do the sort of job we did.

POSTSCRIPT: HILL 339

I hadn't yet turned in my equipment, or gone to eat, when our platoon sergeant stopped me. "You know you've got another mission tomorrow, don't you?" he asked.

Then he explained that Hart and I were slated to take out a team of new men. That was why we had been extracted a day early.

But, he promised, it would be an easy mission.

REPLACEMENTS

We were getting new men every day, because all of us who had come over in August were due for return to the United States soon. Some of the new men were volunteers, but a few of them had simply been told to report to the LRRP platoon, and did not know who we were, or what we did.

I wondered how the platoon would manage after the experienced men were gone.

The LRRP platoon area made up part of the perimeter, that short stretch of wire being our responsibility to defend. Our bunkers were about twenty-five meters uphill from the snarled rolls of concertina, an informal junkpile-garbage dump growing on the inside of the wire itself.

A few nights earlier, a curious mortar barrage had fallen in a good pattern about a hundred meters short of the wire. If it had been on target, it would have devastated the LRRP tents. We figured it had indeed been aimed at us, but that it had been accidentally short.

Life went on.

I was resting on my cot inside my tent, writing a letter home. The sides of my GP medium were rolled high to catch the breeze. The whole platoon area was quiet. Several patrols were out, and the rest of us were relaxing.

"Hey!" yelled one of our men. I looked up to see what he wanted, but before I or anyone else around could respond, he launched himself over a sandbag wall and ran downhill toward the wire. He was shirtless and he carried no weapon.

He ran through the garbage and reached down, pulling up a Vietnamese man like a rabbit out of a magician's hat. He started beating the man before any resistance could be offered by the prisoner.

I put my hand on my carbine.

"Get a weapon! Bring me a weapon!" the LRRP was shouting. I ran out of my tent and saw several others coming with guns, too. We were all at the base of the hill in a few seconds.

"Give me a weapon!" the LRRP was still demanding.

"Why?" asked one of our men, "you've got him under control."

"So I can shoot the bastard!" the LRRP said.

"Wait, let's talk to him," argued another man. Someone ran for an interpreter. The prisoner was weak-kneed and bleeding from his mouth, looking away from his captors.

"Son of a bitch was hiding in the dump!" the LRRP who held the Vietnamese by the throat growled as the interpreter arrived.

The interpreter spoke to the prisoner harshly in Vietnamese, and searched his pockets until he found an identity paper. "This say he was VC, but no more," said the interpreter. "He say he was looking in garbage for something to sell."

"Bullshit!" said the LRRP. "He was probably pacing us off for another mortar attack!"

The interpreter and two of the men took the prisoner away. I went back to my tent and returned to my letter, but found myself glancing from time to time back down at the wire to make sure the infiltrator didn't have a friend.

Crowded into the Huey slick with our heavy rucksacks, my team cringed as the pilot skimmed the treetops, flying under some of the trees rather than over them. The jungle zipped past the doorway too fast to really see anything.

The worst part of many a mission was the ride out. I was worried about getting killed in a chopper crash after all this time. I had seventeen days left in the country.

Hart, our team leader, crouched near me.

The other two men with us were new. This was going to be their first time out. The first mission is the big one, the one that determined if you made it or not in the LRRPs.

You can be the greatest infantryman to ever carry an M-16 with a full company around you, but out depending on only the other three men on your team, it's a different story.

Spec-5 Allen was our RTO this trip. He had come from a commo outfit, so we gave him the radio to carry. Private First Class Cates was from an infantry company. Allen was overweight and soft. Cates looked like he could cut it.

We preferred our volunteers from line units, so Allen was getting a fair shake.

I was almost confident about this mission. It was the same area Rilley, Huxtable, Padilla, and myself had scouted a couple of trips back, and it had been clean then.

The target area was high and flat, part of the plateau region southwest of Pleiku, covered with light jungle and rolling plains of savanna grass. The really rough country, the mountains, were to our west and north.

My apprehension over taking out new men was offset by the relative quiet of the area. If we had expected trouble, we would have only taken out one trainee, or none at all.

Cates and Allen were nervous. They watched the gunships flying escort for us, one on each side. The gunnies had their doors shut against the wind, and sunlight glinted off the ammo-belt guides that snaked out to the twin forward-flying machine guns that were mounted on each side of the ships, just above their ponderous rocket pods.

Captain Clarke, our LRRP platoon commanding officer, was up somewhere over us in the Command and Control helicopter to monitor our insertion.

I checked my M-16 rifle again, thinking about the insanity of going on patrol so close to going home, but I should have thought of that back at base camp.

The doorgunner beside me gave Hart and me the signal that our landing zone was near. Hart tapped Cates, who struggled to a ready position. Allen looked out the door, holding onto his hat and rifle.

We passed the LZ, a long clearing among the trees, and made a steep bank as we circled it. I climbed out on the skid while the pilot steadied the ship and we began to descend, squinting into the airstream, watching the LZ get closer.

The doorgunners raised their machine guns, ready to fire, and I saw embankment and grown-over streambed below, mentally marking it as our assembly point. As point man for the team, it was my responsibility to lead the team off the landing zone and to a safe assembly point so we could gather ourselves, decide on what to do, and move out. The team would automatically follow me once we were on the ground.

On ahead, not far away, was the curving, shallow Ia Tae River, choked by rocks and sandbars.

We dropped quickly, the grass a blur under our skids. The pilot was already increasing power for liftoff.

I jumped.

The helicopter was gone, the rest of the team scattered down the LZ, running for me. I was dashing for the tree line, aiming for the position where I remembered the streambed. I didn't hesitate at the tree line. Silence was sacrificed for speed. I plunged down the hill, breaking through the vegetation, almost falling.

I landed in a swampy streambed. In that moment of stillness, I found myself in the company of several North Vietnamese soldiers.

Two of them were prone in the leaves and another one crouched into the bushes. We were only meters from each other.

One of them leveled his SKS carbine at me. He was dressed in dark green and seemed to have rags tied to his clothing and equipment as camouflage.

I reacted, bringing my M-16 around, but he fired first, and I saw his weapon recoil from the shot. I pulled my trigger almost at the same time, but we both missed.

I fired again, my M-16 jammed, someone else fired from the side, and I yelled, *"Dinks! Dinks!"* at the top of my lungs.

The battle was on.

I was trying to run backward, get a grenade off my belt, and dodge all at the same time. A burst of automatic fire tore through my rucksack and knocked me down. I rolled, pulled the grenade free, and heaved it behind me as I regained my feet. Rifle fire was cracking from all around now.

My grenade hit a tree, bounced back, and exploded too close. I clawed through the vines and ran as hard as I could back uphill, remembering to veer to the side so my own team wouldn't shoot me.

Automatic fire hammered from the left and right flanks. I knew we were in the middle of something too big for a recon team.

As I ran, I pumped the bolt back and forth on my M-16, trying to clear the jam, stopping for no natural obstacles in my escape. I plowed through the underbrush as fast as I could under the circumstances, and ran into my second big surprise of the day.

An NVA soldier was hidden in the very thicket I was trying to charge through.

He twisted in the bushes to face me, but the vines prevented him from quickly bringing his rifle—a U.S. M-16 like mine—to bear. I imagine the last thing either of us were expecting at the time was a face-to-face confrontation.

He began firing (his M-16 *worked)* as he turned, and I felt bullets slam into the canteen and ammo pouch on my right side. The concussion from his muzzle blast stung my stomach and groin.

I rammed the flash suppressor of my M-16 into his belly and fired, and literally ran right over his body.

My ammo pouch was shot open, the magazines spilling out, and the new two-quart flexible canteen I had fastened beside the ammo pouch had taken a couple of hits and was blown open.

I reached the crest of the hill, seeing blue sky through the foliage, and dived for cover behind the first tree over the hump . . . then something unexplainable happened.

I was suddenly surrounded by thick, green, chemical smoke.

For a wild second I was completely confused, but the heat and the taste of the smoke identified the source. My pack was on *fire* from one of my own smoke grenades.

I executed the quick backpack jettison only used in dire emergencies, rolling in the grass to extinguish any of the fire on my clothing. My pack was flaming, issuing a column of green smoke up through the trees.

I didn't know it at the time, but up on the LZ our new RTO had done only one thing so far in this fight. When the shooting began, he had dropped and made radio contact with the helicopters, and upon seeing the plume of green smoke rising from the streambed, he concluded I had marked the enemy position with smoke before being killed.

He told the gunships to fire at the smoke.

I was right beside the smoke.

My smoke grenade had been shot at the bottom of the hill when I had been hit in the rucksack. It had been burning all the time, but I hadn't slowed down enough in my escape for the smoke to catch up with me.

As I lay on the ground, watching my rucksack burn, trying to unjam my M-16, a gunship dropped out of the sky and made a firing pass at me with his four flex-mount M-60 machine guns.

The hillside exploded into falling limbs and splintered bark as the trees took the fury of the automatic fire. With my face buried in the dirt, I could actually hear the bullets as they flailed the earth.

Another gunship was right on the tail of the first. This ship had the turret-mounted automatic 40mm grenade launcher on its nose, and its shells were bursting in the upper parts of the trees over my head. Pieces of the trees were falling all around me. I was trying to mentally calculate the effective kill zone of the 40mm grenades, hoping most of the fragments would lose lethal velocity before they reached me.

The only thing I could really think of coherently was that I was not far enough out of the tree line.

I pulled another frag grenade off my belt and heaved it down the hill to discourage any followers, and tried to fire again, but my M16 was jammed again. After every round I ejected bent, double-fed cartridges, cursing the Colt arms company with real venom. I resorted to another grenade, my next-to-last one, and tried again with the rifle.

At that point heavy firing erupted from all sides around the LZ. The clearing had been a trap. It was actually a giant ambush.

The North Vietnamese had obviously gambled we might use this clearing for a large-scale infantry assault. If they knew we had patrolled through this area before, they might have taken it to mean we were doing it prior to an airmobile assault.

But instead of an infantry company charging down in dozens of helicopters, only four LRRPs were caught in the trap.

We had exposed the ambush the hard, hard way.

Bullets chopped through the trees. Explosions were close and rapid. Tracers flashed across the open LZ, just over the grass. Gusts of dirty high-explosive smoke blossomed from mortar hits.

AK-47s cracked zealously everywhere, and I couldn't

move an inch. This was it. The truth struck. I was going to
die on this LZ.

I'm not saying I was *afraid* I was going to die, or that
I might die. I was *going* to die. It was a fact, and I accepted
it with a strange resignation and sadness.

I lay on my back, looking up at the sky. It was a clear
blue, marred only by the smoke rising from the explosions.
God, I thought, there's only four of us. It was a short
prayer but to the point.

I moved, grabbing for my smoldering rucksack,
crawling for the open LZ. My physical will to live carried
me when my mental will had failed.

I made it to the tall grass of the landing zone, hoping
that if any of my team saw me they wouldn't mistake me
for an enemy soldier. "Hart!" I yelled, trying to be heard
over the gunfire, "Hart!"

Hart's face popped up nearby, his soft hat pulled
down tight over his forehead. Allen was lying close to him,
looking at me but not moving.

Hart was firing. He would rip off a burst from his
CAR-15, roll to another spot, rise and fire again. He was
changing magazines as fast as he could. I couldn't see
Cates or hear his M-16.

I crawled quickly to Allen and took the radio handset
from him. He had his head buried in his arms as if dead. I
discovered why. As soon as I had the handset in my hand,
bullets began to strike close to me.

A sniper had Allen zeroed. I threw down the handset
and rolled away, but Hart was screaming, "Get on the
radio, get on the radio!" I grabbed for the handset again,
and again dirt sprayed in my face as the sniper's bullets hit
in front of me. This time I held onto the handset, aware
that my entire body was a target.

Allen hadn't moved at all. My rifle wasn't working
and *he* wasn't firing. "Shoot, goddamn it!" I pleaded with
him, and wanted to take his weapon, but knew he would
probably shoot me if I tried.

The sniper was peppering the ground around Allen

and me. I was both afraid to move and afraid not to. One thing seemed sure. I couldn't talk on the radio.

Cates, our missing man, was alive. He was on his end of the LZ, removed from the rest of us, also with a jammed M-16. This time it was not the manufacturer's fault. Cates had cleaned his rifle before the mission and had disassembled the trigger group. This is not authorized for the average soldier to do, and he had replaced the hammer spring without sufficient tension to fire the weapon.

He aimed, pulled the trigger, heard a light click, but the weapon did not fire, ejected the round, and did it again. He was emptying magazines doing this drill, and he could clearly see an enemy soldier in a tree.

My own rifle was still jamming regularly. It would fire one or two rounds on semi and jam, or short bursts of automatic and jam. I tried changing magazines, switching back and forth from full to semi, but nothing worked.

In order for any of us to fire down the embankment, it was necessary to rise slightly. I was firing from a kneeling position, going flat to clear my jams, getting up to fire again.

Hart was right beside me, crouching, raking the streambed with his CAR-15, and waving one arm at me, shouting, "Get down! Get down!" as if he were immune to bullets but not I.

In the battle for the LZ, with my fear of the sharpshooter that had Allen and me targeted, trying to make my weapon shoot back, I wasn't getting a great deal of radio communication accomplished with our air support. My one message so far to Captain Clarke had been brief and to the point: "Get us out! They're all around us! Get us out!"

One of the gunships was working the tree line over to our rear, and the enemy fire there, including the mortar, slacked off, but the rifle and machine-gun fire from our flanks and front was still considerable.

With their positions known, and air strikes on the way (if Clarke was doing his job), the enemy should have been rapidly pulling out his heavy weapons.

Captain Clarke, flying around up there in relative

safety, was trying to calm me down so I could give him something straight on the radio.

"We can't help you if you don't use correct radio procedure," he said.

I admit my transmissions were garbled, but every time I tried to talk into that handset, a bullet slammed into the ground close enough to sting me with dirt.

The gunships had been cutting it a bit close. The tree line to our front was their target now, and since we were almost in those trees, we were catching a lot of spray fire directed at them.

We had a problem. If we moved too far into the clearing, the NVA could blow us away, but if we moved too far into the trees, the helicopters would blow us away.

I was scared of the NVA and mad at the helicopters. I didn't want to die pinned down on the LZ with a rifle that wouldn't fire, a fear-frozen, inexperienced radioman, and seventeen days left in Vietnam.

I continued to ask for extraction, and heard a pilot come on the radio and tell Clarke that as long as the ground fire was as heavy as it was, he wasn't going to land and pick up *anybody*.

I pulled the pin on a smoke grenade and threw it back onto the LZ, telling Clarke the smoke marked our position and to get the gunships straight on that fact. As soon as the smoke burned out I threw another.

The enemy fire was getting sporadic. My personal antagonist, the sniper who had Allen and me so well plotted, stopped shooting. The gunships were forcing the NVA to withdraw.

I didn't blame them. If I'd been in there, I'd have gone too.

Cates saw the guy he had been trying to shoot jump down off his tree stand and run. The two gunships were now circling the LZ like hawks ready to pounce on anything that moved.

I threw my sixth smoke grenade. I had tossed reds, greens, violets, and whites, every smoke Allen, Hart, and I owned. The LZ downwind of us was fogged with multicolored smoke.

We watched nervously to our rear for infiltrators, casting long looks through the smoke haze. We had stopped firing, and now the only shots were from distant rifles, the retreating enemy firing at the gunships.

A Huey slick, the same one we had ridden out on, came ponderously sailing in over the treetops, both doorgunners blasting furiously into the trees and underbrush.

I stood and waved, hoping I wouldn't be mistaken for an enemy soldier by the helicopter. The pilot glided the ship toward us, the wind from the rotors beating down the grass.

We met it, running under its skids. Cates and Allen jumped aboard, their bush hats lost. I climbed in as Hart covered us, and I pulled him aboard as the pilot lifted us out and up into the sky we had come down from just a few minutes—a lifetime—ago.

Allen quit the LRRPs as soon as we arrived back at base camp, dropping his radio, tiger fatigues, and weapon beside his cot and going back to his unit so fast he didn't even say good-bye. Cates stayed with the platoon.

21 May 1967: Casualties

Weapons Platoon, 1st Battalion, 8th Infantry, part of the 1st Brigade, was ambushed and wiped out down to a single man, who escaped because he faked death as the enemy stripped and searched the bodies.

When the U.S. counterattack came and reached the slaughtered platoon's position, all of the corpses were found naked, their weapons and equipment missing.

Another unit with the 1st of the 8th was mortared heavily following the massacre, and another dozen Americans were killed, plus seventy wounded.

The battles on 18, 19, and 20 May were taking place just slightly southwest of The Oasis.

I was told that since I was so close to being sent home, my Silver or Bronze Star award paperwork would be sent on to the United States and handled there.

24 May 1967: One More Mission

I was asked to volunteer for another mission, this one to go back to Hill 339 and sit out another week of radio relay. That was reasonable, so I agreed.

For this mission, I would be taking three new men, one of them a sniper with an M21-type rifle. I took my carbine. The other two men took an M-16 and a CAR-15.

I figured a stay on 339 would do me good, give me time to think, to consider, to plan. It was as quiet up there as a monastery, and invited introspection.

We packed our personal equipment, filled our water cans, and boarded a helicopter the morning of the 24th, taking the flight out across the jungle, going past infantry battalions still locked in sporadic skirmishes, and were delivered atop 339 like mice deposited by an eagle in a mountaintop nest.

It was almost good to be back on the peak. The new men found it breathtakingly beautiful. I showed them how to pitch their shelters and organize the camp.

We erected the tall antenna for the radio, and made all of our communications checks with the teams that were out, one team a special consideration.

They were a stay-behind ambush at a firebase being abandoned by the artillery and infantry. They had hidden themselves in the main bunker as the Chinook helicopters flew in and carried out the 105mm howitzers and gun crews, and the infantry walked away in column back to the jungle.

* * *

Enemy action came not long after I made contact with the stay-behind team and arranged what we would do if the enemy came into the firebase.

The team had been waiting for three days in the command bunker at the firebase, watching the perimeter, keeping their weapons ready.

One of the men in the stay-behind ambush wasn't a LRRP. He was a Brigade Headquarters and Headquarters Company sergeant from one of the staff sections. I knew him. He was a considerate man, always polite in his daily work.

Having never seen any action, he had asked to go out with one of our teams on something easy, and had been obliged with the stationary ambush.

He was going to get his war story to tell, but he wasn't aware of it just yet.

They had a new type of experimental mine laid around their bunker, which was unusual in that it was a long, 24mm-diameter rubberized tube filled with plastic explosive, and wrapped at regular intervals with heavy coils of fragmentation wire.

The team had unrolled this "linear mine" in the ditches and between the bunkers of the firebase, with the mine detonators inside their bunker.

I received the first call from them late in the afternoon.

"We've got NVA coming out of the tree line," their team leader said. "I count one . . . two . . . three . . . four . . . five . . . six . . . you better let me call you back."

I relayed the message to The Oasis, who alerted the battery of 8-inch howitzers that had been standing by, their guns preaimed at the firebase.

The team, as I learned later, grabbed their weapons and went to their firing positions. The slow, careful squad of North Vietnamese walked directly into the firebase,

AK-47s ready, as the LRRPs weapons were being drawn on them.

The LRRP team leader had a shotgun. He told his men to hold their fire until he began shooting. The NVA walked boldly into the perimeter, heading for the command bunker where the LRRPs were hiding.

The team leader shotgunned the North Vietnamese point man, and the two men behind the stricken point went down to a full magazine from another LRRP's M-16.

As the NVA dived and rolled for cover, the team detonated the linear mines, explosions smashing between the sandbag walls and bunkers, throwing huge clouds of dust and smoke up into the sky.

Then while the surviving North Vietnamese were still stunned, the LRRP team ran like hell, racing out of the firebase, going for the safety of the jungle.

When they stopped running, they radioed me again.

"Okay!" the team leader shouted in his excitement, "we're out! Bring in the artillery!"

I called the artillery and they laid a barrage of big, powerful 8-inchers on and around the firebase, destroying the NVA there along with the sandbags and old barbwire.

On the morning of the 25th, we noticed what seemed to be smoke from campfires coming off the mountains closest to us, part of the Chu Pong range.

I radioed The Oasis again and described the target to them, and they diverted a spotter plane to fly over and take a closer look. What he saw caused my team to cluster to the radio.

"I've got trucks down there in the valley," the pilot told me, "their road leads back into Cambodia. I also have a visual on the campfires, I see them up the ridgeline. Is that a roger for you?"

"Affirmative," I said.

"Okay," replied the pilot. "There is a flight of Vietnamese Al-Es on their way from New Pleiku now."

The Al-Es were old U.S. propeller-driven fighter-bombers that were put into service just after World War II.

They had been used in Korea, and retired from most U.S. service afterward, on the premise that jets would replace them.

Vietnam required a close air-support fighter-bomber like the Al-E, which carried a heavy load of bombs and rockets, and could stay on target for hours, while the faster, sexier jets had to get there, drop their bombs, and fly home. The Skyraiders, as the Al-Es were called, were slow enough to be more accurate with their bombing, a point appreciated by the American and South Vietnamese infantry.

The flight of Skyraiders droned in, meeting the little canvas-covered spotter plane, and watched where the spotter's white-phosphorus marker rockets hit.

We sat on top of 339 and watched, given the best seat for the spectacle to follow.

The Skyraiders circled, coordinated their plans, and began to attack, coming in over the Chu Pong Mountains with 20mm cannons cracking wickedly, then releasing 500-pound bombs as they passed the target.

The bombs shattered the stands of trees along the ridgeline, and after several passes had been made, there was a deep, powerful blast, smoke billowing from under the trees, and a surprised "That was a secondary!" from the spotter pilot.

The explosion seemed to come from out of a cave, because we saw the smoke jet out horizontally from the hillside before it billowed and spread upward.

The Skyraiders were apparently hitting a cache of North Vietnamese munitions.

The spotter pilot was talking rapidly with the Skyraider pilots, and we were taking questions from The Oasis.

Our team laughed and congratulated each other as the Skyraiders flew away, and we watched the smoke on the ridgeland across the valley for hours, feeling not one bit sorry for the men there who would be trying to salvage what they could of their ammunition and their lives.

* * *

We prepared for the night, assigning fields of fire, emergency actions, repacking equipment, and moving slightly off the very top of the hill to a safer break in the rocks on one of the sides of 339 where it was virtually straight down.

We strung a poncho overhead as a shelter in case of rain, and just before midnight the man on guard woke me but said nothing.

I knew the moment I saw his face, he had heard something serious. He pointed toward the crest. "I heard them kicking rocks," he whispered.

Silently, I made sure everybody was awake. Then I heard it. People were indeed walking around above us, pebbles crunching under their feet.

I picked up my carbine, and motioned for the other men to get their weapons. I quietly instructed the radioman to stay with the set and call The Oasis immediately if the enemy was on the hill with us.

I indicated for the man with the M-16 to move around to one side of the crest and come up slowly. The sniper was to stay near the radioman. I began to creep up the rocky slope, holding my carbine in my right hand and supporting myself with my left.

At the edge, I lay still for a moment and listened. There was nothing. I raised my head and carbine and looked over the top.

Directly in front of me was the silhouette of a North Vietnamese soldier holding his rifle in a relaxed stance, but looking right where my head stuck above the rocks.

I pulled the trigger of the carbine. The hammer fell against the firing pin with a loud snap, but the chamber was empty. I had cleared and not rechambered a round in my weapon after being inserted on the hill, a safety precaution that was now likely to get me killed.

I reached rapidly over the carbine with my left hand and snapped the bolt handle back, feeding a cartridge into the chamber.

The enemy soldier reacted, swinging his rifle around toward me and fired. The shot went by my ear.

I fired, my burst staggering him, and I kept the trigger down, sweeping the muzzle across the crest. The soldier stepped back, sat down awkwardly, then fell over.

He had two friends. One dark form moved an arm, his grenade falling over my shoulder, rolling down the hill, and exploding somewhere below. I fired at him, and he jumped off the opposite side of the peak. It was at least one hundred meters to the first rocks he would hit. The man with him dashed away from me, down the ridgeline, but my carbine was empty.

My partner fired at the retreating man with his M-16, his bullets breaking the rocks and tossing leaves and dirt into the air across the peak.

I rolled down to the radioman. "Get brigade on the radio," I said, "now."

The sniper was wide-eyed with fear. The radioman stammered out the message. It wasn't fast or clear enough for me. I grabbed the handset from him, and described the contact.

I was furious. I knew what was happening. The North Vietnamese had guessed where all their grief had been coming from, and sent a recon team up 339. If we had laid low, and let them leave, maybe we could have gotten away without a fight, but not after this.

The recon team would not be alone. They probably had a platoon somewhere near, and that platoon would have a company.

We were in real trouble.

"Get up on the landing zone," I said to the radioman and the sniper. We scrambled to the peak, and each of us covered a side.

The sniper with his special rifle guarded the south drop, the M-16 and CAR-15 covering the sides. I took the north approach. The only way they could come up was by that ridgeline.

The man I had shot lay near me, still on his side. I

had put at least a three-round burst into his chest. I wasn't worried about him.

I laid my hat beside me, took all of my carbine magazines and grenades, and put them in the hat so I could reach my ammunition easily.

Brigade radioed again, asking for our current situation, offering assistance.

North Vietnamese rushed up the slope, firing as they dodged from tree to tree. I dropped the radio handset and fired back, the muzzle flash of my own carbine blinding me.

The new man with his M-16 rolled over my way and took cover near the body of the man I had killed, snapping off aimed bursts into the trees.

I picked the handset up again, telling brigade we were under attack. They could hear our rifle fire as I spoke to them. I asked for helicopter gunships, artillery, Puff the Magic Dragon, and fighter-bombers. We had nowhere to run off 339. We were at the very top, on a tiny rocky flat spot, and I had no doubt we had NVA coming up all around us. It was last-stand time.

The sniper began to fire, shouting to me, and the other man with the CAR-15 started to crack off rounds down his slope. I didn't know if they were firing because they were scared, or because they had targets.

The enemy soldiers coming up the ridgeline were trying to keep our heads down with rifle fire as they crawled forward, but their fire was too high.

I put the carbine on semiauto, hoping to conserve my ammunition as long as possible, aiming at the flashes of the enemy weapons in the jagged ridges below me.

The dead man jumped up to run away.

My man with the M-16 gaped for an instant, then cut the man down with a burst that started at his ankles and went up his back. This time the man fell hard off the peak, down into the beginning of the bushes.

I threw a grenade down the ridgeline, watching the trees frame the flash of the explosion. My M-16 rifleman was doing fine, aiming, keeping up steady fire at the enemy in the trees.

I heard a voice over the radio handset telling me a spotter plane was on the way, and to mark our position with a strobe light. I took my strobe out of its pouch and turned it on, twisting to place it by my feet.

It began to flash methodically.

The enemy rushers went to ground, and for a moment, their firing stopped. It was oddly quiet. I looked at the faces of my men in the surrealistic flashes of the strobe. They seemed astonished.

With a determined, steady drone, the spotter aircraft passed just over the tops of the trees that rose above the ridgeline. The pilot banked the ship, and stuck his M-16 out his window, firing tracers down on the NVA. I was struck with the bravery and futility of his gesture.

The firing began again. Rifles from the ridge started cracking, and grenades were exploding as both we and the enemy threw them at each other.

The sniper flipped over toward me, badly shaken, trying to get my attention as I fired my carbine. I felt him beating my shoulder and looked at him.

"A grenade just landed beside me, but it didn't explode!" he said, then rolling exactly back where he had been before, resumed firing down his dropoff, almost having to hold the entire rifle over the edge to do so.

I wanted artillery fast, and called the 42nd Artillery. They said they could only reach me with their 175mm guns, and at my range from them they had a thousand-meter error.

"You shoot, I'll correct it," I said, then turned to the team and shouted, "One-seven-fives coming in! One-seven-fives!"

The first shell hit like the artillery officer had said, about a thousand meters away in the valley. The blast echoed off the Chu Pongs and the sound rumbled along the valley floor.

I corrected, telling them to shift fire one thousand meters along the gun-target line, in my direction.

The second shell hit near the base of the northern end of the ridgeline, and the trees vibrated all the way up to us. The 175mms were very powerful. The enemy rifle fire slacked for a moment as they turned to look down the ridge.

The third shell crashed into the valley beside the hill, and I knew then that just hitting the hill was a matter of luck for the artillery. We were on the extreme rim of their total range, beyond their effective range.

For the moment, close was good enough for me. I told the gunners to fire for effect, and hugged the ground. There were two 175mm guns firing, and they alternated, one firing and one loading, their super-velocity, extreme-range loads propelling the high-explosive shells toward 339.

The shells came down on the ridge, past 339, and on both sides of 339. The terrific explosions from all around our hill gave us courage, knowing the North Vietnamese would not know of our accuracy problems.

"Lift the artillery," radioed the spotter plane, "I've got help up here."

I called off the artillery support, talking to the spotter, who was having our new assistance switch to our frequency. It was a C-47 dragonship with miniguns. I had the equivalent firepower of a division of riflemen now.

The sky seared with the brilliant white light of the dragonship's one-million-candlepower parachute flares.

The Chu Pong Mountains, the valley beside us, the distant hills, everything became visible in the stark black-and-white world the magnesium sun of a flare produces.

"Where do you want it?" the pilot of the dragonship asked me.

"They're all around my hill, but put what you can on the north approach. We've got people coming up that way," I said.

"I can't give you fire any closer than five hundred meters from your position," said the pilot, "or we stand too good a chance of hitting you."

"They're closer than that," I argued. "I need it directly at the base of the hill!"

"Can't do it," the pilot said again. "These guns spray a hell of a wide pattern."

"Okay," I said, "do the best you can, but give me some fire now!"

With a screeching roar, the sky split and hell came down like the breath of an avenging god. The noise of the miniguns alone was terrifying, but each time the dragonship belched flame and tracers, I could see the treetops below in the beaten zone disentegrate.

I had been close to the fire from a dragonship before, but never directly under it. The rumbling motors from the old cargo plane droned on for half an hour, new flares dropping just as the old ones burned out, keeping our section of Vietnam bathed in the tilting, unreal world of flare-light.

Finally, the dragonship wished us good luck and pointed itself east, flying away from 339, back home to an airstrip somewhere, for its gunners to shovel out belt links and empty cartridge cases by the truckload.

"Hang in there," said the spotter to me, "but get your heads down. Your fighters are on the way." I could hear his little engine, but not see him in the dark.

I didn't have time to tell my team.

There was a streak of something silver across our front, moving so fast there was yet no noise. The sound of the aircraft came at the same instant the blast did. Before I could draw a breath, the ridgeline directly before me exploded with an expanding cloud of flame. It was napalm.

I clearly saw the impact; the ridgeline was engulfed in red-orange fire. I saw the flamefront roar across the ridge, striking trees, and saw the splash of napalm as it spattered off bark and branches.

The heat was searing. I buried my face in my arms to try and protect myself. For a time that had to be short— but in my memory has no limits at all—all I could see, feel, or smell was fire.

The top of the hill was illuminated like day, if day were blinding orange. I realized my skin had become absolutely dry, the sweat steamed off me, and my clothes were very hot.

The worst of the fireball burned away, and I looked up, hearing a distinctive sound. One of the fighter-bombers was diving toward us. It was one of the few times in combat that I heard a sound that resembled almost precisely a sound effect I had heard in films.

It came from behind us. I looked over my shoulder and into the night sky. Brilliant in every detail, reflecting the napalm fire, precisely aligned so I was looking at it front-on, came another Skyraider. Under each wing was a tapered aluminum tank.

The tanks dropped off the wings. They were napalm bombs.

I saw them begin to flip slowly in the air, coming my way.

The radio was right beside me, tall antenna up. The aircraft itself was still on course, and now I could see the outline of the canopy frame and the pilot's face. He was going to hit my radio antenna. I knocked the radio flat.

The Skyraider passed over my head by what seemed only a few meters. I saw the rocket racks under his wings and the rivets in the polished metal of the fuselage. The suction actually bounced me, and the screaming roar of the engine was deafening.

The napalm canisters hit just down the back south slope, boiling a spread of petroleum-based fire upward, towering over us, streamers of flame falling onto the crest.

The four of us were too shaken to speak, not knowing what to expect next.

I began shouting to the team, trying to find out what was happening at their sides of our little defense perimeter. The napalm in front of us had burned low now; only the underbrush was still on fire. Behind us, on the dropoff, the two canisters that had hit there were still going strong, making a solid wall of fire that lit the smoke clouds over us with yellow heat.

One of the Skyraiders came back again, and dropped a bomb on one side of 339 not burning in napalm. It was a

CBU (cluster-bomb unit), which opened in the air and spewed hundreds of small bombs all along the side of the hill and down the slope.

Most of them exploded in a group, making a resounding crash, but dozens bounced and spun into the air, coming down to detonate on the second impact, resembling multiple grenade explosions.

One thudded on top of the crest, skipped a short distance, and blew away the poncho shelter we had erected in the crevice.

I lifted my face off the rocks. The CBU had been incredible.

Another one hit the opposite side.

As it blasted through the trees, the tightly packed bomblets scattered, and exploded individually and in bunches. It seemed as though the Vietnamese pilots were willing to sacrifice our team in order to kill the enemy.

We could not see much from the crest any longer because of the smoke, but I could still hear the Skyraiders powering past; now they were firing their 20mm cannons.

"Look!" one of the team yelled, pointing down below the smoke cover.

The darkness of the jungle floor was broken by pinpoints of muzzle flashes. There were hundreds of them, from a large unit of North Vietnamese in the valley below us, between 339 and the Chu Pong Mountains, and they were firing up at the Skyraiders.

I estimated them at battalion strength, and put together a sequence. The battalion was moving at night, off the Chu Pongs, down the valley and toward The Oasis.

If the assault on us after we shot the first three men off the peak was indicative of their strength, about two infantry squads had come our way.

They had tried to climb around us, coming up the drops on the sides, and throw grenades, but most of their grenades had gone entirely over us, falling down the opposite sides, so small was our peak.

The radio told me there were helicopters on the way. I acknowledged, telling the team. None of us were hurt. One

of the men who had been using his pack as cover discovered the pack had been burned on one side by a napalm
splash from the second set of canisters. I found small waxy
pieces of unburned napalm fuel near me, bits of the bombs
that had been thrown away from the main cell before complete ignition.

I received a call from one of the helicopters who asked
me about ground fire. I told him there was no more, and in
a few minutes a Huey appeared in the smoke, flying in
sideways to our landing zone, the small fires from burning
trees lighting up the underside of the helicopter.

We climbed aboard, leaving the strobe light, the water
cans, and our ponchos, and at 2310 hours on May 25th, we
flew into the darkness, off Hill 339.

At brigade headquarters in The Oasis, I saw the
crowd coming toward our helicopter even before it landed.
It was men from all over Brigade Headquarters Company,
cheering us, pulling us out of the cabin of the Huey, and
carrying us into the tactical operations center. We were
met like heroes. They were laughing, shouting, grabbing,
and clapping for us.

My feet were not allowed to touch the ground until
the men who had me on their shoulders eased me down
inside the operations bunker. My team members were right
behind me. The crowd had taken away our weapons and
equipment, stacking it in a corner.

The brigade commander and several of the infantry
battalion commanders were grinning at us. We were directed to stand in front of the warboard, the same one I
once had kept posted with unit locations as a brigade clerk.

"Here's to you!" saluted the officers, downing glasses
of whiskey, and refilling them quickly. The brigade commander walked up to me. I realized the man was drunk,
and the officers with him were drunk.

"I'm goddamned proud of you boys," he said, "real
goddamned proud. We showed them bastards a thing or
two tonight! Now, tomorrow, I've got to commit a battal-

ion to the field. I want to ask you, where should I put them? You tell me where they ought to go."

I was still shaken from the battle on the hill. Being in the operations center, up against the mapboard, with all the electric lights and staring clerks, I felt nervous. The fact my brigade commander was so drunk he could not speak to me without slurring his words was another shock. He was making a fool of himself.

"Those stupid sons of bitches don't know where to commit troops," the brigade commander said, motioning toward the operations and intelligence shops. "All they do is fuck up! I want you to tell me where to put my infantry!"

"Here," I said loudly, pointing to the Chu Pongs on the map, "from here to the border. You'll find them. The NVA are out there, I swear."

"I'll do it, by God, in the morning, I'll do it," said the colonel. "Your captain tells me you go home in a week, is that right?"

"Yes, sir," I said.

"Well, you're too damn short to be pulling any more missions. I want you off those patrols now, understand?"

"Yes, sir," I said.

"Okay, go get some sleep!" the colonel said, and the four of us picked up our equipment and walked out of the operations center, through the crowd outside, trying to smile at the men slapping our backs and asking us questions.

29 May 1967: Base Camp

I sold my carbine to one of the new LRRPs and gave a friend my survival knife. I could have taken it back with me, but I told him I wanted it to stay in Vietnam where it could do some good. "I hope you kill a dozen NVA with it," I told my friend.

With my rucksack packed, and each good-bye said, I

walked to the landing zone in front of brigade to wait for a
helicopter to base camp.

As I was leaving the company area, I heard the news a
LRRP had been killed. I stopped. What teams were out?

The dead man wasn't one of the veterans of the platoon. It was one of the new men. He had been killed by one
of the other new men. It had been an accident.

I waited by the LZ, and soon, a helicopter came, and I
was waved by the loading sergeant there to get aboard.

A body wrapped in a poncho was taken off the Huey.
The trouser legs sticking out of the poncho were clad in
tiger fatigues. It was the man I had just learned of. A
group of infantrymen carried him. His boots bounced life-
lessly as they passed me.

Many of the original LRRP platoon were already in
base camp, back at their units, arranging to get out of
Vietnam. Most of the unit now, except for a very few veterans still on their last patrol, was all new.

At basecamp, I learned a new name had been applied
again.

The 4th Division Dragon Mountain Base Camp was
now officially Camp Enari. I heard some of the base-camp
clerks at personnel using the name. For a moment I listened.

"What the fuck kind of name is Enari?" a soldier
asked a clerk.

"Beats me," said one of the clerks.

"How long you been here?" I asked him.

"Four months," he said.

"Enari was the name of one of our lieutenants that
originally came over with the 2nd Brigade headquarters," I
said.

"Yeah?"

"He left headquarters and went to a line company like
I did," I told the clerk, who might or might not have
wanted to know, but I didn't care. I was going to tell him.
"Enari was killed taking his people in on an assault against
a tree line."

"Did you know this Enari?" the clerk asked me.

"Yes, I knew him," I said, feeling angry and sad. "We used to talk together at Fort Lewis before we shipped out. Enari was a nice guy, he liked sports cars, he was married, he had just bought a new Alfa GTZ before we left . . . it was white."

"I'm sorry," said the clerk. "I had never heard the name."

"Well," I said, disturbed and wanting to leave, "it was Lieutenant Enari's name. If you say it now, you know who he was."

I walked around the expanse of base camp. It was a real town now. Electric power lines ran from building to building on poles, there were telephone lines, road signs to control the traffic, piped water, glass windows, and concrete-block walls.

Grass grew on lawns, and walkways were marked with painted rocks. Music played from wooden barracks. There were air conditioners in the windows.

I needed to find C Company because I had to get to the personnel and supply offices to process some of my paperwork.

Approaching a formation of soldiers standing in front of a new row of white wooden-frame barracks, I decided to asked about C Company because I knew I had to be close.

"This is C Company," said one of the soldiers. He looked very young, and his jungle fatigues were new.

"I need C, Second of the Eighth," I said.

"That's us," he said.

I looked up and down the formation. I didn't believe it. I couldn't see anyone I knew.

"Hey, Camper!" yelled a voice from the ranks, and one of the veterans pushed his way out to me. "Good to see you! You must be processing out!"

"That's right!" I said, then nodded toward the company. "Who are these guys?"

"Well, we got a lot of new replacements," the veteran said. "Everybody in 1st Platoon is new, and over half of us in 2nd Platoon are new. It's about half and half in 3rd. Weapons is still pretty much intact."

"I didn't recognize anybody," I said.

"It was a rough year," my friend explained.

I made the rounds to finance, medical, personnel, and supply, carrying a clipboard with my files and other paperwork on it, letting Vietnam slip away from me with each waking morning.

It was near 2nd Brigade headquarters in base camp where I saw two LRRPs. They were dressed in tiger fatigues, carrying their rucksacks, apparently just out of The Oasis.

"Who's out there winning the war?" I asked, walking up to them with the first smile I had managed in days. The clerks had been harassing me, and the more false base-camp war stories I heard, the closer I was coming to smashing a cook or orderly with his own typewriter.

The LRRPs turned wearily, glad to see me, then a change came over their faces.

"Did you hear about Harmon and Bonnert?" one of them asked.

"No," I said. "I thought they'd be coming out with you guys. They're going home the same time as me."

"They're dead," the LRRP told me.

I took a deep breath. "What happened?" I asked.

The man told me the story. I stood and listened to it, then waved good-bye to them, pointing the way to the outprocessing station in brigade.

I walked back to the transit barracks, quiet and thoughtful.

Harmon, whom I had met first in the LRRP platoon, and whom I had seen lying wounded on the dirt floor of an aid tent during the heavy mortar attack on 3 Tango, was dead. He was an Alaskan Indian, and he kept a sharp knife in his equipment all the time. He was dead.

Bonnert I had not met until he had come back from the hospital in Japan. He had been shot through the thigh while walking point for his team. They had presumed him dead, and left him there while they dropped back. He threw off his rucksack, and crawled back to them, in agony all the way, afraid they would leave him. He had been seasoned when we met, and we had been friends. He was dead.

Harmon and Bonnert had taken out a team of two new men, going into a lightly forested area. It was near a developing infantry battle, and their team had been under the control of an infantry battalion.

When the fighting spread so quickly it engulfed the LRRP team, they had pulled in with the infantry. A column of tanks, tracks, and trucks had pushed out through the plateau region, and the LRRP team was riding one of the M-60 tanks.

The column was ambushed.

The tank was hit with rockets, and the two new LRRPs were blown off it. Both of them were wounded. Coon, one of the new men, looked up at the tank. He was the one to come back and tell the tale.

Coon said Bonnert was badly wounded, and Harmon was trying to hold him on the deck of the tank, which was starting to burn from the rocket hit.

Then, Coon said, the North Vietnamese attacked.

The infantry ran away. They left the trucks and the tracks, and they ran.

Harmon did not run. He held onto Bonnert, and pointed his CAR-15 over the turret of the tank, firing at the enemy.

Bonnert was hit several times, Coon said, as Harmon held him, pulling to get him behind cover. He was probably dead, Coon said, and Harmon didn't know it.

The Alaskan Indian died like that, firing his weapon over the turret, holding his friend, the tank beginning to burn fiercely.

But he didn't run, and he didn't leave his friend.

And in the first week of June 1967, he did not go home.

I flew out of New Pleiku Air Base in a Boeing 727 chartered to the army, every seat filled. We left the airstrip at max power, nose up, climbing for altitude to get out of ground-fire range as fast as possible.

Like most everyone else on board, I wore wrinkled, ill-fitting khakis issued to me by a base-camp quartermaster. The khakis I'd brought over a year before had long since mildewed and rotted away.

I did not even have an AWOL bag of personal items. The one I had packed was missing, lost, or stolen in the shuffle at the outprocessing center. My money, orders, and ID card were in my pockets.

Our first stop was Cam Ranh Bay, a short jet flight from Pleiku. As we let off a few shuttling passengers and picked up replacements, I watched the sand dunes and long stretches of scrub brush from my window, cruising tracks plowing across the beaches like Panzers in North Africa.

As we took off again, some of the men cheered, but the elation I expected to feel when our tires left Vietnam's soil wasn't there. I just felt tired and a little sad. I almost expected to wake up from this dream, exhausted on patrol somewhere.

We flew to Clark Air Force Base in the Philippines and landed there along rows of neatly parked, camouflage-painted F-4 Phantom fighter-bombers and C-130 cargo planes. I saw no gun bunkers alongside the runways, and had to remind myself there didn't need to be. We were not in Vietnam, but the combat aircraft around us twisted such reason. Our perimeter was unprotected. They should have bunkers, I thought, just in case.

Once parked, we were briefly allowed off the 727 to go into the air terminal, where military families in brightly colored civilian clothes waited for their own flights. I found a snack bar and ordered cold milk, something I had wanted and promised myself for a long time, providing I got out alive.

The snack bar only sold reconstituted milk, the same type sent to Vietnam. I wasn't far enough away from the war yet.

Soon we were all back aboard our plane and airborne again, aimed this time for Japan, and a longer stopover and change of planes.

It was night over Yokote by the time we arrived, massed neon advertising signs in Japanese idiograms making a blaze of color below as we approached for landing.

After Vietnam, the early June night in Japan seemed cold to me as we filed off the 727 and were led to a hangar outfitted as a mass waiting area for troops in transit. Inside, hundreds of soldiers milled around or sat crouched on benches, listening to loudspeaker announcements for their flight times and numbers.

I changed to a 707 there, boarding the bigger plane with an anxious crowd of troopers. This was it. The next stop was the United States, The World.

Tired now, I slept during most of the flight across the Pacific, trying to adjust my mind to the fact I was on my way home, at altitude, suspended between realities.

When I woke later, having slept all I could, most of the men around me were still slumped in their seats. Even the stewardesses were resting. In the quiet dimness of the long cabin it was peaceful. Outside my window was blackness. I studied it. You have to learn to see through darkness.

Slowly, a suggestion of gray appeared ahead of us in the night sky, and the gray began to glow. It became purple, thinning to yellows and oranges, a stratospheric dawn.

Here comes the sun, I thought. First, it flickered ahead in the atmosphere, a rim of light that illuminated the edges of our wings, a filling brightness that transformed the sky into vast glory.

We were flying into morning. Darkness was behind us. In the light I saw the coastline and hills of California. Men were stirring, being shaken awake by their friends. Faces were pressed to the windows. No one cheered like they had leaving Vietnam. There was too much of a sense of awe in the twin spectacles of dawn and America appearing together before us like a vision.

We landed at Travis Air Force Base, near San Francisco, and were bussed to Oakland Army Terminal to be quickly processed in and out, authorized leave, given new dress-green uniforms with all the proper insignia, and turned loose.

It was the "Summer of Love" in San Francisco. I went downtown briefly, just to see the sights before going on to the airport. The hippies and flower children were in their uniforms of ragged clothes, long hair, love beads, and sandals. I looked at them and they looked at me, in my uniform of summerweight green, service ribbons, polished brass, and military insignia. There were VW vans painted with peace signs; and hashish, pot, and LSD were staples of the streets. The latest music was a Beatles album, *Sgt. Pepper's Lonely Hearts Club Band,* released just that week.

I said nothing to anyone downtown, and they said nothing to me, and by noon, I was at the airport. I finally found my fresh milk there, and at a snack bar in the terminal, I drank glasses of it and ate hot dogs with mustard, my first meal Stateside.

On the way to the departure gate for my plane home, I passed a newspaper vending machine. The headlines stunned me.

JERUSALEM MORTARED, it read.

The words didn't even have a relationship in my mind. *Mortared* was a term I knew too well. Someone was always getting mortared, but *Jerusalem?* It made as much sense to me as if it had read DISNEYLAND MORTARED. I had to stop and read that story. There were massive battles breaking out in the Middle East between Israel and her border countries. What we would later know as the famous Six-Day War was beginning.

Boarding my flight, a commercial 707, I was realizing my war was not the only one around. There were other places.

I was seated beside a young businessman dressed in a suit, and in front of us sat two pretty college-age girls. Once we were in the air, and the stewardess had served us soft drinks, the businessman and I began to talk. Our conversation was polite, really just generalities. Soon, the two girls in front of us turned to comment on something, and all of us were talking together.

I honestly was charmed, realizing how I'd missed such kind social words, and the iced drinks and informality made the small talk an event for me. I told the businessman and the girls I was going home on leave, having just come out of Vietnam.

"You mean *you* were in Vietnam?" asked one of the girls, "In the *fighting?*"

"I just left yesterday," I said.

"How long were you there?"

"About a year."

"You were there in the fighting and you were *killing* people?"

The way she said "killing people" had a very wrong ring to it, as if I had been killing for fun or committing murder. I was searching for an appropriate answer when both girls turned away from me and spoke no more.

For a moment, I didn't understand. The businessman also lowered his head and became absorbed in a magazine. The party was over. I sat quietly, drinking my soda, studiously ignored by the salesman and the girls.

I had just left the protesters and hippies in San Francisco's parks. These passengers were just average people to me, not freaks waving Vietcong flags. My God, were things that bad?

I stood and edged past the salesman, apologizing for disturbing him, and he grunted a superficial reply. Up the aisle, in an empty row of seats, I sat down alone, confused and hurt. It was a personal hurt.

When the stewardess noticed me, she came over and offered to refill my glass. "Are you all right?" she asked.

"I'm fine," I lied. I wanted to go back and tell those girls and that salesman about the village the NVA had burned down with flamethrowers, about the starved baby we buried, about so much. I wanted to, but I didn't, because they had made up their minds on Vietnam without really knowing anything about it. They wouldn't want to know what I would tell them. It would upset their preconceptions, and soon I might be screaming at them, and I didn't think I could control it.

After we had landed and the door of the 707 opened, I exited with the other passengers down the stairs into the afternoon sun of Birmingham Airport, seeing my wife and father waiting for me on the ground.

For that moment, I forgot the incident on the flight and we embraced; I was truly happy. I was alive. I had made it.

POSTSCRIPT: END OF MISSION

I went home with infected leech bites on my knee, serious skin-fungus problems on my feet and lower legs, a badly weakened digestive system, and as soon as my thirty-day supply of supressant pills ran out, a good case of vivax malaria.

Someone tried to tally the platoon's kills the week I left. It was a figure that stood between fifty and eighty, depending on who you believed.

The 4th Division LRRP company grew stronger and better, and the brigade LRRPs—only provisional anyway —withered away.

I would rebel against the Stateside army, and eventually get discharged following many bouts in the stockade. After a time of trying to live the straight and narrow life of a civilian, I would give it up and take employment as a mercenary. There were other wars ahead, Yemen, El Salvador, Guatemala, and many covert operations.

But those are other stories.